Questions & Answers
Professional Responsibility

CAROLINA ACADEMIC PRESS
QUESTIONS & ANSWERS SERIES

Questions & Answers: Sales & Leases
Aviva Abramovsky

Questions & Answers: Administrative Law,
Third Edition
Linda D. Jellum, Karen A. Jordan

Questions & Answers: Antitrust
Shubha Ghosh

Questions & Answers: Bankruptcy
Bruce A. Markell, Mary Jo Wiggins

Questions & Answers: Business Associations,
Second Edition
Douglas M. Branson

Questions & Answers: Civil Procedure,
Fourth Edition
William V. Dorsaneo, III, Elizabeth Thornburg

Questions & Answers: Constitutional Law,
Third Edition
Paul E. McGreal, Linda S. Eads, Charles W. Rhodes

Questions & Answers: Contracts, Second Edition
Scott J. Burnham

Questions & Answers: Copyright Law
Dave Fagundes, Robert C. Lind

Questions & Answers: Criminal Law, Third Edition
Emily Levine, Paul Marcus

Questions & Answers: Criminal Procedure—
Police Investigation, Third Edition
Neil P. Cohen, Michael J. Benza, Wayne A. Logan

Questions & Answers: Criminal Procedure—
Prosecution and Adjudication, Third Edition
Neil P. Cohen, Michael J. Benza, Wayne A. Logan

Questions & Answers: Environmental Law
Dru Stevenson

Questions & Answers: Evidence, Third Edition
David P. Leonard, Paul Giannelli

Questions & Answers: Family Law, Second Edition
Mark Strasser

Questions & Answers: Federal Estate & Gift
Taxation, Second Edition
Elaine Gagliardi

Questions & Answers: Federal Income Tax
David L. Cameron

Questions & Answers: Intellectual Property,
Second Edition
Gary Myers, Lee Ann W. Lockridge

Questions & Answers: International Law
Rebecca Bratspies

Questions & Answers: Patent Law
Cynthia Ho

Questions & Answers: Payment Systems,
Second Edition
Timothy R. Zinnecker

Questions & Answers: Professional Responsibility,
Fourth Edition
Patrick Emery Longan

Questions & Answers: Property, Second Edition
John Nagle

Questions & Answers: Remedies
Rachel Janutis, Tracy Thomas

Questions & Answers: Secured Transactions,
Second Edition
Bruce A. Markell, Timothy R. Zinnecker

Questions & Answers: Taxation of Business Entities
Kristofer Neslund, Nancy Neslund

Questions & Answers: The First Amendment,
Third Edition
Russell L. Weaver, William D. Araiza

Questions & Answers: Torts, Third Edition
Anita Bernstein, David P. Leonard

Questions & Answers: Trademark and
Unfair Competition
Vince Chiappetta

Questions & Answers: Wills, Trusts, and Estates,
Third Edition
Thomas Featherston

Questions & Answers
Professional Responsibility

FOURTH EDITION

Multiple-Choice and Short-Answer
Questions and Answers

Patrick Emery Longan

WILLIAM AUGUSTUS BOOTLE CHAIR IN ETHICS AND
PROFESSIONALISM IN THE PRACTICE OF LAW
WALTER F. GEORGE SCHOOL OF LAW
MERCER UNIVERSITY

CAROLINA ACADEMIC PRESS
Durham, North Carolina

ISBN 978-1-53100-644-0
e-ISBN 978-1-53100-645-7

Carolina Academic Press, LLC
700 Kent Street
Durham, North Carolina 27701
Telephone (919) 489-7486
Fax (919) 493-5668
www.cap-press.com

Printed in the United States of America

Contents

Preface

This all-new Fourth Edition makes some significant changes from prior editions. First and foremost, the organization and emphasis of the book now mirrors the organization and emphasis of the Multistate Professional Responsibility Exam (MPRE). The multiple-choice questions are written in the same format as the MPRE questions (the MPRE is entirely multiple choice), and the questions are approximately the same length and difficulty as the questions you will face on the MPRE. You should find the book to be a useful tool in your preparation and practice for the MPRE.

The book is also intended, of course, to help you in your required Professional Responsibility course. It is not a substitute for the materials assigned by your professor, nor is it a "short course" on Professional Responsibility. It is intended rather to enable you to test your understanding and adapt your study strategies accordingly. You may want to use the book at several discrete intervals during the semester. For example, once you have studied conflicts of interest, it would be a good time to review that material and then use the book to test your command of that subject. You should then have a good idea about the strengths and weaknesses of your understanding as the semester goes on and the final exam approaches.

Regardless of how you use the book, for the MPRE, for your Professional Responsibility course, or both, it will be most useful if you study the applicable Model Rules of Professional Conduct or the applicable provisions of the Model Code of Judicial Conduct before attempting to answer the questions. You will find the official comments to these various rules to be essential reading as well. Read the questions carefully and attempt to answer them before you read the suggested answer. You will learn much more from that active endeavor than you will from the passive exercise of reading the question and then flipping to the suggested answer.

The questions and answers in this book are based upon the American Bar Association's Model Rules of Professional Conduct and the ABA's Model Code of Judicial Conduct. Your state's rules for lawyers and judges will differ somewhat from these, but the model provisions have proven to be quite influential in the development of many states' rules. The questions and answers in this book reflect the text and interpretations of the Model Rules and Model Code as of May 1, 2017.

I wish you well as you undertake the study of your responsibilities as a member of your chosen profession and as you prepare to pass the MPRE, the next step on the journey to the beginning of your legal career.

Patrick Longan
Macon, Georgia
May, 2017

About the Author

Patrick Emery Longan holds the William Augustus Bootle Chair in Ethics and Professionalism in the Practice of Law at the Mercer University School of Law and is the Director of the Mercer Center for Legal Ethics and Professionalism. Professor Longan is a 1983 graduate of the University of Chicago Law School, which he attended after obtaining his undergraduate degree from Washington University in St. Louis and his master's degree in economics from the University of Sussex. Upon his graduation from law school, Professor Longan clerked for Bernard M. Decker, Senior United States District Judge for the Northern District of Illinois. He practiced law for seven years and became a full-time law teacher in 1991. In his academic career, Professor Longan has taught at Southern Methodist University School of Law, Stetson University College of Law, the University of Florida College of Law, Charleston School of Law, John Marshall (Atlanta) Law School, Georgia State University College of Law, and Mercer University School of Law. Professor Longan lives in Macon, Georgia with his wife, Gretchen.

Questions

Regulation of the Legal Profession

1. Lawyer appeared for a court hearing. Lawyer's Opposing Counsel, who was elderly, appeared at the hearing but was visibly confused. Opposing Counsel could not remember the facts of the case, the applicable law, or even his own client's name. Lawyer agreed with Opposing Counsel to postpone the hearing. This was the third time that Lawyer had interacted with Opposing Counsel on litigated matters and found Opposing Counsel to be utterly unable to discharge his duties to his clients because of confusion. Each time, Lawyer agreed to postpone the proceeding. Opposing Counsel was a solo practitioner. Lawyer suggested to Opposing Counsel that he should seek medical help and perhaps close or suspend his practice. Opposing Counsel refused and continued to represent clients. Lawyer's clients gave Lawyer informed consent to reveal all of this information to an appropriate professional authority. Lawyer decided not to do so and did not do so.

   Did Lawyer violate the Model Rules of Professional Conduct?

   (A) Yes, because Lawyer knew that Opposing Counsel was violating the rules of conduct by not withdrawing from the representation of his clients.

   (B) Yes, because Lawyer was obliged to report all misconduct of other lawyers to an appropriate professional authority.

   (C) No, because Lawyer had the option but not the duty to report the misconduct of Opposing Counsel.

   (D) No, because Lawyer did not know that Opposing Counsel had committed misconduct.

2. Lawyer was licensed only in State A. Lawyer went into State B to advise Client about a lawsuit that had been filed against Client in State B. At that time, Lawyer did not expect to be admitted pro hac vice in the case, but Lawyer's Supervisor (who was also licensed only in State A) reasonably expected to be admitted pro hac vice in the case against Client in State B. Lawyer did not regularly engage in any conduct in State B or hold herself out as being licensed in State B.

   Did Lawyer violate the Model Rules of Professional Conduct?

   (A) Yes, because Lawyer practiced law in a state where she was not licensed to do so.

   (B) Yes, because Lawyer did not expect to be admitted pro hac vice in Client's case in State B.

   (C) No, because Lawyer did not appear in court for Client in State B.

   (D) No, because Lawyer's Supervisor reasonably expected to be admitted pro hac vice in Client's case in State B.

3. At a cocktail party, Junior Associate heard Older Lawyer (in another firm) brag that Older Lawyer had withdrawn client funds from his firm's trust account and used the funds to pay the rent on the firm's office space. Junior Associate asked a friend at Older Lawyer's firm and confirmed that what Older Lawyer had said was true. Junior Associate went to her Supervisory Lawyer in her own firm. Junior Lawyer asked her Supervisory Lawyer whether she had to report Older Lawyer to the bar. Supervisory Lawyer said, "no—this was just one of those 'technical' violations of the rules that don't hurt anybody and that they don't teach you about in law school. You don't have to tell anybody." Junior Lawyer relied on Supervisory Lawyer's advice and did not report Older Lawyer to the bar. Older Lawyer's client eventually found out about the conversation at the cocktail party and filed grievances against Older Lawyer for taking the money and against Junior Associate for not reporting it.

   Did Junior Associate violate the Model Rules of Professional Conduct?

   (A) Yes, because Supervisory Lawyer's instructions were not a reasonable resolution of an arguable question of professional duty.

   (B) Yes, because Junior Associate relied on the advice of Supervisory Lawyer rather than exercising independent professional judgment.

   (C) No, because Junior Associate and Older Lawyer were not in the same firm.

   (D) No, because Junior Associate relied on the instructions of Supervisory Lawyer.

4. Lawyer was licensed only in State A. Lawyer specialized in negotiating contracts for baseball players who had been drafted by major league teams. Lawyer's first dozen baseball clients were players from State A. Lawyer's reputation grew, and recently, Lawyer was asked to represent Player in negotiations with a team in State B. Lawyer was not licensed in State B. Lawyer informed Player that Lawyer was not licensed in State B, and Player gave informed consent to Lawyer's representation in State B. Lawyer conducted negotiations with the general manager of this team over the phone, by email, and in person in State B. Lawyer successfully negotiated a contract for Player.

   Did Lawyer violate the Model Rules of Professional Conduct?

   (A) Yes, because Lawyer practiced law in a state where he was not licensed.

   (B) Yes, because Lawyer did not obtain pro hac vice admission to practice in State B.

   (C) No, because the temporary representation of a client in State B arose from Lawyer's practice in State A.

   (D) No, because Player gave informed consent to Lawyer's representation in State B.

5. Lawyer wanted to organize her practice in such as way as to maximize her profit. She decided to offer a "one-stop shop" for clients who needed her estate planning services and who also needed the services of her brother, a certified financial planner who was not a lawyer. Lawyer set up the firm as a professional corporation. She and her brother were the only shareholders. The shareholder agreement specified that Lawyer's brother would have no right

to control or direct Lawyer's judgment and that all fees from Lawyer's estate planning services would be strictly segregated, accounted for, and not shared directly or indirectly with her brother.

Did Lawyer violate the Model Rules of Professional Conduct?

(A) Yes, because Lawyer practiced law with a professional corporation in which a nonlawyer owned an interest.

(B) Yes, because Lawyer's firm offered non-legal services.

(C) No, because Lawyer's brother had no right to control or direct Lawyer's judgment.

(D) No, because Lawyer did not share her legal fees with a nonlawyer.

6. Bar Applicant completed his fitness questionnaire as part of the bar admission process. The questionnaire asked Bar Applicant to reveal in writing the date, place and circumstances of all arrests of Bar Applicant. In college, Bar Applicant had been arrested for aggravated assault at a college party. Bar Applicant actually committed the aggravated assault (it was caught on cell phone video), but Bar Applicant was intoxicated at the time. Bar Applicant completed a court diversion program and was granted "first offender" status in his state, which meant that there was no adjudication of guilt. Bar Applicant took this to mean that the record of his arrest and charge would be "expunged" and no one would be able to discern that he had ever been arrested or charged. In response to the question on the bar questionnaire regarding the date, place or circumstances of any arrest, Bar Applicant wrote: "None." Bar Applicant was admitted to the bar.

Is Bar Applicant subject to discipline by the bar?

(A) Yes, because Bar Applicant committed aggravated assault, a criminal act that reflected adversely on his fitness to practice law.

(B) Yes, because Bar Applicant knowingly made a false statement of material fact in connection with his bar application.

(C) No, because Bar Applicant was not a member of the bar at the time he completed the questionnaire.

(D) No, because Bar Applicant was never adjudicated guilty.

7. Lawyer represented Client against Corporation and alleged that Corporation had manufactured and distributed a dangerous drug. Client's case was the first of its kind, but the drug had been distributed to thousands of people. Through the litigation, Lawyer developed a unique knowledge of the drug and its dangers, as well as of how Corporation internally handled the development and distribution of the drug. In settlement negotiations with Corporation on behalf of Client, Lawyer offered to keep Client's recovery confidential and never to sue Corporation on behalf of another client who had taken this particular drug. In the end, the parties finalized a settlement that did not contain any limit on Lawyer's future representation of other clients but did contain the confidentiality clause.

Did Lawyer violate the Model Rules of Professional Conduct?

(A) Yes, because Lawyer agreed to keep the settlement amount confidential.

(B) Yes, because Lawyer offered to restrict his right to practice as part of the settlement of Client's case.

(C) No, because confidential settlements are permitted.

(D) No, because Lawyer merely offered but did not agree not to sue Corporation about the drug in the future.

8. Lawyer handled personal injury cases. In order to generate more business, Lawyer made an agreement with Podiatrist. Lawyer agreed to refer clients she had who were in need of podiatry to Podiatrist. In return, Podiatrist agreed to refer patients who needed a lawyer to Lawyer. Both parties agreed that the referral arrangement would not be exclusive, and Lawyer always informed her clients of the existence and nature of the referral agreement with Podiatrist. As additional incentive for Podiatrist to refer cases, Lawyer agreed to pay Podiatrist a "convenience fee" of 10% of the legal fees that Lawyer received as a result of representing clients referred by Podiatrist. Any clients in this category gave informed consent in writing to the fee for Podiatrist and to the amount, which came solely from Lawyer's contingent fee.

Did Lawyer violate the Model Rules of Professional Conduct?

(A) Yes, because Lawyer entered into a reciprocal referral arrangement with Podiatrist.

(B) Yes, because Lawyer shared legal fees with a nonlawyer.

(C) No, because all clients whose cases resulted in a sharing of the fee gave informed consent to the arrangement and the amount.

(D) No, because the referral agreement was not exclusive.

9. Lawyer was a solo practitioner. Lawyer used the same standard form engagement agreement with all of Lawyer's clients. That agreement provided that clients would be responsible for all reasonable and necessary out-of-pocket expenses that Lawyer incurred on behalf of clients. Lawyer employed Office Manager to handle the administrative operations of Lawyer's law office. To increase the profitability of the practice, Office Manager "marked up" by 10% the actual costs of expenses incurred on behalf of clients and billed clients for the larger amount without revealing the "mark up." Lawyer had provided no training to Office Manager regarding lawyer's professional responsibilities. Lawyer did not know that Office Manager "marked up" expenses until clients had been billed for inflated expenses for years. When Lawyer found out, Lawyer immediately fired Office Manager and stopped the practice of "marking up" expenses.

Did Lawyer violate the Model Rules of Professional Conduct?

(A) Yes, because Lawyer failed to properly train Office Manager to ensure that Office Manager's conduct was compatible with the professional obligations of Lawyer.

(B) Yes, because Lawyer was vicariously responsible for Office Manager's actions.

(C) No, because there was nothing improper about charging clients slightly more than the actual out of pocket expenses associated with the Clients' cases.

(D) No, because Lawyer did not know that Office Manager was charging clients more than the actual out-of-pocket cost for expenses.

10. Associate supervised Law Clerk in connection with a lawsuit for Client about a breach of contract. Associate was not a partner in the firm and had no managerial responsibility for the firm. Associate made reasonable efforts to ensure that Law Clerk's conduct was compatible with Associate's professional obligations. Despite those efforts, Law Clerk took it upon herself during discovery to delete a relevant, unprivileged but damaging email from Client's account so that the email would not have to be produced in response to an outstanding proper document request from the opposing party. Ten days later, Law Clerk told Associate what Law Clerk had done. Associate knew from experience with Client's email system that all messages in the "Deleted Items" folder would be permanently deleted from the system, and irretrievable, fourteen days after being deleted. Associate scolded Law Clerk for deleting the email but did not retrieve it before the email was deleted and became permanently irretrievable.

Is Associate vicariously liable, as a matter of discipline, for Law Clerk's conduct?

(A) Yes, because Associate was Law Clerk's supervisor.

(B) Yes, because Associate was Law Clerk's supervisor and had time to take remedial action but did not do so.

(C) No, because Associate was not a partner and did not have managerial authority in the firm.

(D) No, because Associate did not order Law Clerk to delete the email.

11. Law Firm decided to make some contingency plans in case one of the partners died unexpectedly. One of the partners suggested that part of the plan should be for Law Firm to pay to any deceased partner's estate the partner's share of the firm profits for a period of one year, as a type of self-insurance. Another partner raised the concern that Law Firm potentially would be sharing legal fees with a nonlawyer executor, in violation of the prohibition in the Model Rules of Professional Conduct on lawyers sharing legal fees with nonlawyers. Respond to this partner's concerns.

12. Lawyer needs help to deal with the volume of business that her practice is attracting. Lawyer has a law school Classmate who recently had the misfortune of being suspended from the practice of law for one year. During Classmate's period of suspension, Lawyer wishes to hire Classmate to interview and screen potential clients. Classmate offers also in those interviews to provide some preliminary basic advice for clients to follow before Lawyer has the chance to meet with them. Lawyer comes to you for advice about her professional responsibilities. How would you counsel Lawyer about this proposition?

13. Lawyer just graduated from law school and passed the bar. In a tough job market, Lawyer was able to secure a job offer from Law Firm, which has a highly specialized practice. Law Firm offered Lawyer a position as an associate and offered to train associate in its highly specialized

field of law. In conjunction with the training, Law Firm also offered to introduce Lawyer to the small set of clients who use Law Firm's highly specialized services. In exchange for the training and the introductions, Law Firm has asked Lawyer to agree not to compete in its locality for a period of six months if Lawyer left Law Firm in the first three years. How must Lawyer respond to this offer?

14. Lawyer's business plan for her practice is to advertise extensively in order to represent large numbers of persons who have been hurt in car accidents. Lawyer anticipates that most of the clients who will respond to her advertising are clients whose claims are not large. Lawyer believes that she will be able to build a profitable firm based upon a high volume of low value cases, but the economics of the practice will work only if Lawyer employs a large number of paralegals to draft pleadings, gather information from clients, and convey settlement offers to and from clients and insurance companies. What must Lawyer do to make sure that in executing this business plan she is complying with her responsibilities under the Model Rules of Professional Conduct?

The Client-Lawyer Relationship

15. Lawyer represented Client, a doctor who had been fired by Hospital. Doctor sued Hospital and alleged that her termination was wrongful. Lawyer consulted with Client about how many depositions to take. Lawyer and Client agreed that Lawyer would take the deposition of every member of Hospital's staff without having to consult with Client about each one. Once Client saw how much this strategy cost and how much it antagonized members of the staff, Client told Lawyer not to take any more depositions of staff members without talking to Client first. Lawyer continued to take the depositions of the staff members.

    Did Lawyer violate the Model Rules of Professional Conduct?

    (A) Yes, because Lawyer did not consult with Client about the cost of each deposition of a staff member.

    (B) Yes, because Client revoked Lawyer's authority to take the depositions of all the staff members without consultation.

    (C) No, because Client gave Lawyer the authority to take the depositions of the staff members without consultation.

    (D) No, because Lawyer had the professional discretion to decide how many depositions to take.

16. Lawyer represented Defendant in a criminal case. Defendant expressed to Lawyer a desire to testify. Lawyer reasonably believed, but did not know, that the proposed testimony would be false. In Lawyer's professional judgment, presenting such testimony would not be an effective means of achieving Defendant's objective (acquittal). Lawyer firmly believed that Defendant should not testify. Lawyer consulted with Defendant about the wisdom of testifying, particularly in light of the implausibility of the proposed testimony and Defendant's extensive criminal record. Despite Lawyer's best efforts, Defendant insisted on testifying. Lawyer concluded that he had no choice but to put Defendant on the witness stand. Defendant testified and was convicted.

    Was Lawyer's conclusion that he had no choice correct under the Model Rules of Professional Conduct?

    (A) Yes, because the client was a criminal defendant.

    (B) Yes, because the decision whether to testify always belongs to the client.

    (C) No, because Lawyer reasonably believed that Defendant would testify falsely.

    (D) No, because Lawyer's professional judgment was that testifying would not be an effective means of achieving Defendant's objectives.

17. Lawyer represented Daughter in connection with her divorce from Son-in-Law. Daughter's Father agreed to pay Lawyer to represent Daughter. The fee agreement was that Father would pay Lawyer a cash fee equal to 33% of the value of the property that Daughter would receive in the divorce (the Daughter would keep 100% of the property, and the fee would be paid separately by Father). Daughter gave informed consent to this arrangement, and Lawyer and Father agreed that Father would not interfere with Lawyer's attorney-client relationship with Daughter or with Lawyer's professional judgment. Lawyer and Father agreed further that Lawyer would protect Daughter's confidential information, even from Father.

Did the fee agreement conform to the Model Rules of Professional Conduct?

(A) Yes, because the agreement protected Daughter's confidential information and Lawyer's independent professional judgment.

(B) Yes, because Daughter gave informed consent to the agreement.

(C) No, because Lawyer agreed to accept payment of a fee from someone other than the client.

(D) No, because Lawyer agreed to accept a contingent fee in a divorce case.

18. Client was charged with murder. Client asked Lawyer to represent Client but could not pay Lawyer's fee in cash. Client met with Lawyer and offered in writing to convey a penthouse condominium to Lawyer as payment of the fee. Lawyer immediately accepted that offer and signed the written agreement. The market value of the condo was less than the amount that would have been a reasonable fee for Lawyer to charge under the circumstances.

Did Lawyer violate the Model Rules of Professional Conduct?

(A) Yes, because Lawyer did not give Client the opportunity to seek the advice of independent counsel before entering into the fee agreement.

(B) Yes, because Lawyer accepted property in payment of a legal fee.

(C) No, because the fee, measured by the market value of the property conveyed, was reasonable.

(D) No, because Client agreed to the transaction.

19. Lawyer represented Father in a divorce action against Mother. Father told Lawyer that it would be a good strategy to seek custody of the young children that Father had with Mother, primarily as a "bargaining chip" to use in negotiations over a financial settlement. Father wanted custody and had a legal right to seek it but did not have any significant chance of winning it. Lawyer fundamentally disagreed with Father about whether this would be a good strategy. The strategy also was repugnant to Lawyer because of the effects a custody fight could have on the children. Lawyer explained Lawyer's objections to Father. Father insisted on the strategy. Lawyer followed Father's instructions and sought custody of the children on Father's behalf.

Did Lawyer violate the Model Rules of Professional Conduct?

(A) Yes, because Lawyer was required to seek to withdraw once it became clear that Lawyer and Father had a fundamental disagreement over strategy.

(B) Yes, because Lawyer assisted with an action that Lawyer found to be repugnant.

(C) No, because Lawyer consulted with Father about the strategy.

(D) No, because decisions about means that might adversely affect third persons belong exclusively to clients.

20. Real Estate Lawyer was asked by Client to file a personal injury case. Real Estate Lawyer referred the case to Trial Lawyer, who practiced in a different firm. The two lawyers made a written agreement to split the fee for the personal injury case evenly between the two of them. The total fee was reasonable. Real Estate Lawyer agreed to be jointly responsible for the representation but agreed not to do any work on the case. Client agreed to the sharing of the fees, although Client was not advised that the split would be even between the two lawyers.

Did the fee-sharing arrangement conform to the Model Rules of Professional Conduct?

(A) Yes, because the lawyers agreed to be jointly responsible for the case.

(B) Yes, because Client consented to the sharing of the fee.

(C) No, because the lawyers did not share the fee in proportion to the work performed.

(D) No, because Client was not advised of the share that each lawyer would receive.

21. Lawyer represented Plaintiff in a civil case in which Lawyer and Plaintiff had agreed to a contingent fee. In the fee contract, Plaintiff and Lawyer agreed that Lawyer would advance all of the expenses of the case, including filing fees, court reporter fees, and expert witness fees, and that Plaintiff's responsibility to reimburse Lawyer was contingent upon a recovery by the Plaintiff by judgment or settlement. Without consulting with Client, Lawyer hired an expert witness. Lawyer paid the expert's fee. When the case settled, Plaintiff objected to reimbursing Lawyer for the expert's fee out of the settlement proceeds. Plaintiff claimed that Lawyer violated the Model Rules of Professional Conduct by hiring the expert under these circumstances.

Did Lawyer violate the Model Rules of Professional Conduct?

(A) Yes, because Lawyer did not consult with Client about retaining the expert.

(B) Yes, because Lawyer provided improper financial assistance to Plaintiff in connection with the case.

(C) No, because hiring the expert was a matter of professional judgment that belonged to Lawyer.

(D) No, because Lawyer was permitted to advance expenses and make repayment contingent upon the outcome of the case.

22. Client was injured at work and retained Lawyer. Lawyer and Client agreed that Lawyer would represent Client only in connection with Client's worker's compensation claim. The limit on

the scope of the representation was reasonable, and Client gave informed consent to it. In the course of representing Client on the worker's compensation claim, Lawyer learned that Client's objective was to maximize Client's financial recovery for injuries Client sustained at work. In the course of representing Client, Lawyer also learned of possible causes of action in tort that Client might pursue for the same injuries. Those claims were outside Lawyer's area of practice and expertise and outside the limited scope of Lawyer's representation of Client. Lawyer did not tell Client about those possible causes of action.

Did Lawyer violate the Model Rules of Professional Conduct?

(A) Yes, because Lawyer limited the scope of his representation of the client.

(B) Yes, because Lawyer had a duty of communication to reveal information relating to the client's known objectives.

(C) No, because the information was not relevant to any matter within the limited scope of the representation.

(D) No, because the limit on the scope of representation was reasonable and the client gave informed consent.

23. Lawyer represented Client in a civil case. After years of litigation and months of negotiation, Client agreed to a settlement with Opposing Party. One part of that settlement was a Clause that Client fought hard to keep out of the settlement. Opposing Party kept insisting on the Clause and would not settle without it. Eventually, Client very reluctantly agreed to the Clause. Counsel for Opposing Party sent Lawyer a copy of the settlement agreement that Opposing Party had signed and asked for Client's signature on the agreement to finalize the settlement. Lawyer reviewed the settlement agreement carefully and determined that the Clause had been inadvertently omitted from the settlement agreement by counsel for Opposing Party. Without consulting Client, Lawyer informed counsel for Opposing Party of the omission.

Did Lawyer violate the Model Rules of Professional Conduct?

(A) Yes, because Lawyer violated his duty of communication with Client.

(B) Yes, because Lawyer violated his duty of loyalty to Client.

(C) No, because Lawyer owed a duty of civility and cooperation to counsel for Opposing Party.

(D) No, because Client had already agreed to the Clause.

24. Lawyer had three clients in personal injury cases, each of whom agreed to compensate Lawyer on an hourly basis at the rate of $200 per hour. Lawyer attended a court calendar call that lasted four hours. The cases for all three clients were on the docket for the calendar call. The judge required Lawyer to be present at the beginning of the calendar call, but it just so happened that the judge placed all three of Lawyer's cases at the very end of the four-hour period. Lawyer, therefore, was required by the judge to be present for the entire four-hour calendar call on behalf of each of her three clients. Lawyer billed each of the three clients $800 for the four hours that Lawyer necessarily spent attending the calendar call, for a total of $2400. None of the clients paid Lawyer's bills.

Did Lawyer violate the Model Rules of Professional Conduct?

(A) Yes, because Lawyer did not earn twelve billable hours.

(B) Yes, because Lawyer billed on an hourly basis for personal injury cases.

(C) No, because the clients did not pay Lawyer's bills.

(D) No, because Lawyer had to be present for the calendar call for the benefit of all three clients.

25. Lawyer represented Client One and Client Two in two unrelated transactional matters. In the course of representing Client Two, Lawyer learned information that Client One needed in order to make an informed decision regarding the matter for which Client One had engaged Lawyer. Lawyer sought the informed consent of Client Two to the revelation of this information to Client One. Client Two refused to consent. Lawyer withdrew from representing Client One but continued to represent Client Two.

Did Lawyer violate the Model Rules of Professional Conduct?

(A) Yes, because Lawyer continued to represent Client Two.

(B) Yes, because Lawyer violated Lawyer's duty of communication with Client One.

(C) No, because Lawyer had the option to withdraw from representing Client One.

(D) No, because Lawyer was required to withdraw from representing Client One.

26. Lawyer assisted Client with a series of transactions and prepared and delivered to Client the documents necessary to complete another similar transaction with Buyer. Lawyer then learned that all of the transactions, including the one that had not yet closed, were part of an elaborate fraud perpetrated by Client with Lawyer's (heretofore unknown) assistance. Lawyer withdrew from representing Client and sought Client's permission to reveal the fraud to Buyer before Buyer closed the next transaction. Client refused to give informed consent to this revelation. Lawyer gave notice to Buyer of Lawyer's withdrawal and disaffirmed the documents. Buyer withdrew from the transaction. Client filed a grievance and alleged that Lawyer had violated the Model Rules of Professional Conduct.

Did Lawyer violate the Model Rules of Professional Conduct?

(A) Yes, because Lawyer did not reveal to Buyer that the transaction was a fraud.

(B) Yes, because Lawyer gave Buyer notice of Lawyer's withdrawal and disaffirmed the documents necessary for the transaction.

(C) No, because Lawyer had the option but not the duty to reveal that the transaction was a fraud.

(D) No, because Lawyer was required to withdraw as soon as Lawyer knew that the earlier transactions had been fraudulent.

27. Lawyer represented Client, who was a defendant in a serious criminal matter. Prosecutor presented a plea offer to Lawyer under which Client would plead guilty to one charge and Pros-

ecutor would dismiss all other charges. Under the deal, Client would serve a prison sentence of 10 years and would serve an additional 10 years on probation. If Client went to trial and was convicted, Client faced life in prison. Lawyer promptly conveyed the plea offer to Client. Lawyer and Client had not discussed what an acceptable plea bargain would be. When Client asked Lawyer what Client should do, Lawyer responded that this decision belonged only to Client and that Lawyer's job was to convey the offer. Client went to trial, was convicted, and was sentenced to life in prison.

Did Lawyer violate the Model Rules of Professional Conduct?

(A) Yes, because Lawyer did not accept the plea offer on behalf of Client.

(B) Yes, because Lawyer did not consult with Client about the plea offer.

(C) No, because Lawyer promptly conveyed the plea offer to Client.

(D) No, because the decision to reject the plea offer belonged solely to Client.

28. Lawyer represented Client under a written contingent fee contract that initially complied in every respect with the Model Rules of Professional Conduct. After years of litigation, on the eve of trial, Lawyer received a settlement offer from the opposing party and recommended strongly that Client accept it. Client refused to do so. Because Lawyer believed that the settlement offer was good, and because Lawyer feared the prospect of losing at trial and receiving no fee for years of effort, Lawyer proposed that Client agree instead to compensate Lawyer on an hourly basis for all hours the Lawyer had spent and would spend at trial. Lawyer threatened to withdraw as counsel if Client did not agree to this arrangement. Client agreed, but after trial, Client refused to pay Lawyer's hourly fees.

Was the revised fee agreement enforceable against Client?

(A) Yes, because Client agreed to it.

(B) Yes, because Client declined a reasonable settlement offer.

(C) No, because the revised fee agreement changed the basis of Lawyer's fee.

(D) No, because Client agreed to the revised fee agreement under duress.

29. Lawyer represented Client, who was a defendant in a criminal case. Client told Lawyer that Client would not plead guilty under any circumstances and that Client wanted only to have his fate decided "by a jury of my peers." At a pretrial conference at which Client was not present, the judge presiding over the case asked whether Client would agree to a bench trial. Without consulting with Client, Lawyer told the judge immediately that Client would not agree to waive jury trial and that Client insisted on having his fate decided by a jury of his peers.

Did Lawyer violate the Model Rules of Professional Conduct?

(A) Yes, because the decision to waive a jury trial belonged to Client.

(B) Yes, because Lawyer failed to communicate with Client about the judge's inquiry.

(C) No, because the decision to waive a jury trial or not was a tactical decision that belonged to Lawyer.

(D) No, because Client had already instructed Lawyer not to waive a jury trial.

30. Lawyer represented Client in connection with the promotion of a series of oil and gas exploration joint ventures. Lawyer prepared the required disclosures for Client, who then presented the disclosures along with a sales pitch to potential investors. Client obtained many investors and millions of dollars through this process. Lawyer formed a reasonable belief that Client was defrauding all of these investors. Lawyer did not, however, know whether the transactions were fraudulent. Lawyer assisted with several more of the transactions but then withdrew from representing Client in connection with them.

Did Lawyer violate the Model Rules of Professional Conduct?

(A) Yes, because Lawyer assisted with transactions that lawyer reasonably believed to be fraudulent.

(B) Yes, because Lawyer had neither the duty nor the option to withdraw under these circumstances.

(C) No, because Lawyer had the option but not the duty to withdraw under these circumstances.

(D) No, because Lawyer had the duty to withdraw under these circumstances.

31. Lawyer represented Client, a plaintiff in a personal injury case. Client was unable to work because of her injuries. Client had young children and no source of income. Client faced eviction. Lawyer firmly believed that Client eventually would recover, by settlement or judgment, a very substantial sum in the case. The insurance company for the defendant knew about Client's financial problems and sent Lawyer a settlement offer that was much less than what Lawyer reasonably expected Client to recover if the case had gone forward. Lawyer feared that Client would accept the low offer of settlement in order to avoid eviction. Lawyer conveyed the settlement offer to Client but assisted Client by guaranteeing a bank loan to Client from which Client was able to pay her rent and other living expenses until a better offer was received. Did Lawyer violate the Model Rules of Professional Conduct?

32. Estate Lawyer represents Husband and Wife in connection with the preparation of wills for each client respectively. In a meeting with Lawyer, Husband and Wife each agree to leave his or her estate entirely to the other. While Estate Lawyer is drafting the wills, Estate Lawyer receives a call from Husband instructing Estate Lawyer to change the terms of Husband's will to leave Husband's estate to Husband's mistress, about whom Wife knows nothing. Husband instructs Lawyer not to reveal this change to Wife. Estate Lawyer is unable to change Husband's mind. May Estate Lawyer do as Husband instructs?

33. Lawyer received a voicemail from a regular Client, who left a detailed message about Client's latest proposed business venture. Client was asking Lawyer for assistance in putting the venture together. Lawyer recognized immediately that what Client wanted to do, and what Client wanted Lawyer's help with, was a crime in their state. Lawyer called Client back and discussed

the proposed venture. Lawyer explained why the venture would be a crime and explained that Lawyer could not help put it together. Lawyer declined to help Client with the venture. Did Lawyer comply with the Model Rules of Professional Conduct?

34. Lawyer first represented Client in a small civil suit. About six months after that case settled, Lawyer represented Client in connection with the sale of Client's business. Two months after the sale closed, Client was arrested for driving under the influence, and Lawyer represented Client in connection with that matter. A year passed. Client hired Lawyer to pursue collection of a debt for Client. That matter took more than a year. When it ended, five months passed before Client called again, this time to ask Lawyer to handle Client's divorce. Lawyer did so. Four months have passed since that matter ended. Lawyer has no open matters for Client. Neither Client nor Lawyer ever discussed or documented the beginning or end of their attorney-client relationship. Now Lawyer has been asked to file suit against Client for a new client. The new suit would be unrelated to anything Lawyer has ever handled for Client. Lawyer believes she can accept this case because Client is now a former client, and the new matter is not substantially related to anything Lawyer did for Client. Client protests that Lawyer is currently Client's lawyer and therefore cannot sue Client on any matter, even an unrelated one, without informed consent. Who is right?

35. Lawyer represented Corporation in a case in which Plaintiff had sued Corporation for $100,000,000 in damages. Such a judgment would have bankrupted Corporation. Lawyer and Corporation reasonably anticipated that the case would take years to litigate and that the result was uncertain. Lawyer and Client agreed that, if Plaintiff prevailed, the $100,000,000 prayer for relief was not unreasonable. Corporation had cash flow issues that made payment of Lawyer's hourly rate throughout the pendency of the case a problem. Lawyer and Client agreed in writing that Corporation would pay Lawyer a contingent fee of 10% of the difference between $100,000,000 and the amount of the final judgment. After several years of litigation, Lawyer obtained a summary judgment for corporation and billed Client for $10,000,000, 10% of the difference between $100,000,000 and zero. Corporation refused to pay Lawyer's contingent fee and claimed that the contract between Lawyer and Corporation was illegal under the Model Rules of Professional Conduct because it called for a "reverse" contingent fee. Did the contract between Lawyer and Corporation violate the Model Rules of Professional Conduct for that reason?

Client Confidentiality

36. Lawyer represented Client, who was charged with murder. In the course of investigating the case, Lawyer came upon information from a witness that Client had committed the murder. The police did not find this witness and dismissed the charges against Client. Lawyer's attorney-client relationship with Client ended. Later, a person other than Client was wrongfully convicted of the murder and sentenced to death. The sentence was to be carried out within days. Lawyer asked Client (now a former client) for permission to reveal what Lawyer had learned about the Client's involvement in the murder because Lawyer reasonably believed that an innocent person would be killed if the information were not revealed. Client refused. Lawyer nevertheless revealed the information to the district attorney. The execution was delayed, and eventually the wrongfully convicted person was exonerated.

    Did Lawyer violate the Model Rules of Professional Conduct?

    (A) Yes, because Lawyer revealed privileged information.

    (B) Yes, because Lawyer revealed confidential information without authorization to do so.

    (C) No, because Lawyer reasonably believed that revealing the information was reasonably necessary in order to prevent the death of the person who had been wrongfully convicted.

    (D) No, because the attorney-client relationship had ended when Lawyer revealed the information.

37. Lawyer represented Client, an elderly man who resided in a nursing home. Lawyer reasonably believed that Client had diminished mental capacity. Client's primary caregiver, an employee of a local nursing service, told Lawyer that Client wanted to leave the caregiver a significant bequest. Client had grown children who had always been close to Client and visited him often in the nursing home. Lawyer asked Client about the bequest, and Client instructed Lawyer to revise his will to include the bequest to the caregiver and not to reveal the new will to the children. Lawyer reasonably concluded from these events that Client could not protect himself and was at substantial risk of financial harm from the caregiver. Lawyer determined that revealing the information would be in Client's best interests and told Client's children about the impairment and the instructions to prepare a new will. The children went to court to obtain the appointment of a guardian for Client.

    Did Lawyer violate the Model Rules of Professional Conduct?

    (A) Yes, because Lawyer revealed confidential information to the children despite Client's instructions.

(B) Yes, because Lawyer revealed privileged information to the children despite Client's instructions.

(C) No, because Lawyer determined that revelation of the information was in Client's best interests.

(D) No, because Lawyer was impliedly authorized to reveal the information to the children.

38. Acme Insurance Co. hired Lawyer to represent one of its policyholders in the defense of a claim about a catastrophic automobile accident. In Lawyer's jurisdiction, a lawyer who was hired by an insurance company to represent an insured represented only the insured and not the insurance company. As to Lawyer, the insurance company was merely a third-party payor of Lawyer's fees. The policyholder (Client) told Lawyer that the accident occurred while the policyholder's employee was on a personal errand (a detour) while he was conducting business for Client. Lawyer knew that this fact meant that Client was using Lawyer's services in an attempt to perpetrate insurance fraud by getting the Acme Insurance Company to pay a claim for which it was not contractually liable. Without seeking the consent of Client, Lawyer made a motion to withdraw as counsel for Client and informed Acme Insurance Company that the accident occurred while Client's employee was on a personal errand rather than conducting business for Client.

Did Lawyer violate the Model Rules of Professional Conduct?

(A) Yes, because Lawyer revealed information relating to the representation without Client's consent.

(B) Yes, because Lawyer sought to withdraw as counsel for Client.

(C) No, because the Acme Insurance Company was paying Lawyer's fees.

(D) No, because Lawyer revealed information to prevent Client from using Lawyer's services to perpetrate a fraud that would cause substantial financial injury to the insurance company.

39. Client retained Lawyer to defend Client on criminal charges of assault. Client told Lawyer that Client was addicted to opiates and as a result did not recall the events that led to the charge of assault. Lawyer told Lawyer's Associate (a full-time employee in Lawyer's firm) that Client was addicted to opiates. Associate performed legal research to determine whether being under the influence of opiates might be a defense to the charge of assault.

Did Lawyer violate Lawyer's duty of confidentiality under the Model Rules of Professional Conduct by telling Associate that Client was addicted to opiates?

(A) Yes, because the information was protected by the attorney-client privilege.

(B) Yes, because Lawyer did not obtain informed consent of Client.

(C) No, because the Associate was a privileged person for purposes of the attorney-client privilege.

(D) No, because Lawyer was impliedly authorized to share that information with Associate.

40. Lawyer represented Client in connection with Client's divorce. During the representation, Client told Lawyer that Client planned to kill her husband after the divorce was final. Lawyer reasonably believed that Client was serious and that Client had the means to carry out the threat, but Lawyer did not reveal the threat to anyone. Once the divorce became final, Lawyer's attorney-client relationship with Client ended. Lawyer still did not reveal the threat to anyone. Client then killed her ex-husband.

Did Lawyer violate the Model Rules of Professional Conduct?

(A) Yes, because Lawyer had the duty to reveal confidential information to prevent the death of another.

(B) Yes, because Lawyer was no longer bound to keep the threat confidential once the attorney-client relationship ended.

(C) No, because Lawyer had the option but not the duty to reveal the threat.

(D) No, because Lawyer had no choice but to keep the threat confidential.

41. Lawyer undertook to represent Sleazy Client in connection with certain real estate development deals. In the course of preparing the necessary documents, Lawyer discovered that Sleazy Client defrauded Buyer in a recent transaction that was handled by another lawyer. That earlier deal had closed, but not all of the money had been paid by Buyer. Lawyer revealed the fraud to Buyer, who promptly refused to make the remaining payment to Sleazy Client.

Did Lawyer violate the Model Rules of Professional Conduct?

(A) Yes, because the only harm that Buyer would have suffered was financial.

(B) Yes, because Lawyer's services were not used in connection with the fraud.

(C) No, because the information that Lawyer revealed related to a time before Lawyer represented Sleazy Client.

(D) No, because disclosure was reasonably necessary to prevent further financial harm to Buyer from the fraud.

42. Lawyer represented Client in connection with the development of a planned community for the elderly. In the course of that representation, Lawyer was investigating whether Client had sufficient assets to secure bank financing for the project. Lawyer learned that Client owned a tract of vacant land on which Client had separate (but still secret) plans to build an indoor shopping mall. The shopping mall project was outside the scope of Lawyer's representation of Client. Lawyer's representation of Client ended when the project for the planned community was over. Lawyer then purchased for himself a tract of land adjacent to the proposed shopping mall, because Lawyer knew that Client would need that land for parking spaces for the mall. Lawyer then sold that land to Client (now a former client) and made a sizeable profit on the sale.

Did Lawyer violate the Model Rules of Professional Conduct?

(A) Yes, because Lawyer entered into a business transaction with a former client.

(B) Yes, because Lawyer used confidential information of Client to the disadvantage of Client.

(C) No, because lawyer's duty of confidentiality ended when Lawyer's attorney-client relationship with Client ended.

(D) No, because the information about the mall concerned a matter that was outside the scope of Lawyer's representation of Client.

43. Lawyer met with Elderly Client about estate planning. Elderly Client's Son attended the meeting in order to help Elderly Client understand what Lawyer was saying about the estate plan. Given the state of Elderly Client's health, Son's participation in the meeting was necessary and helpful. Later, Elderly Client's Daughter filed a civil suit to have a guardian appointed for Elderly Client. Elderly Client testified about the terms of Elderly Client's will and was asked what was said between Lawyer and Elderly Client in the estate-planning meeting. Elderly Client refused to answer on the basis of attorney-client privilege. Daughter claimed that Son's presence in the meeting negated any claim of privilege. The judge ruled that Elderly Client could refuse to answer.

Was the judge correct on the basis of the attorney-client privilege?

(A) Yes, because Son was present to assist Elderly Client communicate with Lawyer.

(B) Yes, because Son was present with the permission of Elderly Client.

(C) No, because Son's presence meant that the communications between Lawyer and Elderly Client were not made in confidence.

(D) No, because Son was not a privileged person for purposes of the attorney client privilege.

44. Lawyer regularly represented Railroad in connection with accidents at railroad crossings. One of railroad's trains struck Plaintiff's car at a rural crossing. Lawyer's investigator immediately went to the scene and took numerous photographs, including photos that accurately depicted the proximity of a stand of trees to the crossing (and therefore accurately depicted Plaintiff's limited sight line, something that would be important in any litigation over the accident). Plaintiff later sued Railroad about the accident. By then, the stand of trees had been harvested. Plaintiff sought discovery of the photographs taken by Lawyer's investigator immediately after the accident. Lawyer resisted on the basis of the work product doctrine. The judge issued a protective order to protect against production of the photos because, the judge concluded, they were work product.

Was the judge correct to issue a protective order to prevent discovery of the photos?

(A) Yes, because the photos were taken in anticipation of litigation.

(B) Yes, because the photos contained Lawyer's mental impressions.

(C) No, because the photos were important evidence that Plaintiff could not obtain otherwise.

(D) No, because the photos were taken by Lawyer's investigator rather than Lawyer.

45. Lawyer specialized in representing plaintiffs in suits against their employers for employment discrimination. Lawyer and Client met and entered into an attorney-client relationship with the objective of pursuing such a case against Plaintiff's Employer. Lawyer received a long email from Plaintiff's work email address setting forth the factual bases for Plaintiff's claims of discrimination and asking several questions that revealed the substance of advice that Lawyer had given Plaintiff face-to-face. Lawyer responded directly to Plaintiff's email. More such email exchanges followed. Lawyer treated all communications with Plaintiff as confidential. The emails were unencrypted. Consistent with its corporate policy regarding email, Employer accessed Plaintiff's work email account and obtained all of Plaintiff's emails back and forth with Lawyer. Employer defeated Plaintiff's claim of employment discrimination.

Did Lawyer violate the Model Rules of Professional Conduct?

(A) Yes, because Lawyer used unencrypted email to communicate with Client about her case.

(B) Yes, because Lawyer did not advise Client not to use her work email for communications with Lawyer about the case.

(C) No, because Lawyer did not reveal any information that related to the representation of Client.

(D) No, because Lawyer and Client had a reasonable expectation of privacy when they communicated by email.

46. Lawyer represented Client in a divorce action. At the conclusion of the case, Client was very unhappy with the result and with Lawyer's representation. Client filed a grievance with the state bar disciplinary board and alleged the Lawyer violated several rules of conduct. Under the state bar disciplinary board's procedures, no disciplinary case commences until a lawyer has an opportunity to respond to a grievance and the disciplinary board investigates it. In response to Client's grievance, Lawyer wrote a detailed letter to the disciplinary board in which Lawyer defended herself by revealing information relating to the representation of Client.

Did Lawyer violate the Model Rules of Professional Conduct?

(A) Yes, because Client did not give informed consent to the revelation of Client's confidential information.

(B) Yes, because no disciplinary proceeding had begun.

(C) No, because the disclosures were impliedly authorized.

(D) No, because Lawyer was responding to allegations concerning Lawyer's representation of Client.

47. Lawyer represented Client is a high-profile criminal case. In the course of investigating the matter, Lawyer came upon evidence that caused Lawyer to form a reasonable belief that Client's planned testimony at the trial would be false. Lawyer called Ethics Professor and told Ethics Professor what Lawyer had learned and what Client planned to testify to at trial. Lawyer asked Ethics Professor whether Lawyer would be violating the rules of conduct by offering

Client's testimony in light of what Lawyer had learned while investigating the matter. Did Lawyer violate the Model Rules of Professional Conduct?

48. Lawyer represented Corporation as outside counsel. Lawyer did not represent any employees or officers of Corporation personally. Corporation's General Counsel told Lawyer confidentially that the Occupational Health and Safety Administration (OSHA) was investigating Corporation. General Counsel told Lawyer the particular concerns of OSHA and instructed Lawyer to conduct a parallel investigation. Lawyer interviewed employees to determine whether anyone was engaged in any violations of health and safety regulations. To further his investigation, Lawyer told the employees about the kinds of heath and safety concerns that General Counsel had described to Lawyer. Did Lawyer violate his duty of confidentiality by doing so?

49. Lawyer represented Client, a prominent elected official. Client told Lawyer privately that some associates of Client had been arrested and that these associates had damaging information about Client. Lawyer and Client discussed whether Client could raise sufficient funds to bail out Client's associates and to "take care of" Client's associates through and beyond the case for which they had been arrested. Lawyer and Client discussed the logistics of collecting sufficient funds and paying them to Client's associates in exchange for a promise by the associates not to reveal to law enforcement any damaging information about Client. Assume that paying a witness not to talk to law enforcement is obstruction of justice, a crime. Lawyer is called to testify before a grand jury and is asked to reveal the content of Lawyer's conversation with Client, as just described. Lawyer invokes the attorney-client privilege. Is Lawyer's discussion with Client protected by the attorney-client privilege?

Conflicts of Interest

50. Lawyer commenced a consensual sexual relationship with Paralegal, who at the time was a married man. Paralegal decided to seek a divorce, and Lawyer agreed to represent Paralegal in connection with the divorce. Throughout Lawyer's representation of Paralegal, their sexual relationship continued. Lawyer never sought Paralegal's consent to any possible conflict of interest.

    Did Lawyer violate the Model Rules of Professional Conduct?

    (A) Yes, because Lawyer represented Paralegal despite a conflict of interest to which Paralegal had not given informed consent.

    (B) Yes, because Lawyer continued a preexisting sexual relationship with Paralegal during the representation.

    (C) No, because the sexual relationship between Lawyer and Paralegal predated the commencement of the attorney-client relationship.

    (D) No, because the sexual relationship between Lawyer and Paralegal was consensual.

51. Law Firm represents a defendant in a personal injury case. Law Firm wants to hire an associate who works for the firm that represents the plaintiff in that case. The associate has not worked on the case or otherwise acquired any confidential information about the case. If necessary, Law Firm is ready, willing and able to screen the associate from any involvement in the case if the associate joins Law Firm. The plaintiff will not consent to any conflict of interest that might be created by the associate switching firms in the midst of the litigation.

    May Law Firm hire the associate and continue to represent the defendant, consistent with the Model Rules of Professional Conduct?

    (A) Yes, because the associate will not bring a conflict of interest when he joins the firm.

    (B) Yes, because Law Firm can screen the associate from any involvement in the matter.

    (C) No, because the associate will bring a conflict of interest into the firm, and that conflict will be imputed to other members of the firm.

    (D) No, because the associate would be switching sides in the case.

52. Lawyer represented Client A in connection with a personal injury case that settled. The lawyer notified Client A that, upon completion and signing of the settlement documents, the attorney-client relationship between them terminated. A year later, Lawyer was asked to represent Client B against Client A in connection with a will contest. Client A was a named beneficiary

in a will that Client B claimed was signed only because of Client A's undue influence over the testator. Lawyer undertook the representation of Client B and sued Client A.

Did Lawyer violate the Model Rules of Professional Conduct?

(A) Yes, because Lawyer learned confidential information about Client A while serving as Client A's attorney.

(B) Yes, because Lawyer sued his former client without informed consent.

(C) No, because the two matters were not substantially related.

(D) No, because Client A was a former client of Lawyer and not a current client.

53. Lawyer is asked by Client #1, Client #2, and Client #3 to represent all of them in connection with the formation of a joint venture. Client #1 will be financing the venture, while Client #2 brings management expertise. Client #3 is the salesman. The clients ask Lawyer to advise all of them about the best way to structure the business. The scope of the representation would include the negotiation of shares of ownership, dissolution rights, buyout provisions, and salary and benefits for each of them. The clients are prepared to give Lawyer informed consent to the joint representation, and relations among the clients are amicable.

May Lawyer undertake the joint representation of Client #1, Client #2 and Client #3?

(A) Yes, because all three clients are prepared to give informed consent to Lawyer's conflict of interest.

(B) Yes, because there is only a potential for a conflict of interest and not an actual conflict of interest.

(C) No, because Lawyer would have a conflict of interest and would have to withdraw from representing all three clients if disputes arise among them later.

(D) No, because the conflict is not consentable.

54. Lawyer was asked to represent Defendant One and Defendant Two in connection with the killing of Victim. Defendant One and Defendant Two allegedly were robbing Victim at gunpoint when Defendant One shot and killed Victim. Defendant One had a long record of violent felonies. Defendant Two had no criminal record and was much younger than Defendant One. Defendant One was charged with malice (intentional) murder, and Defendant Two was charged with felony murder (because the Victim died during the commission of a felony in which Defendant Two participated). Lawyer obtained informed consent of both clients to represent both of them despite the risk that his representation of one might materially limit his representation of the other. Prosecutor made a motion to disqualify Lawyer, and the trial court granted the motion.

Did the trial court err when it granted Prosecutor's motion to disqualify defense counsel?

(A) Yes, because Prosecutor did not have standing to complain about Lawyer's alleged conflict of interest.

(B) Yes, because Defendant One and Defendant Two consented to the dual representation.

(C) No, because one lawyer may not represent two criminal co-defendants.

(D) No, because the dual representation raised a serious potential for conflict.

55. Lawyer is asked to represent Client in a notorious criminal case. Client has no money but does own a valuable home. Also, the literary rights to Client's story may eventually be worth millions. Client proposes to give Lawyer a promissory note for the lawyer's reasonable fee, with the proviso that the note will be secured by a lien on Client's home and by an assignment of any compensation Client receives for the literary rights to the story of Client's prosecution, up to the value of the reasonable fee. Client is independently represented in connection with the fee contract.

May Lawyer agree to this proposal?

(A) Yes, because the fee is reasonable.

(B) Yes, because Client is being independently represented in connection with the fee contract.

(C) No, because Lawyer may not contract for a lien on Client's home.

(D) No, because Lawyer may not enter into a contract that gives Lawyer any literary rights to the story of the case while Lawyer represents Client.

56. Lawyer has strong religious beliefs that include the belief that abortion is a sin in all circumstances. Lawyer's Firm is asked to represent Client, who is challenging new state law restrictions on the availability of abortion services. Firm asks Lawyer to represent Client in this matter. Lawyer considers her religious beliefs and thinks about what she would be called upon to accomplish for Client. Lawyer concludes that she could not provide competent and diligent representation to Client in this matter. Other lawyers in Firm do not share Lawyer's views on abortion and could render competent and diligent representation to Client.

May Firm undertake the representation of Client?

(A) Yes, because personal religious beliefs do not create conflicts of interest.

(B) Yes, because Lawyer's conflict of interest will not be imputed to other lawyers in Firm.

(C) No, because Lawyer's conflict will be imputed to all other lawyers in Firm.

(D) No, because Lawyer's conflict is not consentable.

57. Husband went to see Lawyer, a solo practitioner, to discuss the possibility that Lawyer would represent Husband in divorce from Wife. Lawyer asked Husband to tell Lawyer just enough information to enable Lawyer to determine whether to represent Husband and not to reveal significant details of the dispute. Husband nevertheless revealed to Lawyer information that could be significantly harmful to Husband in the divorce. Lawyer ultimately declined to represent Husband. Wife asked Lawyer to represent her in divorce from Husband. Husband would not consent to Lawyer's representation of Wife. Lawyer nevertheless undertook to represent Wife against Husband.

Did Lawyer violate the Model Rules of Professional Conduct?

(A) Yes, because Lawyer learned information that could be significantly harmful to Husband.

(B) Yes, because Lawyer undertook to represent Wife against a former prospective client of Lawyer.

(C) No, because Lawyer undertook reasonable measures to avoid exposure to more disqualifying information than was reasonably necessary to determine whether to represent Husband.

(D) No, because Husband never became a client of Lawyer.

58. Lawyer undertook to represent Plaintiff One and Plaintiff Two in a tort case in which both clients were injured as a result of an automobile accident. Lawyer obtained informed consent to the joint representation. The conflict at the outset of the representation was consentable. In the midst of the litigation, it became clear that it would be in the best interest of Plaintiff One to file a cross-claim against Plaintiff Two. Because Plaintiff Two's insurance company would have paid any damages on the cross-claim, Plaintiff One and Plaintiff Two both gave informed consent to Lawyer bringing the cross-claim. Lawyer brought the cross-claim for Plaintiff One against Lawyer's other client in the case, Plaintiff Two.

Did Lawyer violate the Model Rules of Professional Conduct?

(A) Yes, because Lawyer became an advocate for one client against another current client.

(B) Yes, because the conflict between Plaintiff One and Plaintiff Two was not consentable.

(C) No, because both clients gave informed consent.

(D) No, because there was no conflict of interest.

59. Lawyer represents Small Client (which generates small fees) in a matter. This is the first and only matter in which Lawyer ever represented Small Client. Big Client (which generates big fees) asks Lawyer to represent Big Client in a suit against Small Client. This matter would be unrelated to the matter in which Lawyer represents Small Client. Lawyer knows that Lawyer could withdraw from the matter for Small Client without material adverse effect on the interests of Small Client. Lawyer withdraws from representing Small Client and sues Small Client on behalf of Big Client. Small Client files a motion to disqualify Lawyer from representing Big Client.

Is Lawyer subject to disqualification?

(A) Yes, because Lawyer is suing a former client on behalf of a new client.

(B) Yes, because Lawyer dropped one client to represent a more lucrative client.

(C) No, because the new matter is unrelated to anything Lawyer ever handled for Small Client.

(D) No, because Lawyer was permitted to withdraw from the matter in which Lawyer represented Small Client.

60. Lawyer represented Client and prepared an estate plan. Client's Son knew that Client would not allow Lawyer to prepare the estate plan if Lawyer charged Client Lawyer's usual fee.

Lawyer's usual fee was reasonable, but Client was known to be stingy. Client's Son offered to secretly pay one-half of Lawyer's customary fee. Lawyer accepted this arrangement. At the request of Client's Son, Lawyer did not inform Client that Client's Son would be paying any of Lawyer's fee. Lawyer did not share any of Client's confidential information with Client's Son and did not allow Client's Son to influence Lawyer's work for Client in any way.

Did Lawyer commit misconduct?

(A) Yes, because Lawyer accepted payment for her services from a third party.

(B) Yes, because Lawyer did not obtain informed consent of Client to the payment by Client's Son of part of Lawyer's fee.

(C) No, because Lawyer did not share any of Client's confidential information with Client's Son and did not allow Client's Son to influence Lawyer's work for Client in any way.

(D) No, because Lawyer's fee was reasonable.

61. Lawyer formerly worked for the United States Department of Homeland Security (DHS). In that capacity, Lawyer personally and substantially participated in the drafting of legislation about the collection and storage of data collected by DHS from cell phone companies. Lawyer left her position at DHS and joined Law Firm. Law Firm has been asked to represent a cell phone company to defend a case in which the plaintiffs are, among other things, seeking to have the legislation Lawyer drafted declared to be unconstitutional. Although Lawyer will not personally participate in the case, Law Firm does not intend to screen Lawyer.

May Law Firm undertake the representation?

(A) Yes, because the drafting of legislation is not a "matter" for purposes of conflicts of interest.

(B) Yes, because Law Firm would be defending the legislation that she helped to draft and so would be on the same side of the issue as Lawyer was when she worked for the government.

(C) No, because Lawyer participated personally and substantially in the drafting of the legislation.

(D) No, because Law Firm does not intend to screen Lawyer.

62. Lawyer represented the American Cola Company (ACC) in connection with a lawsuit. While Lawyer was engaged in that representation, Lawyer was asked by the National Cola Company (NCC) to represent NCC in connection with an unrelated lawsuit. The case on which Lawyer worked for ACC did not involve NCC, nor would NCC's confidential information have been useful in any way in that case. Likewise, the case on which Lawyer worked for NCC did not involve ACC, and none of ACC's confidential information would have been useful in that case. ACC and NCC were economic competitors for the same markets. Lawyer agreed to represent NCC while he continued to represent ACC. Lawyer obtained informed consent to do so from ACC (his existing client) but not from NCC.

Did Lawyer violate the Model Rules of Professional Conduct?

(A) Yes, because Lawyer obtained informed consent from only one of his two clients.

(B) Yes, because the simultaneous representation of the clients presents a nonconsentable conflict.

(C) No, because the two clients were merely economic competitors.

(D) No, because Lawyer obtained informed consent from his existing client.

63. Lawyer represented Client One in opposition to a motion for a new trial in a case in which one crucial issue was whether the time to make the motion ran from the date the judge signed the judgment or whether it ran instead from the date on which the clerk entered the judgment in the court's file. Lawyer argued that the time to make the motion ran from the date the judge signed the judgment. That same week, in another case in another trial court in another county, Lawyer represented Client Two in support of a motion for new trial in an unrelated case. Lawyer argued in that case that the rule should be that the time to make a motion for new trial ran from the date the clerk entered the judgment in the court's file. Lawyer did not obtain informed consent of Client One or Client Two to argue these inconsistent positions on this question of law.

Did Lawyer violate the Model Rules of Professional Conduct?

(A) Yes, because Lawyer did not obtain informed consent of both clients.

(B) Yes, because the chance that Lawyer's advocacy for Client One might create precedent adverse to the interests of Client Two, and vice versa, created a nonconsentable conflict.

(C) No, because there was no conflict of interest.

(D) No, because this situation presented only a "positional" conflict of interest.

64. Lawyer represented Client in a dispute between Client and Client's Sister over ownership of a "skybox" at a major league baseball stadium. Client claimed that he inherited the license to use the skybox from Client's father. Sister claimed that their father left the license for the skybox to her. Client could not pay Lawyer's reasonable and customary fees for representation of this type. Lawyer proposed that Client agree to a contingent fee in which Lawyer would receive a one-third undivided interest in the license to the skybox if Client prevailed in the litigation. The value of such an interest would be less than a reasonable fee for the representation. Lawyer advised Client in writing that Client should seek independent counsel and gave Client a reasonable opportunity to do so. Client agreed to the fee arrangement.

Did Lawyer violate the Model Rules of Professional Conduct?

(A) Yes, because Lawyer entered into an agreement for a contingent fee in an estate case.

(B) Yes, because Lawyer acquired an interest in the cause of action that Lawyer was asserting for Client.

(C) No, because Lawyer may contract for a contingent fee in an estate case.

(D) No, because Lawyer advised Client in writing that Client should seek independent counsel and gave Client a reasonable opportunity to do so.

65. Law Firm represented Client against Opposing Party in a large antitrust case in federal court. Law Firm hired Law Clerk as an associate. Law Clerk had served as law clerk to the trial judge who was presiding over the antitrust case. Law Clerk did not work on the antitrust case. Law Firm screened Law Clerk from the antitrust case in a timely manner. Law Firm agreed to pay Law Clerk a salary while the antitrust case was pending and Client was paying fees to Law Firm, but Law Firm made sure that Law Clerk would not receive any compensation directly related to the antitrust case. Law Firm immediately gave all parties and the court written notice that Law Firm had hired Law Clerk and had instituted these screening measures. Opposing Party filed a motion to disqualify Law Firm from participating in the antitrust case because Law Firm had hired Law Clerk.

Was Law Firm subject to disqualification because Law Firm hired Law Clerk?

(A) Yes, because Law Clerk received a salary while Law Firm was receiving fees related to the antitrust case.

(B) Yes, because all of Law Firm's lawyers were subject to imputed disqualification because of Law Clerk's conflict of interest.

(C) No, because Law Firm timely screened Law Clerk and gave appropriate notice.

(D) No, because Law Clerk did not serve as an adjudicative officer in the matter.

66. Lawyer was a partner in Law Firm. Associate worked for Law Firm. Associate worked on a case for Client. Associate and Client then fell in love and decided to commence a sexual relationship. Before doing so, Associate asked to be removed from representing Client. Lawyer took over the representation of Client but did not report Associate to the bar. Lawyer continued to represent Client while Associate and Client maintained a sexual relationship. Associate was at all times employed by Law Firm.

Did Lawyer violate the Model Rules of Professional Conduct?

(A) Yes, because Associate was prohibited from representing Client and that prohibition was imputed to Lawyer.

(B) Yes, because Lawyer did not report Associate to the bar.

(C) No, because the prohibition of Associate's representation of Client was not imputed to other lawyers in Law Firm.

(D) No, because Associate was not prohibited from representing Client, and thus there was nothing to impute to Lawyer.

67. Lawyer represented Client for many years. Lawyer and Client were not related. Client was elderly and held Lawyer in great esteem. Client suggested to Lawyer that Client wanted to change Client's will to establish an educational trust for the benefit of Lawyer's Grandson. The trust would provide sufficient funds for Grandson to attend the college of his choice, without con-

cern about the cost. Lawyer advised Client that Client should seek independent advice before making a testamentary gift for the benefit of a member of Lawyer's family, and Lawyer gave Client ample opportunity to secure such advice. Client insisted on going forward with the plan, and Lawyer gratefully drafted a new will for Client with the trust provisions in it.

Did Lawyer violate the Model Rules of Professional Conduct?

(A) Yes, because Lawyer did not obtain informed consent to Lawyer's conflict of interest in preparing an instrument that gave a substantial gift to a member of Lawyer's family.

(B) Yes, because Lawyer prepared a will giving Lawyer's Grandson a substantial gift from a client to whom Lawyer was not related.

(C) No, because Lawyer advised Client to seek independent counsel and gave Client ample opportunity to do so.

(D) No, because Lawyer did not personally receive a gift.

68. Law Firm formerly represented Corporation in zoning matters and other matters. Two weeks ago, the lawyer in Law Firm who did all of Corporation's zoning work left Law Firm to form her own firm. The departing lawyer took with her all of Corporation's zoning matters. Law Firm still represented Corporation in one unrelated "slip and fall" case. There were no lawyers left in Law Firm who did any work for Corporation in zoning matters. Law Firm was then asked to represent New Client in a zoning matter against Corporation. Under what circumstances, if any, could Law Firm accept representation of New Client in the zoning matter against Corporation?

69. Your firm wants to hire Lawyer, who currently is an attorney for the federal National Cookie Safety Administration (NCSA). Your firm currently represents Mr. Cookie, Inc. (MCI) in connection with litigation in which NCSA has sued MCI to force the recall of certain MCI cookies. Lawyer currently supervises other lawyers who are conducting that litigation for the NCSA against MCI but has had no personal or substantial involvement in it. If your firm hires Lawyer, will it be necessary to screen Lawyer from any involvement in the NCSA v. MCI?

70. Law Firm formerly represented Corporation as a defendant in Class Action. Partner in Law Firm was lead counsel for Corporation. Partner decided to leave Law Firm to join another firm. Corporation decided that Partner would continue to represent Corporation in Class Action. Law Firm had no other matters for Corporation. One lawyer and five paralegals with confidential information about Class Action stayed with Law Firm after Partner and Corporation left. New Client opted out of Class Action and asked Law Firm to represent him in an individual case against Corporation in which New Client would assert exactly the same claims as were being presented in Class Action. Under what circumstances, if any, may Law Firm agree to represent New Client against Corporation in this matter?

71. Lawyer represents Client A in connection with Client A's purchase of a hotel. A new client, Client B, asks Lawyer to represent Client B in an unrelated transaction in which Client B is purchasing a resort. Coincidentally, the seller of the resort would be Client A. Does Lawyer have a conflict of interest in representing Client B in this transaction?

72. Lawyer represented multiple clients who had been injured as a result of their use of the drug Morphodax, which had been manufactured and distributed by Pharma, Incorporated (Pharma). Counsel for Pharma made a settlement offer to Lawyer to resolve by one cash payment all of the claims of Lawyer's Morphodax clients. Lawyer believed that the amount of the settlement offer was fair and that her clients should accept the offer. If the cases settled for this aggregate amount, Lawyer intended to distribute the settlement funds in accordance with a formula that Lawyer developed. The formula would give more money to clients who had been more seriously injured by their use of Morphodax. What steps must Lawyer take to be sure that she complies with her obligations under the Model Rules of Professional Conduct in connection with this aggregate settlement?

73. Lawyer represented Client in connection with the preparation of Client's will. In the course of that representation, Lawyer learned about Client's lake house. Lawyer wished to purchase a lake house, and Lawyer knew that Client wished to sell his. What steps must Lawyer take to make sure that, in purchasing the lake house from Client, that Lawyer complies with his obligations under the Model Rules of Professional Conduct?

Competence, Legal Malpractice, and Other Civil Liability

74. Lawyer had just been admitted to the practice of law and went into private practice by himself. Client came to Lawyer and asked Lawyer to handle Client's divorce and child custody case. Lawyer had never handled a divorce or child custody case before, but Lawyer had no other clients. Lawyer had no contacts with older lawyers in the community to whom Lawyer could turn for guidance or assistance. Lawyer agreed to represent Client. Lawyer then devoted hours of study and learned how to handle each stage of a divorce and child custody case before Lawyer acted for Client in each such stage. Lawyer did not charge Client for these hours of self-education.

    Did Lawyer violate the Model Rules of Professional Conduct?

    (A) Yes, because Lawyer agreed to represent Client at a time when Lawyer was not competent to handle Client's matter.

    (B) Yes, because Lawyer did not associate a lawyer of established competence in divorce and child custody.

    (C) No, because Lawyer undertook the matter only after being duly admitted to the bar.

    (D) No, because Lawyer became competent through necessary study.

75. Lawyer represented Client in connection with Client's claim for worker's compensation benefits. Client had suffered a brain injury on the job. The injury affected Client's judgment and Client's ability to control impulses. Lawyer recovered 100% of the benefits to which Client was entitled as a result of the injury. During the representation of Client, Lawyer initiated and maintained a consensual sexual relationship with Client. After the termination of Lawyer's attorney-client relationship with Client, Client's husband discovered the sexual relationship between Lawyer and Client. Client filed a civil suit for damages against Lawyer for initiating and maintaining the sexual relationship at a time when Client's judgment and impulse control were impaired.

    Would Lawyer be liable for damages to Client under these circumstances?

    (A) Yes, because Lawyer committed legal malpractice.

    (B) Yes, because Lawyer breached his fiduciary duties to Client.

    (C) No, because Lawyer recovered for Client 100% of what Client was entitled to receive as a result of Client's injury at work.

    (D) No, because the sexual relationship was consensual.

76. Lawyer found that his need for filing cabinets to maintain client files was growing and that the expense of renting enough space for the files was becoming prohibitive. Lawyer researched his options and decided to store his client files electronically on remote servers not directly under Lawyer's control, a practice usually known as "cloud computing." Lawyer was not familiar with the technical aspects of cloud computing but hired a Vendor to handle his "cloud." Lawyer did not know of the need to put in place special safeguards to protect confidential client information. Vendor had never worked with a lawyer before and did not advise Lawyer of how to safeguard the information once it was in Lawyer's "cloud." Third parties were able to access Lawyer's clients' confidential information because of the lack of security.

Did Lawyer violate the Model Rules of Professional Conduct?

(A) Yes, because Lawyer did not maintain his competence with respect to the benefits and risks of technology.

(B) Yes, because Lawyer stored client files on remote servers not directly under Lawyer's control.

(C) No, because Lawyer was permitted to use "cloud computing" for the storage of client files.

(D) No, because Lawyer did not reveal or use the confidential client information to the detriment of his clients.

77. Lawyer represented Client in a contentious divorce case. Client was very unhappy with the result of the case and blamed Lawyer. Client fired Lawyer and threatened to sue Lawyer for malpractice. Lawyer went to see Client face-to-face to discuss Client's threat to file a malpractice action before Client had time to hire a lawyer to represent Client in connection with such a claim. Lawyer proposed that Lawyer would refund to Client all of the fees that Client had paid Lawyer for the matter, and in exchange, Client would sign a release of any malpractice claims against Lawyer. Lawyer told Client that Client should seek independent legal counsel before agreeing to this proposal and told Client to get back with Lawyer after Client had had to opportunity to do so. Client declined to seek independent counsel and immediately agreed to the proposal and signed the release. Lawyer refunded all the fees that Client had paid Lawyer in connection with the divorce.

Did Lawyer violate the Model Rules of Professional Conduct?

(A) Yes, because Client was not represented in connection with the agreement.

(B) Yes, because Client was not advised in writing of the desirability of seeking the advice of independent counsel.

(C) No, because Client was advised of the desirability of seeking the advice of independent counsel and given an opportunity to do so.

(D) No, because this was a settlement of a malpractice claim after the representation ended rather than a prospective limit on the attorney's malpractice.

78. Prospective Client consulted with Lawyer about the possibility of Lawyer representing Client in a claim for medical malpractice against Doctor. Lawyer did not agree to represent Prospec-

tive Client but did agree to review the relevant medical records. Lawyer reviewed the medical records but did not have the requisite expertise to understand how Prospective Client was treated and how Doctor might have committed medical malpractice. Lawyer nevertheless told Prospective Client that Prospective Client "did not have a case" and that, therefore, Lawyer was declining to enter into an attorney-client relationship with Prospective Client. Prospective Client relied on Lawyer's advice about the claim and did nothing until after the applicable statute of limitations had run. Then Prospective Client consulted another lawyer who had a medical specialist review the records. That review revealed that Doctor had committed medical malpractice. Prospective Client's claim against Doctor, however, was barred by the statute of limitations.

Is Lawyer liable to Prospective Client for malpractice?

(A) Yes, because Lawyer gave advice without conducting an adequate investigation of Prospective Client's claim.

(B) Yes, because Lawyer did not file Prospective Client's claim before the statute of limitations ran.

(C) No, because Prospective Client never became a client.

(D) No, because Lawyer would be protected from malpractice liability by the doctrine of judgmental immunity.

79. Professor was a full-time law professor and did not actively practice law, even though Professor had an active law license. Professor taught Property and Land Use. Before going into law teaching, Professor had never represented anyone accused of a crime or been to court in any capacity. Late one night, Professor received a call from the father of one of Professor's students. The student had just been arrested and would be appearing before a judge for a first appearance early the next morning. The student's father had not had time to find a criminal defense lawyer but did not want his son to be unrepresented at the first appearance. The father asked Professor to appear and represent the student at the first appearance pro bono. Professor did so.

Did Professor violate the Model Rules of Professional Conduct?

(A) Yes, because Professor represented the student even though Professor was incompetent to do so.

(B) Yes, because Professor did not associate an attorney with criminal law experience.

(C) No, because Professor had an active law license.

(D) No, because Professor represented the student only on an emergency basis.

80. Lawyer represented Client against Client's partners in a "business divorce" case to dissolve a partnership. Client was angry with his partners and resentful of the cost and distraction that resulted from the need to be involved in litigation with them. Lawyer sent written interrogatories to counsel who represented the partners. Just before the responses to the interrogatories were due, opposing counsel asked Lawyer for a 15-day extension for submitting responses.

The extension did not affect any other deadlines or scheduled events in the case. Without consulting with Client, Lawyer agreed to the extension. Client was angry when Client found out that Lawyer had accommodated opposing counsel and threatened to file a grievance against Lawyer.

Did Lawyer violate the Model Rules of Professional Conduct?

(A) Yes, because Lawyer violated Lawyer's duty of diligence by agreeing to the delay.

(B) Yes, because Lawyer did not consult with Client about the postponement.

(C) No, because Lawyer was permitted to agree to reasonable requests for postponements that did not prejudice Client.

(D) No, because decisions about the means of achieving Client's objectives belonged to Lawyer.

81. Lawyer represented Client in connection with charges of criminal conspiracy. Lawyer believed that Prosecutor's case was extremely weak and that it was highly unlikely that Client would be convicted. On the basis of that judgment, Lawyer rejected Prosecutor's plea offer of a one-year prison sentence for Client in exchange for a guilty plea. Lawyer and Client had not discussed what an acceptable plea agreement would be. Lawyer believed that the plea offer was so bad, and the chances of conviction so low, that Lawyer did not convey the offer to Client. The case went to trial. The jury convicted Client, and the judge sentenced Client to serve ten years in prison. The conviction and sentence were upheld on appeal, and Client's attempts to attack the conviction collaterally were all unsuccessful. Client sued Lawyer for malpractice.

Will Client be able to recover from Lawyer for malpractice?

(A) Yes, because Lawyer failed to convey Prosecutor's plea offer to Client.

(B) Yes, because Lawyer was wrong about the likely outcome of trial.

(C) No, because Lawyer had professional discretion to not convey the plea offer.

(D) No, because Client will be unable to prove that any damages resulted from Lawyer's malpractice.

82. Trustee hired Lawyer to assist Trustee in the fulfillment of Trustee's fiduciary obligations to Ward, an incapacitated adult nephew of Trustee. Lawyer assisted Trustee with a number of transactions involving the property in Ward's estate. Lawyer learned that one of those transactions was fraudulent and was solely for the benefit of Trustee to the detriment of Ward. Lawyer learned these facts after Lawyer had completed Lawyer's assistance with the transaction but before the transaction closed. Lawyer could have prevented the transaction from closing. Lawyer did nothing, and the transaction closed. A Successor Trustee for Ward was appointed later and discovered the fraudulent transaction. Successor Trustee sued Lawyer on behalf of Ward for professional negligence for failing to prevent the fraud of Trustee.

Will Lawyer be liable for professional negligence?

(A) Yes, because Lawyer knew about Trustee's fraud in time to prevent the harm to Ward.

(B) Yes, because Ward was Lawyer's client when the fraud occurred.

(C) No, because Lawyer did not knowingly assist in the fraud.

(D) No, because Ward was never a client of Lawyer.

83. Lawyer represented Client in connection with the sale of Client's business to Buyer. One important issue in the negotiations with Buyer's counsel was whether Buyer would acquire as part of the sale certain valuable tax credits that belonged to Client. If the tax credits could have been conveyed, then the price that Buyer paid to Client would have been higher. The tax credits would have been more valuable in Buyer's hands than in Client's. Lawyer concluded that the tax credits would not and could not be conveyed as part of the sale and so advised Client. Lawyer did not, therefore, raise the issue in negotiations with Buyer's counsel. Even if Lawyer had sought to increase the purchase price because of the tax credits, and Buyer had refused, Client would have agreed to the deal anyway. Client needed to sell the business regardless. The deal closed. Client later discovered that Lawyer was wrong. The tax credits absolutely without question could have been part of the sale. Client sued Lawyer for malpractice for not attempting to include the tax credits in the deal and thereby raise the purchase price that Client would have received. Buyer has refused to cooperate in the malpractice action.

Will Lawyer be liable to Client for malpractice?

(A) Yes, because Lawyer was not diligent in the negotiations with Buyer when Lawyer failed to include the tax credits as part of the negotiation.

(B) Yes, because Lawyer gave incorrect advice about whether the tax credits could be conveyed as part of the sale.

(C) No, because proof of Client's damages would be too speculative.

(D) No, because Lawyer's breach of the standard of care occurred in a transactional context.

84. Lawyer agreed to represent Client, even though Client had fired three other lawyers who had undertaken to represent him in the matter. As a condition of agreeing to represent Client under these circumstances, Lawyer required Client to sign an agreement in advance that Client would be able to sue Lawyer for malpractice only if Lawyer engaged in gross negligence or reckless or intentional misconduct. When Lawyer presented this proposal to Client, Lawyer advised Client of the advisability of obtaining independent counsel before Client signed it and gave Client plenty of opportunity to obtain such counsel. Client did not obtain independent counsel but did sign the agreement limiting Lawyer's liability for malpractice. Did Lawyer violate the Model Rules of Professional Conduct?

85. Lawyer represented Client in connection with Client's claim for medical malpractice. In Lawyer's jurisdiction, the state legislature had passed legislation that capped the damages that plaintiffs in medical malpractice cases could recover. The Governor signed the bill after Client's claim was filed but before it had been adjudicated. The defendant in Client's case obtained a partial summary judgment that struck Client's claims for damages in excess of the statutory

cap. Lawyer considered whether to file an interlocutory appeal to argue that the statutory cap did not apply to claims that were pending before the Governor signed the bill. Lawyer did exhaustive research. There was no definitive case law on this question. Lawyer advised that Client's chances of winning an appeal were slim, and Client settled his claim for the statutory cap. Six months later, the State Supreme Court held that the statutory cap did not apply to cases that were already pending when the cap went into effect. Client sued Lawyer for malpractice. Is Lawyer liable to Client for malpractice under these circumstances?

86. Lawyer worked for a firm for several years but decided to start her own firm. Because of the expense, and her faith in her own competence, Lawyer decided not to carry any malpractice insurance. She considered herself "self-insured," which simply meant that she would be personally responsible for the costs of defending any claims and for settling or paying any claims. Lawyer did not reveal to clients or prospective clients that she did not carry malpractice insurance. When one client asked if she was insured against malpractice, Lawyer responded, "yes," because Lawyer considered herself to be self-insured. How, if at all, did Lawyer violate the Model Rules of Professional Conduct?

87. Lawyer represented Client in connection with Client's will. Lawyer did not represent Client's Girlfriend or Client's Wife. Lawyer knew that Client's objective was to make sure that Client's entire estate went to Girlfriend and not to Client's Wife upon Client's death. Lawyer negligently prepared the will in such a way that the will was invalid under state law. As a result of Lawyer's negligence, Client's entire estate went to Client's Wife. Girlfriend inherited nothing. Girlfriend sued Lawyer. Is Lawyer liable to Girlfriend even though Lawyer was never in an attorney-client relationship with Girlfriend?

Litigation and Other Forms of Advocacy

88. Lawyer represents Client, a celebrity who has been accused of child molestation. A local news station reported that Client's DNA was found on the clothing of the victim. This information did not come from the prosecutor in the case. Lawyer knew this statement was untrue and that in fact the DNA sample obtained from that clothing did not match Client's DNA. Lawyer had the report of the test to prove it. This report will definitely be admissible at trial. Lawyer called a news conference and shared the report that Client's DNA was not on the victim's clothing.

Did Lawyer violate the Model Rules of Professional Conduct?

(A) Yes, because the prosecutor in the case had not made any public statement that had a substantial likelihood of materially prejudicing Client's case.

(B) Yes, because Lawyer publicized the results of a test connected to an adjudicative proceeding.

(C) No, because the test will be admissible evidence at trial.

(D) No, because Client was the victim of substantial undue prejudice not caused by Client and the result of the real test was necessary to counteract the effects of that publicity.

89. Lawyer represented Client, who had been accused of the murder of her boyfriend. Client testified that she was 500 miles away from the murder scene at the time of the murder. At the time of the presentation of this testimony, Lawyer had no reason to believe that it was untrue. After Client testified but before a verdict, Client told Lawyer privately that Client lied on the stand and was in fact near the scene of the murder the day it happened. Lawyer told Client to correct the record, and Client refused. Lawyer sought court permission to withdraw as counsel for Client and was refused. Lawyer decided not to reveal Client's false testimony to the court. The jury acquitted Client of all charges.

Did Lawyer violate the Model Rules of Professional Conduct?

(A) Yes, because Lawyer came to know of the falsity of evidence he had presented and did not tell the court.

(B) Yes, because Lawyer presented false evidence.

(C) No, because disclosure under these circumstances was optional rather than mandatory.

(D) No, because Lawyer learned of Client's false testimony in a privileged conversation.

90. Lawyer represented Client, who had been accused of battery in a bar fight. Client's objective was to be acquitted. Client's Best Friend was prepared to testify that Client acted in self-

defense. Lawyer knew that Best Friend had an extensive criminal record and had been drinking heavily the night of the bar fight. Lawyer reasonably believed that Best Friend's testimony would be false and that having Best Friend testify would be a very bad strategy. Lawyer consulted with Client and informed Client of Lawyer's judgment. Client insisted that Lawyer offer the testimony of Best Friend. Lawyer refused. Client was convicted of battery.

Did Lawyer violate the Model Rules of Professional Conduct?

(A) Yes, because Lawyer did not abide by Client's decision regarding the means of achieving Client's objective.

(B) Yes, because, as a defendant in a criminal matter, Client had the right to decide who would testify on his behalf.

(C) No, because Lawyer had the discretion to refuse to offer evidence that Lawyer reasonably believed was false.

(D) No, because Lawyer was not permitted to present evidence that Lawyer reasonably believed was false.

91. Lawyer was representing Client, a prominent politician who was on trial for corruption. In the course of preparing one of the witnesses (not Client), Lawyer learned that one of Client's political supporters had made arrangements to meet secretly with one of the jurors. The plan was for the juror to be paid a certain sum in exchange for guaranteeing at least a hung jury. Lawyer decided to tell no one and took no action as a result of receiving this information. Client eventually was convicted on all charges.

Did Lawyer violate the Model Rules of Professional Conduct?

(A) Yes, because Lawyer had a duty to take reasonable remedial measures once Lawyer learned of the plan to bribe a juror.

(B) Yes, because Lawyer had a duty to report the planned crime to law enforcement.

(C) No, because the information that Lawyer had about the bribery plot was confidential.

(D) No, because Client was convicted.

92. Lawyer represented Client in a deportation proceeding before the United States Immigration Court. In that proceeding, Lawyer argued that Client should receive asylum in the United States because of the likelihood that Client would suffer grave economic privation in Client's home country. The U.S. Immigration Court had never accepted grave economic privation as a basis for asylum. Lawyer had a good faith argument to reverse this existing and prevailing view of the law. Lawyer did not yet possess factual evidence to support the allegation of grave economic privation. Lawyer personally believed that the case for Client ultimately would succeed.

Did Lawyer violate the Model Rules of Professional Conduct?

(A) Yes, because Lawyer did not yet possess evidence to support the allegation of grave economic privation.

(B) Yes, because Lawyer made a legal argument that was unsupported by existing law.

(C) No, because Lawyer had a good faith basis to argue to change the prevailing law.

(D) No, because Lawyer believed that the case for Client ultimately would succeed.

93. Lawyer represented Defendant in a personal injury case. Lawyer interviewed Witness and learned that Witness might testify to facts that would harm Defendant. Lawyer asked Witness not to agree to talk voluntarily to Plaintiff's Counsel about the accident. Witness was not re-lated to Defendant, and Witness was not an employee or other agent of Defendant. Lawyer reasonably believed that the interests of Witness would not be adversely affected by refusing to talk to Plaintiff's Counsel. Witness agreed not to talk voluntarily to Plaintiff's Counsel.

Did Lawyer violate the Model Rules of Professional Conduct?

(A) Yes, because Witness was not a relative, employee or other agent of Client.

(B) Yes, because Lawyer asked a witness not to cooperate with opposing counsel.

(C) No, because Lawyer reasonably believed that the interests of Witness would not be ad-versely affected by refusing to talk to Plaintiff's counsel.

(D) No, because Lawyer merely asked Witness not to talk to Plaintiff's Counsel.

94. Lawyer represented Client in a case of first impression in Client's state's Supreme Court. Client's case depended entirely on how the state Supreme Court decided one issue of law. An-other state's Supreme Court had recently decided that exact issue in a published opinion in Smith v. Jones. That result was the opposite of what Lawyer was seeking on behalf of Client. Lawyer's Opposing Counsel for some reason did not cite the Smith v. Jones opinion in Client's case. Because Lawyer did not want to harm Client's chances, Lawyer decided not to cite Smith v. Jones.

Did Lawyer violate the Model Rules of Professional Conduct?

(A) Yes, because the result in Smith v. Jones was directly adverse to Lawyer's legal position.

(B) Yes, because Smith v. Jones was persuasive authority, and Opposing Counsel did not cite the case.

(C) No, because Smith v. Jones was not from a controlling authority.

(D) No, because citing Smith v. Jones would have hurt Lawyer's Client.

95. Lawyer served for many years as the District Attorney. After Lawyer retired as District Attorney, a heinous crime was committed. The police arrested a suspect, and the new District Attorney charged the suspect with the crime. The lawyer for the suspect repeatedly went on television to talk about the case and excoriated the police for arresting the suspect and claimed that the arrest and prosecution were parts of an ongoing pattern of years of corruption in the police department and the District Attorney's office. Lawyer resented the implication that he had been corrupt as District Attorney and called a press conference to refute the claims of corrup-tion. During the press conference, Lawyer talked about the suspect in the pending case. Lawyer

stated his personal opinion that the suspect was "guilty as hell" and would be convicted and sentenced to death.

Did Lawyer violate the Model Rules of Professional Conduct?

(A) Yes, because Lawyer publicly expressed his personal opinion as to the guilt of the accused.

(B) Yes, because Lawyer held a press conference about a pending case.

(C) No, because Lawyer was responding to the substantial undue prejudicial effect of recent publicity.

(D) No, because Lawyer did not represent, and had not represented, anyone in the proceeding or the related investigation.

96. Lawyer was appointed to represent Client in a civil case involving termination of Client's parental rights. Client gave testimony at a deposition that Lawyer reasonably believed was false. Lawyer attempted unsuccessfully to persuade Client to correct the record. Lawyer sought to withdraw from the case, but the court refused to allow Lawyer to withdraw. Lawyer revealed to the court that Lawyer reasonably believed that Client had testified falsely at the deposition.

Did Lawyer violate the Model Rules of Professional Conduct?

(A) Yes, because Lawyer sought to withdraw from the case.

(B) Yes, because Lawyer revealed confidential information to the court.

(C) No, because the testimony was given at a deposition rather than in court.

(D) No, because Lawyer was appointed counsel rather than retained counsel.

97. Lawyer represented Teenager in a case of malice murder. Lawyer had secured an expert who was prepared to testify that Teenager's actions were the result of a psychological condition known as "Affluenza," a psychological disability caused by the wealth of Teenager's family. Lawyer intended to try to introduce the expert's testimony at trial to explain Teenager's state of mind and at least to try to mitigate Teenager's culpability for the victim's death. There was no evidence of the "Affluenza" defense other than the expert. Lawyer did not believe that the trial judge would allow the expert to testify but had few choices in defending Teenager. Lawyer did reasonably believe that the argument for admitted the testimony was not frivolous. In Lawyer's opening statement to the jury, Lawyer explained "Affluenza" defense and described how it affected Teenager, but Lawyer did not state any personal opinion regarding the "Affluenza" defense as it applied to Teenager. During trial, the trial judge, as expected, ruled that the expert's testimony was inadmissible.

Did Lawyer violate the Model Rules of Professional Conduct?

(A) Yes, because Lawyer did not reasonably believe that the "Affluenza" defense would be supported by admissible evidence.

(B) Yes, because the evidence of the "Affluenza" defense was not admitted.

(C) No, because Lawyer did not express any personal opinion regarding the "Affluenza" defense as it applied to Teenager.

(D) No, because Lawyer reasonably believed that the argument for admitting the testimony of the expert was not frivolous.

98. Lawyer represented Client in a jury trial. As the case progressed, Lawyer became increasingly concerned about Juror Smith, whose facial expressions and body language indicated that Juror Smith was not reacting to the evidence in a way that favored Client. Lawyer had an account with, and a profile posted on, an electronic social media site (ESMS) for business professionals. Lawyer accessed ESMS and searched to determine whether Juror Smith also had an account and a profile. Lawyer discovered that Juror Smith did have an account and a profile on ESMS. Lawyer clicked on the link to Juror Smith's public profile and reviewed the information that Juror Smith had posted there. Unbeknownst to Lawyer, ESMS automatically sent a message to Juror Smith that Lawyer was reviewing his profile. Juror Smith complained that Lawyer was "cyber-stalking" him.

Did Lawyer violate the Model Rules of Professional Conduct?

(A) Yes, because Lawyer communicated ex parte with Juror Smith.

(B) Yes, because Lawyer reviewed Juror Smith's ESMS profile.

(C) No, because Lawyer did not know that by clicking on the link she would be communicating with Juror Smith.

(D) No, because the notification that Lawyer had reviewed Juror Smith's profile was not a communication from Lawyer.

99. Lawyer was an alcoholic and regularly attended meeting of his state's Approved Lawyer's Assistance Program. Prosecutor was also an alcoholic and also attended these meetings. During one such meeting, Prosecutor admitted that she had knowingly allowed a police officer to commit perjury during the recent prosecution of a notorious drug kingpin. Lawyer was not involved in that case in any way. The case resulted in a conviction and was on appeal. Lawyer did not reveal this information to anyone. The conviction eventually was affirmed.

Did Lawyer violate the Model Rules of Professional Conduct?

(A) Yes, because Lawyer failed to report the information to the appropriate professional authority.

(B) Yes, because Lawyer knew of a criminal act related to a proceeding and failed to take reasonable remedial measures.

(C) No, because Lawyer did not represent anyone in the proceeding.

(D) No, because the case was on appeal when Lawyer learned what had happened.

100. Lawyer represented Client, who had been accused of assault. Client told Lawyer that Client wanted to testify that Client was in another city the night the assault happened. Lawyer had

seen evidence on surveillance video that clearly showed Client in the vicinity of the assault within minutes of the crime. Lawyer had also seen evidence that Client had withdrawn money from an ATM machine around the corner from the assault just minutes after it happened. Client still insisted that Client was in another city that night. Lawyer refused to present Client's testimony about Client's whereabouts and sought to withdraw for "professional reasons." Judge denied the motion to withdraw and ordered Lawyer to put Client on the stand to testify. Lawyer did as Judge instructed, and Client testified that Client was in another city the night of the assault. Client was acquitted of the assault.

Did Lawyer violate the Model Rules of Professional Conduct?

(A) Yes, because Lawyer refused to present Client's testimony without knowing that it would be false.

(B) Yes, because Lawyer knowingly presented false evidence.

(C) No, because Lawyer only did what Judge ordered Lawyer to do.

(D) No, because Lawyer was permitted to knowingly present false evidence from a criminal defendant.

101. The Supreme Court of Lawyer's state adopted a rule for cases involving the denial of a bar applicant's application for a certificate of fitness to practice law. For all applicants who became the subject of proceedings in the Supreme Court on such a matter, the rule required applicants to reveal whether they had ever committed a crime, regardless of whether they had ever been arrested or charged for it. Lawyer believed that this rule was unconstitutional because it required applicants to incriminate themselves. Assume that Lawyer was clearly correct in that assessment. Lawyer consulted with Client and learned that Client in fact had committed crimes for which he had not yet been arrested or charged. Lawyer and Client reached an agreement that Lawyer would not provide this information to the Supreme Court as part of a proceeding before the Supreme Court related to Client's bar application. Lawyer did not inform the Supreme Court of Lawyer's decision not to comply with the Supreme Court's rule.

Did Lawyer violate the Model Rules of Professional Conduct?

(A) Yes, because Lawyer refused to follow a rule of the tribunal.

(B) Yes, because Lawyer's refusal to follow the rule was not an open refusal.

(C) No, because Lawyer consulted with Client about whether to reveal the crimes.

(D) No, because the Supreme Court's rule was unconstitutional.

102. Defendant was charged with kidnapping. Prosecutor participated in the investigation that led to Defendant's arrest but was no longer involved personally and substantially in the prosecution of Defendant. After Defendant had been indicted, Defendant escaped from the jail where Defendant was incarcerated pending trial. Prosecutor immediately held a press conference at which Prosecutor warned the public that Defendant was dangerous and that no member of

the public should render any assistance to Defendant or attempt to apprehend him. The police caught Defendant and returned him to jail to await trial for kidnapping and for the escape.

Did Prosecutor commit misconduct by what he said at the press conference?

(A) Yes, because the remarks had a substantial likelihood of heightening public condemnation of the Defendant.

(B) Yes, because the remarks had a substantial likelihood of materially prejudicing Defendant's right to a fair trial.

(C) No, because Prosecutor was no longer participating personally and substantially in the prosecution of Defendant.

(D) No, because the remarks were necessary to protect the public.

103. Lawyer represented Client in a binding arbitration regarding Client's claim for medical malpractice against Doctor. Client suffered complications from a back surgery performed by Doctor. During a proceeding, Lawyer stated to Arbitrator that Client had had no back problems before the problem that led Client to consult Doctor. When Lawyer made this statement, Lawyer had reason to believe it was true and in fact believed it to be true. Later in the case, Lawyer learned to Lawyer's surprise that Client in fact had had earlier back problems. Assume that the issue whether Client had earlier back problems was a material issue in the case. Lawyer did not correct Lawyer's earlier misstatement on this point.

Did Lawyer violate the Model Rules of Professional Conduct?

(A) Yes, because Lawyer made a false statement of fact to a tribunal.

(B) Yes, because Lawyer failed to correct a false statement of fact to a tribunal.

(C) No, because Lawyer did not knowingly make a false statement of fact to a tribunal.

(D) No, because an arbitrator is not a tribunal.

104. Lawyer met with Client while Client was incarcerated on charges of possession of child pornography. Client told Lawyer that his "stash" of child pornography was in a box buried in Client's backyard. Client asked Lawyer to get the box and destroy it before the police could find it once they executed a search warrant on Client's property. Lawyer did not want to destroy evidence. Instead, Lawyer dug up the box and anonymously sent it to the police who were investigating Client. Nothing about the box or its contents tied Client or Lawyer to possession of the box. Did Lawyer violate the Model Rules of Professional Conduct?

105. Lawyer represents Client in a lawsuit involving the ownership of real property. Opposing counsel has sent a notice for Client's deposition next week. Client has secret plans to sell the property that is the subject of the case, and surprisingly, opposing counsel has not taken steps to impede such a secret sale. Such a sale would be to Client's strategic advantage in the case. Lawyer and Client fear, however, that opposing counsel will ask at the deposition about any plans to sell the property. Client will be unable to close the secret sale before the deposition but will be able to do so soon afterwards. Lawyer has a good relationship with opposing coun-

sel and knows that opposing counsel will agree to postpone the deposition if Lawyer asks him to do so. Will Lawyer be committing misconduct under the Model Rules of Professional Conduct if Lawyer requests a short postponement of the deposition in order to enable Client to sell the property?

106. Several years ago, Lawyer represented Client in a complex antitrust case. Client finally obtained a favorable judgment, which was affirmed at every level of available appeal. The case has now been over for more than a year. Lawyer just learned that one of Client's business associates (not a lawyer), unbeknownst to Client, had threatened one of the witnesses that would have testified against Client. That witness never testified. Such intimidation constituted the crime of obstruction of justice in Lawyer's state. What obligation, if any, does Lawyer now have with respect to the obstruction of justice?

107. Lawyer lost a jury verdict and was surprised by the result. Lawyer suspected that there was juror misconduct and wanted to speak with the jurors in order to investigate that suspicion. In Lawyer's jurisdiction, the law did not forbid contact with jurors after the conclusion of a case. The judge in Lawyer's case had not forbidden it by court order. Lawyer called all of the jurors on the phone. Juror Ten called back and left a voicemail for Lawyer that said, "Leave me alone, I do not want to speak with you." Lawyer suspected she was on the right track in her investigation and waited for Juror Ten outside Juror Ten's place of employment. Lawyer approached Juror Ten and began asking questions about the jury's deliberations. Did Lawyer violate the Model Rules of Professional Conduct?

108. Lawyer participated face-to-face with Client and Opposing Party in the negotiation of a business transaction. Years later, Opposing Party sued Client for fraud based upon something that Client allegedly said during those face-to-face negotiations. Client meanwhile had suffered a stroke and became unable to testify about what happened in the face-to-face negotiations years before. Only Lawyer is available to testify about that, and Lawyer's testimony will be favorable to Client and consistent with what Client would have testified to. Lawyer's law firm would like to represent Client in the fraud case but recognizes that Lawyer will be disqualified as an advocate because he will be a necessary witness. May Lawyer's law firm represent Client in the fraud case?

Transactions and Communications with Persons Other Than Clients

109. Lawyer represented Client in connection with Client's case against Acme, Inc., which Lawyer knew was represented by counsel in the matter. Lawyer was contacted by a former employee of Acme, Inc., who offered to give Lawyer copies of emails that would reveal how Acme's lawyer had evaluated the case for Acme's most senior management, the corporate officers who guided and integrated Acme's operations. Lawyer's jurisdiction used the "control group" test for determining when communications between counsel and constituents of a corporation were privileged. Lawyer spoke with the former employee and obtained the emails. Lawyer did not obtain the permission of Acme's counsel before communicating with the former employee or before obtaining the emails.

Did Lawyer violate the Model Rules of Professional Conduct?

(A) Yes, because Lawyer used means of collecting evidence that violated the rights of Acme.

(B) Yes, because Lawyer spoke with a former employee of a represented party.

(C) No, because the emails were not privileged under the "control group" test.

(D) No, because Lawyer had the right to communicate with a former employee of Acme.

110. Lawyer received an email from opposing counsel that contained an attachment titled "Research memo re claims of joint privilege.docx." This e-mail appeared to be the latest in a string of emails among all counsel to a hotly contested case in which Lawyer represented a plaintiff. Two different law firms represented Defendant One and Defendant Two, respectively. Lawyer had been seeking the production of emails sent between the two law firms representing the defendants, but both defendants asserted a "joint defense privilege" to producing them. Lawyer realized immediately upon receipt of the latest email that the message and its attachment were inadvertently sent to Lawyer as a result of the sender hitting "Reply All" by mistake.

In order to comply with her obligations under the Model Rules of Professional Conduct, must Lawyer delete the memorandum from her computer without reading it?

(A) Yes, because the memorandum was inadvertently sent.

(B) Yes, because the memorandum is opinion work product and thus not subject to discovery.

(C) No, because Lawyer's only obligation under the rules of conduct is to notify the sender of the lawyer's receipt of the document.

(D) No, because the sender waived any objection to discovery of the memorandum by sending it to Lawyer.

111. Lawyer represented Client in a series of business transactions. Lawyer prepared and delivered to Client the paperwork necessary to close the next transaction in the series, with Next Buyer. Lawyer learned that Client was engaged in fraud in connection with all of these transactions, past and future. Lawyer withdrew from representing Client and gave notice to Next Buyer that Lawyer had withdrawn. Lawyer also told Next Buyer that Lawyer disaffirmed the paperwork that Lawyer had prepared for Client's imminent transaction with Next Buyer. Next Victim nevertheless expressed the intention of going through with the deal. Lawyer did not warn Next Buyer that the deal was a fraud.

Did Lawyer violate the Model Rules of Professional Conduct?

(A) Yes, because revelation was reasonably necessary to prevent reasonably certain substantial financial harm to another in a transaction in which Client has used Lawyer's services.

(B) Yes, because revelation was necessary in order for Lawyer to avoid assisting Client in a fraud.

(C) No, because revelation to prevent financial harm to another is optional rather than mandatory.

(D) No, because Lawyer undertook reasonable remedial measures by making a noisy withdrawal.

112. Lawyer represented Client and needed to investigate the possibility that Slumlord (an individual) had illegally denied Client the opportunity to rent an apartment because of Client's race. Lawyer had heard about using "testers" to see what a potential defendant does in certain circumstances. Lawyer decided to be a "tester" and pretended to be a renter and spoke with Slumlord. Lawyer did not know that Slumlord knew that Client might sue him and had retained counsel in connection with the matter. Lawyer secretly recorded Slumlord saying several incriminating things. The criminal law of the State where this conversation was recorded required consent of all parties to the recording of a conversation.

Did Lawyer commit misconduct under the Model Rules of Professional Conduct?

(A) Yes, because Lawyer engaged in a criminal act that reflected adversely on Lawyer's honesty, trustworthiness or fitness as a lawyer.

(B) Yes, because Lawyer communicated with a represented party.

(C) No, because Lawyer did not know Slumlord was represented by counsel.

(D) No, because using "testers" is authorized by law.

113. Lawyer represented Husband in divorce from Wife, who was not represented by counsel. Lawyer attempted to negotiate a settlement. Lawyer falsely stated during the negotiations that the offer was the best that Husband would be able to offer. In the course of those negotiations, Wife said to Lawyer, "Thank you for helping us." Lawyer responded, "You are most welcome." Wife signed the settlement as proposed by Lawyer.

Did Lawyer commit misconduct?

(A) Yes, because Lawyer made a false statement of material fact to Wife.

(B) Yes, because Lawyer did not explain his role in the matter.

(C) No, because Lawyer did not misrepresent Lawyer's role in the matter to Wife.

(D) No, because Lawyer was bluffing about what would be an acceptable settlement.

114. Lawyer represented Wife in a divorce proceeding. Lawyer sent an offer of an agreement for temporary support to Husband's Lawyer but received no response for weeks. Lawyer suggested to Wife that she could call her Husband and check on the status of the offer. Lawyer also gave Wife some "talking points" to use when Wife talked to Husband to help Wife convince Husband that Husband should agree to Lawyer's proposal. Lawyer told Wife to tell Husband not to sign the agreement without talking to his lawyer. Wife followed Lawyer's instructions and contacted Husband directly about the settlement offer.

Did Lawyer violate the Model Rules of Professional Conduct?

(A) Yes, because Lawyer had contact with a represented party through the acts of another.

(B) Yes, because Lawyer initiated the idea of Wife contacting Husband and gave Wife "talking points."

(C) No, because Lawyer had reason to believe that Husband's lawyer had not communicated the settlement offer to husband.

(D) No, because represented parties are allowed to speak directly with each other.

115. Lawyer conducted heated negotiations to settle a civil case. As a strategy, Lawyer "bluffed" opposing counsel. Lawyer first lied about the minimum amount his client would be willing to accept in settlement. Lawyer also lied about the length of the applicable statute of limitations. Lawyer knew that the limitations period had expired on his client's claim, but he took a chance that opposing counsel would not know that and would not look it up. Both bluffs worked. Lawyer achieved a good settlement for his client. Did Lawyer violate the Model Rules of Professional Conduct?

116. Lawyer represents Client in connection with Client's divorce from Husband, who is unrepresented. Lawyer has prepared a settlement offer and wishes to present it to Husband. If Husband were represented, Lawyer would feel free to prepare the settlement agreement, present the settlement offer to opposing counsel, explain his view of the meaning of the documents, and articulate his view of the underlying legal obligations. Lawyer is fearful of taking these steps with an unrepresented person (particularly the last of these), for fear of being seen as giving legal advice to an unrepresented person. What may Lawyer do to try to effect the settlement with Husband?

Different Roles of the Lawyer

117. Lawyer represented the ABC Corporation. The Board of Directors of ABC instructed Lawyer to investigate allegations that ABC executives had been bribing executives of foreign-owned businesses in violation of U.S. law (without any involvement by Lawyer). Lawyer conducted the investigation and learned from an ABC Vice President that these allegations were true. The Vice President instructed Lawyer not to report this fact to anyone else in ABC. Lawyer nevertheless reported this fact up the corporate chain of command all the way to the Board of Directors, which refused to take any action and instructed Lawyer to keep the matter confidential. Lawyer took no further action with respect to the matter.

Did Lawyer violate the Model Rules of Professional Conduct?

(A) Yes, because Lawyer had a duty to "report out" what Lawyer had discovered about ABC's violations of U.S. law.

(B) Yes, because Lawyer violated the duty of confidentiality that Lawyer owed to the ABC Vice President.

(C) No, because Lawyer had the option but not the mandate to report the matter outside the company.

(D) No, because Lawyer was required to keep the findings of the investigation confidential once Lawyer had reported up the corporate chain of command.

118. Lawyer represented Corporation. While Lawyer was working on another project for Corporation unrelated to Corporation's power plant, Lawyer learned that Corporation was operating a power plant that was secretly generating harmful pollution far in excess of what the law permitted. Continuation of the pollution was reasonably likely to result in substantial bodily harm to people who lived nearby. Lawyer reasonably believed that there was a good chance that revelation of the pollution to the Environmental Protection Agency would have resulted in action that would have protected Corporation from massive liability in future lawsuits. Lawyer informed Corporation's Board of Directors of the pollution, but the Board of Directors refused to take any action to stop the pollution. The Board of Directors ordered Lawyer not to reveal the pollution, and Lawyer complied with that order.

Did Lawyer violate the Model Rules of Professional Conduct?

(A) Yes, because revelation of the pollution was necessary to prevent substantial injury to Corporation.

(B) Yes, because revelation was reasonably necessary to prevent substantial bodily harm to people who lived nearby.

(C) No, because Lawyer had the option but not the duty to reveal the pollution to protect Corporation and the public.

(D) No, because the Board of Directors of Corporation ordered Lawyer not to reveal the pollution.

119. Prosecutor knew that Killer had been convicted of murder many years ago in a separate part of the State, not in Prosecutor's jurisdiction. Witness knew Prosecutor and trusted Prosecutor to be a fair-minded and responsible public official. Witness contacted Prosecutor and gave Prosecutor evidence that Killer did not commit the offense for which Killer was convicted. Witness told Prosecutor to do with this evidence whatever Prosecutor thought was right, including doing nothing with it. Prosecutor studied the evidence and found it to be new, credible and material and concluded that the evidence created a reasonable likelihood that Killer was innocent. Prosecutor nevertheless believed that Killer was guilty. Prosecutor chose to do nothing with or about the new evidence.

Did Prosecutor violate the Model Rules of Professional Conduct?

(A) Yes, because Prosecutor was under a duty to disclose the evidence to Killer.

(B) Yes, because Prosecutor was under a duty to disclose the evidence to the court that rendered the judgment or other appropriate authority.

(C) No, because Killer was not convicted in Prosecutor's jurisdiction.

(D) No, because Prosecutor still believed that Killer was guilty.

120. Lawyer represented Corporation in a civil case in which the plaintiff alleged that Corporation's General Counsel had engaged in sexual harassment of employees. Eventually the time came for the lawyer for the plaintiff to take the deposition of the General Counsel, who had not retained counsel for himself personally. General Counsel asked Lawyer to represent General Counsel personally at the deposition. Lawyer perceived that there was a consentable conflict of interest in representing both Corporation and General Counsel in this matter. Lawyer sought and obtained informed consent to the conflict of interest from General Counsel personally and from Corporation, by the informed consent of General Counsel on behalf of Corporation. Lawyer then represented Corporation and General Counsel at the deposition.

Did Lawyer violate the Model Rules of Professional Conduct?

(A) Yes, because Lawyer did not have effective consent from Corporation.

(B) Yes, because Lawyer represented an entity and a constituent of the entity in the same matter.

(C) No, because Lawyer obtained informed consent from both affected clients.

(D) No, because Lawyer already represented General Counsel by virtue of representing Corporation, even before the purported consent.

121. Lawyer was a prosecutor and was in the midst of preparing for trial in a double murder case. There had been much public criticism of the police department for arresting the defendant and of the prosecutor for prosecuting the defendant. Police Commissioner brought Lawyer a report from the crime lab. The report recited that the lab had conducted DNA tests on material under the fingernails of one of the victims. The lab concluded that there was a DNA match between that material and the DNA of the defendant, and that there was a one-in-a-billion chance that the material came from someone else. Police Commissioner told Lawyer that Police Commissioner planned to hold a news conference that afternoon to publicize the lab report. Lawyer did not encourage or discourage Police Commissioner from holding the news conference. Police Commissioner held the news conference and publicized the results of the DNA tests.

Did Lawyer violate the Model Rules of Professional Conduct?

(A) Yes, because Lawyer violated the rules of conduct through the acts of another.

(B) Yes, because Lawyer did not exercise reasonable care to prevent the publication of the DNA test results.

(C) No, because Lawyer did not publicize the DNA test results.

(D) No, because the publication of the DNA test results was only done to protect the Police Department from the substantial undue prejudicial effect of recent publicity generated by others.

122. Client was inexperienced in legal matters and hired Lawyer in connection with Client's plan to acquire property next to, and owned by, a church school and develop it as a "halfway house" for drug addicts who were emerging from the criminal justice system. Client instructed Lawyer to "just write up the deal," but, as Lawyer began to do so, Lawyer realized that the courts might consider such a use for property so close to a school a nuisance and order it to be closed. Lawyer volunteered to Client that Client's plans likely would have serious adverse legal consequences and also volunteered that perhaps Client should think anyway about whether it was "the right thing to do" to house recovering drug addicts next to a school.

Did Lawyer violate the Model Rules of Professional Conduct?

(A) Yes, because Lawyer offered advice beyond what Client requested.

(B) Yes, because Lawyer offered moral advice.

(C) No, because Lawyer was required to offer Client moral advice related to Client's legal problems.

(D) No, because Client was inexperienced in legal matters and Client's proposed course of action was likely to have serious legal consequences for Client.

123. Lawyer Smith represented Client in connection with a personal injury matter. When the case settled, Lawyer Smith deposited the settlement funds into his trust account but then immediately disbursed the entire amount, including Client's funds, to himself. When Client learned

what had happened, Client hired Lawyer Jones to recover the settlement funds. Client would not permit Lawyer Jones to reveal the theft to the state bar, and Lawyer Jones did not do so. Lawyer Jones threatened Lawyer Smith that Lawyer Jones would report the theft to the police if Lawyer Smith did not immediately make restitution and pay Client what Client was owed as part of the settlement. Lawyer Smith complied, and Lawyer Jones did not report the theft to the police.

Did Lawyer Jones violate the Model Rules of Professional Conduct?

(A) Yes, because Lawyer Jones threatened criminal prosecution to advance a civil claim.

(B) Yes, because Lawyer Jones did not reveal the theft to the state bar.

(C) No, because the civil claim and the criminal claim arose from the same facts and were warranted by the facts.

(D) No, because the Model Rules encourage but do not require lawyers to report the misconduct of other lawyers.

124. Lawyer represented Client in connection with Client's sworn testimony before the United States House of Representatives Committee on Interstate and Foreign Commerce. Lawyer helped Client prepare Client's Opening Statement, to be read to the Committee as the first part of Client's sworn testimony. To Lawyer's surprise, Client testified to one matter that was not included in the Opening Statement with which Lawyer had assisted. Lawyer did not know Client intended to testify about this matter. Lawyer knew that what Client told the Committee about this matter was false. Lawyer was unsuccessful in persuading Client to reveal the falsity of the testimony to the Committee. Lawyer withdrew from representing Client and revealed the falsity of Client's testimony to the Committee.

Did Lawyer violate the Model Rules of Professional Conduct?

(A) Yes, because Lawyer revealed confidential information to the Committee.

(B) Yes, because Lawyer withdrew from representing Client.

(C) No, because Lawyer did not present or assist in presenting false evidence to the Committee.

(D) No, because Lawyer was obliged to take reasonable remedial measures.

125. Lawyer was appointed by a court to be the mediator in a hotly contested child custody dispute. Father was represented by counsel. Mother was representing herself. Lawyer met with Father, Father's counsel and Mother to discuss the areas of agreement and the areas of dispute between the parents. After this joint meeting, Lawyer asked each side to adjourn to separate rooms where Lawyer could caucus with each side privately. While Lawyer was caucusing with Mother, she asked Lawyer whether she should tell the judge in the case about Father's use of illegal drugs many years ago. What is Lawyer's duty under the Model Rules of Professional Conduct?

126. Client was a developer of commercial real estate and negotiated with Bank for a new line of credit to finance a new venture. Client was prepared to put up Client's interests in various

commercial properties as collateral for the new line of credit. Bank requested from Client a legal opinion that Client's title to the properties that would serve as collateral was unencumbered. Client employed Lawyer to perform the necessary title searches to confirm the information that Bank needed. Lawyer did the necessary searches and learned that Client's title to one of the properties was encumbered by several mechanics' liens, a judgment lien, and a tax lien. Lawyer delivered the report of the status of the titles of the properties to be used as collateral to Bank, which then denied the line of credit. Did Lawyer violate the Model Rules of Professional Conduct?

127. Lawyer represents Client in a criminal case. Lawyer's considered assessment is that Client is highly likely to be convicted. If Client is convicted, then Client will face a long mandatory minimum prison sentence. Lawyer knows that Client dreads prison and is irrationally optimistic about the chances of an acquittal. The prosecutor makes a plea offer to Lawyer. Lawyer and Client have never discussed whether any plea offer would be acceptable. The offer requires Client to spend several years in prison but far fewer years than the mandatory minimum sentence would be upon a conviction at trial. Explain to Lawyer what her professional responsibilities are at this point.

Safekeeping Funds and Other Property

128. Lawyer represented Client in a personal injury case. Lawyer and Client agreed that Lawyer would advance all of the reasonable expenses of the case and that repayment of the expenses would be contingent upon the outcome of the case. Lawyer and Client also agreed in writing that, in the event of a cash settlement, Lawyer would first calculate Lawyer's fee of 33% of the total settlement, with the payment of the expenses to come off the top of the remaining 66% of the settlement. Client would receive whatever was left. After the case settled but before the settlement funds were paid, Client received a list from Lawyer of the expenses to be reimbursed to Lawyer from Client's share of the settlement proceeds. Client objected to the reimbursement of the fee paid by Lawyer to one of Lawyer's experts, because the expert was a close relative of Lawyer. When Lawyer received the settlement funds, Lawyer immediately notified Client and deposited the funds into Lawyer's trust account. Lawyer held all the funds pending resolution of the dispute with Client about the expert's fee.

Did Lawyer violate the Model Rules of Professional Conduct?

(A) Yes, because Lawyer failed to distribute the portions of the settlement funds that were not in dispute.

(B) Yes, because Lawyer provided improper financial assistance to Client.

(C) No, because Lawyer held the settlement funds in trust pending resolution of the dispute.

(D) No, because Lawyer notified Client immediately of Lawyer's receipt of the funds.

129. Lawyer Smith and Lawyer Jones were not in the same law firm. Client asked Lawyer Jones for help, and Lawyer Jones referred Client to Lawyer Smith in exchange for a "referral fee." The "referral fee" was a share of the hourly fees that Lawyer Smith earned on Client's matter. Lawyer Jones did no work on the matter but did assume joint responsibility for the representation. Client agreed to the arrangement, including the share that each lawyer would receive, and that agreement was confirmed in writing. The total fee was reasonable. Lawyer Smith sent Client an invoice for earned fees. Client paid the fees by check to Lawyer Smith, who deposited the check into his operating account, notified Lawyer Jones of its receipt and promptly paid Lawyer Jones her share of the fees from the operating account.

Did Lawyer Smith violate the Model Rules of Professional Conduct?

(A) Yes, because Lawyer Smith paid Lawyer Jones a referral fee.

(B) Yes, because Lawyer Smith did not deposit Client's check into Lawyer Smith's trust account.

(C) No, because Client's check was for earned fees rather than a deposit against future fees.

(D) No, because Lawyer Smith promptly notified and paid Lawyer Jones.

130. Lawyer represented Client in a suit to collect on a promissory note. Lawyer took possession of the original promissory note and kept it in a fireproof safe while the case was pending. Lawyer kept important papers of other clients of Lawyer in the same safe. Client's promissory note was identified as belonging to Client. During the pendency of the case, Client fired Lawyer for no reason. Client did not owe Lawyer any unpaid legal fees. Client hired another lawyer to undertake to complete the suit related to the promissory note. When new counsel remembered years later to request the original promissory note, Lawyer promptly delivered the original promissory note to new counsel.

Did Lawyer violate the Model Rules of Professional Conduct?

(A) Yes, because Lawyer did not promptly deliver the promissory note to Client upon termination of the attorney-client relationship between Lawyer and Client.

(B) Yes, because Lawyer kept the original promissory note in a safe with important papers of other clients of Lawyer.

(C) No, because Lawyer promptly delivered the promissory note to new counsel upon request.

(D) No, because Lawyer's special duties regarding Client property only applied to money.

131. Lawyer established a trust account for Lawyer's personal injury practice. Bank told Lawyer that Bank would charge Lawyer $20 per month to keep the trust account open. Lawyer rarely was in possession of funds that needed to be kept in the trust account. Lawyer knew that an overdrawn trust account would draw the attention of the bar and would put him at risk of discipline. To ensure that his trust account never had a negative balance due to Bank's service charges, Lawyer deposited $960 of Lawyer's own funds to the trust account to take care of four years' worth of service charges. Lawyer kept accurate records of regarding how much of his own money was being held in the trust account.

Did Lawyer violate the Model Rules of Professional Conduct?

(A) Yes, because Lawyer commingled personal funds with client funds in the trust account.

(B) Yes, because Lawyer deposited more personal funds into the trust account than were necessary to cover the bank service charges.

(C) No, because Lawyer kept accurate records of regarding how much of his own money was being held in the trust account.

(D) No, because the purpose of Lawyer's deposit of personal funds was to prevent an inadvertent overdraft on the account.

132. Lawyer represented Client in a personal injury case about an auto accident. Client had tens of thousands of dollars of unpaid bills from Hospital relating to the accident. Lawyer negotiated a settlement of Client's case that included an amount sufficient to cover Client's unpaid

bills to Hospital (the "special damages funds") and an amount to compensate Client for pain and suffering and lost wages. Lawyer deposited the settlement check into Lawyer's trust account. Hospital asserted a right to the special damages funds. Client ordered Lawyer not to pay those funds to Hospital and demanded that Lawyer deliver the special damages funds to Client along with the rest of Client's net proceeds from the settlement. Lawyer held the special damages funds in trust while Lawyer investigated the matter. Lawyer eventually reasonably concluded that Hospital's claim to the special damages funds was superior. Lawyer paid the "special damages funds" to Hospital.

Did Lawyer violate the Model Rules of Professional Conduct?

(A) Yes, because Lawyer unilaterally decided the dispute.

(B) Yes, because Lawyer was required to interplead the special damages funds into court.

(C) No, because Lawyer held the special damages funds in trust until Lawyer decided who was entitled to them.

(D) No, because Lawyer was obliged to pay the special damages funds to Hospital once Lawyer reasonably concluded that Hospital was entitled to them.

133. Client hired Lawyer to protect Client's claim to the negatives of priceless photographs that a world famous photographer took in the 1930s. Client worked as an assistant to the photographer, and Client claimed that the photographer gave Client the negatives as payment for services rendered. The photographer's estate sued to recover the negatives. Client was afraid that the negatives might be stolen and gave them to Lawyer for safekeeping during the case. What should Lawyer do with the negatives?

134. Lawyer represents Brother, in Brother's capacity as executor of Brother's father's estate. By order of the Probate Court, all funds collected by Lawyer on behalf of the estate are to be distributed equally (net of fees an expenses chargeable to the estate) between Brother and Sister, the only two heirs to Father's estate. Lawyer assists Brother in the sale of real property that belonged to the estate. At the closing of the sale of that property, Lawyer receives a check for $400,000 payable to the estate. What are Lawyer's obligations with respect to the $400,000?

135. Lawyer just opened her own practice and entered into her first attorney-client relationship, with Client. Lawyer had $50,000 in startup funds of her own. These funds were on deposit with Bank, in Lawyer's Operating Account. This was the only bank account that Lawyer had. Pursuant to a written engagement agreement, Client paid Lawyer $10,000 as a deposit against Lawyer's hourly charges for legal fees and Lawyer's disbursements for expenses on Client's behalf. What are Lawyer's responsibilities with respect to the $10,000, both initially and as fees and expenses are incurred on behalf of Client?

Communications about Legal Services

136. Lawyer advertised that she was a "certified specialist" in "tractor-trailer accidents." In fact, Lawyer exclusively handled such matters, and had done so for many years. Lawyer had completed numerous hours of continuing legal education related to tractor-trailer litigation. In particular, she held a "Specialist's Certificate in Tractor-Trailer Litigation" from the State Tort Litigation Institute, which had been approved by the State Supreme Court to certify specialists in various types of personal injury litigation, including tractor-trailer accidents. The American Bar Association had not accredited the Institute to certify specialists. Lawyer did not identify the Institute in her advertisements.

Did Lawyer violate the Model Rules of Professional Conduct?

(A) Yes, because the Institute was not accredited by the American Bar Association.

(B) Yes, because she did not name the certifying organization in her advertisements.

(C) No, because the Institute was approved by the State Supreme Court.

(D) No, because Lawyer was a specialist as a result of her many years of experience handling tractor-trailer accidents.

137. Lawyer specialized in mass tort cases, particularly those in which many people are harmed by one catastrophic event. Lawyer read about a coal ash spill that had injured dozens of people in a small rural town. Lawyer recorded the following message, which was transmitted to every listed telephone number in the affected community through auto-dialing technology: "We at [Lawyer's firm] heard about the tragedy that has affected your community. Please accept our deepest best wishes as you deal with the harm that [the coal company] has done to you. We have experience in helping people like you get what you deserve from greedy corporations. Call us at 1-800-555-1212, and we will be there to fight for you. This recording is advertising material for a law firm."

Did Lawyer violate the Model Rules of Professional Conduct?

(A) Yes, because the recorded message did not begin with notice that it was an advertisement.

(B) Yes, because Lawyer solicited members of the community by telephone with the motive of pecuniary gain.

(C) No, because the solicitation was not face-to-face.

(D) No, because the message included the words "advertising material."

138. Part of Lawyer's practice consisted of representing clients who came to Lawyer through a pre-paid group legal service plan (the Plan) in which Lawyer participated but which Lawyer did not own. To drum up business, employees of the Plan engaged in extensive telemarketing. They "cold-called" residents of certain kinds of neighborhoods, usually at dinner time, and tried to sell memberships in the Plan. Lawyer represented several clients who became members as a result of such solicitation.

Did Lawyer violate the Model Rules of Professional Conduct?

(A) Yes, because lawyers are not permitted to participate in prepaid group legal services plans.

(B) Yes, because Lawyer solicited potential clients through live telephone contact through the acts of another.

(C) No, because Lawyer did not engage in the solicitation himself.

(D) No, because solicitation for membership in a group legal service plan is an exception to the general rule against solicitation.

139. Lawyer subscribed to and paid the usual fees of Lead Generator, Inc. (LGI), an independent marketing company that helped lawyers get clients. LGI advertised extensively online that it "matched" people who needed a lawyer with the "right" lawyer in that person's community. In fact, LGI sent the person who sought a lawyer the contact information for all the lawyers who paid LGI's fees in that community. LGI did not send the contact information for any lawyer who did not pay LGI's fees, and LGI did not inform those who were looking for a lawyer that LGI sent all the names, and only the names, of lawyers who paid its fees.

Did Lawyer violate the Model Rules of Professional Conduct?

(A) Yes, because Lawyer paid LGI for referrals.

(B) Yes, because LGI engaged in false and misleading advertising.

(C) No, because Lawyer did not engage in any false or misleading advertising.

(D) No, because Lawyer was permitted to pay the usual and customary charges associated with generating client leads.

140. Lawyer decided to open her own law firm. Because so many firms had names that were similar to her last name, Lawyer decided to use a trade name for her firm and to advertise using the trade name. Because Lawyer specialized exclusively in representing clients before the United States Copyright Office, Lawyer used the trade name "U.S. Copyright Law Office." A lawyer in competition with Lawyer filed a grievance with the state bar and alleged that Lawyer had committed misconduct.

Did Lawyer commit misconduct under the Model Rules of Professional Conduct?

(A) Yes, because Lawyer used a misleading trade name for Lawyer's Law Firm.

(B) Yes, because Lawyer used a trade name for Lawyer's Law Firm.

(C) No, because the trade name that Lawyer used for Lawyer's law firm was not false.

(D) No, because Lawyer was permitted to use a trade name for her law firm.

141. Lawyer represented plaintiffs in cases that sought the desegregation of country clubs. Lawyer did so pro bono as an expression of Lawyer's deeply held beliefs about equality under the law. Lawyer sought out potential plaintiffs who would have standing for such cases. Lawyer learned about and introduced himself face-to-face to Prospective Client and offered to represent Prospective Client for free in a suit to desegregate a country club in Prospective Client's community. Prospective Client was not a member of Lawyer's family and had neither a prior professional relationship nor a close personal relationship with Lawyer. Prospective Client turned down Lawyer's offer.

Did Lawyer violate the Model Rules of Professional Conduct?

(A) Yes, because Lawyer solicited employment as a lawyer face-to-face.

(B) Yes, because Prospective Client was not a member of Lawyer's family and had neither a prior professional relationship nor a close personal relationship with Lawyer.

(C) No, because Lawyer was not motivated by pecuniary gain.

(D) No, because Prospective Client did not hire Lawyer.

142. Law Firm had multiple offices. Under Law Firm's partnership agreement, every partner agreed that, if the partner did not provide the type of service that a prospective client needed, the partner would refer that prospective client only to another firm partner who usually and customarily provided services of the type that the prospective client needed. In every such circumstance, the referring partner agreed to recommend the other partner. The partnership agreement provided that, in return, the partner to whom the prospective client was referred would compensate the referring lawyer in an amount to be agreed upon or determined by Law Firm's Compensation Committee. Lawyer referred Prospective Client to Partner pursuant to the partnership agreement. Partner compensated Lawyer for the referral in an agreed-upon amount. Prospective Client was not apprised of the referral arrangement.

Did Partner violate the Model Rules of Professional Conduct?

(A) Yes, because Partner compensated Lawyer for recommending Partner's services.

(B) Yes, because the referral arrangement was not disclosed to Prospective Client.

(C) No, because Lawyer and Partner are both lawyers.

(D) No, because the referral was within one law firm.

143. Lawyer graduated from law school, passed the bar exam, and was admitted to practice. Lawyer decided to open her own firm and to limit her practice exclusively to the representation of claimants in worker's compensation matters. Lawyer had never handled a worker's compensation matter. Lawyer advertised the opening of her new practice and advertised that she was a "specialist" who limited her practice to the representation of claimants in worker's compensation cases.

Did Lawyer violate the Model Rules of Professional Conduct?

(A) Yes, because Lawyer was not certified as a specialist by an organization that had been accredited by a bar association.

(B) Yes, because Lawyer engaged in misleading advertising.

(C) No, because Lawyer limited her practice to worker's compensation matters.

(D) No, because Lawyer did not claim to be certified as a specialist.

144. Lawyer comes up with a new idea for generating business. Lawyer wants to set up a Twitter account and tweet about every large verdict that she receives. Lawyer hopes to have enough followers on Twitter that these announcements of the big verdicts she receives will cause the word to spread about how successful Lawyer is in getting good results for clients. That, she hopes, will cause prospective clients to seek the services of Lawyer. Under the Model Rules of Professional Conduct, what advice would you give Lawyer about her plan to use Twitter to generate business in this way?

145. Lawyer specialized in representing plaintiffs in auto accident cases. Lawyer's sister was a chiropractor who frequently treated such people. Lawyer tried to convince his sister to solicit her patients face-to-face to hire Lawyer to handle their injury claims. Lawyer's sister refused. Did Lawyer commit misconduct under the Model Rules of Professional Conduct?

146. Lawyer sought clients by paying for billboards with the advertisement, "A Good Lawyer Knows the Law, but A Great Lawyer Knows the Judge—Call me at 1-800-THE FIXER." In fact, Lawyer was well connected to the local judiciary and was able to obtain results for clients outside the bounds of the law based upon those connections (and a few other techniques). In his advertisement, did Lawyer commit misconduct under the Model Rules of Professional Conduct?

Lawyers' Duties to the Public and the Legal System

147. Lawyer represented consumers in bankruptcy cases. The local bankruptcy judge organized a "pro bono" day and invited lawyers who were admitted to practice in her court to show up in a community center on a Saturday morning and answer questions of members of the public for free. Lawyer received his invitation but did not attend. Lawyer reasoned (correctly) that, instead, he could be working for paying clients during that time and that therefore participation in the "pro bono day" would have caused him some mild financial hardship. In fact, Lawyer did not believe that he should have to work any pro bono hours, because he had invested heavily in his legal education and deserved to be compensated for that investment. Lawyer worked no pro bono hours that year.

Did Lawyer commit misconduct under the Model Rules of Professional Conduct?

(A) Yes, because Lawyer did not have good cause for not participating in the pro bono program.

(B) Yes, because Lawyer did not contribute 50 hours of pro bono work for the year.

(C) No, because pro bono work is not required by the Model Rules of Professional Conduct.

(D) No, because Lawyer would have experienced financial hardship as a result of the pro bono work.

148. Lawyer practiced family law and had extensive experience in custody cases. Lawyer had represented parents with drug problems numerous times in the parents' attempts to keep or obtain custody of their children. A local judge appointed Lawyer to represent Mother in a case in which the State was trying to terminate Mother's parental rights to her three children. Because of Lawyer's experience with custody cases, Lawyer was competent to represent Mother in such a proceeding. Mother was indigent and a drug addict in early recovery (again) from her addiction. Mother had "gotten clean" several times before but had always relapsed. When Mother was in active addiction, she neglected her children terribly. Mother told Lawyer that she very much wanted to raise her children and that they would be better off with her than in foster care. Mother lived in public housing and lived mostly on government benefits and charity. Lawyer did not want to represent Mother and asked the judge on that basis to release him from the appointment as Mother's counsel in the termination of parental rights proceeding.

Did Lawyer violate the Model Rules of Professional Conduct?

(A) Yes, because Lawyer did not show good cause for seeking to avoid the court appointment.

(B) Yes, because Lawyer was obliged to accept the appointment to a matter that Lawyer was competent to handle.

(C) No, because acceptance of court appointments is encouraged but not required by the Model Rules of Professional Conduct.

(D) No, because Lawyer's preference not to represent Mother would make it less likely that Lawyer would represent her competently.

149. Lawyer served as a member of the Board of Directors of her local Legal Services Organization (LSO). The purpose of LSO was to provide free legal services to indigent members of the community. A particular focus of LSO was to provide representation to indigent people who were in eviction proceedings. The Board of Directors of LSO met to discuss whether LSO should continue to commit its limited resources to the prosecution of a class action on behalf of tenants who were refusing to pay rent, and were the subject therefore of eviction proceedings, because several landlords had refused to make repairs to their apartments. Lawyer represented Landlord, one of the defendants in the class action, although Lawyer did not represent Landlord in the class action itself. Lawyer revealed to the Board of Directors that Lawyer represented Landlord. Lawyer participated in the decision of the LSO to discontinue funding the class action and argued that the funding should be discontinued.

Did Lawyer violate the Model Rules of Professional Conduct?

(A) Yes, because Lawyer was a member of a legal services organization whose mission was antagonistic to the interests of Lawyer's client, Landlord.

(B) Yes, because Lawyer participated in a decision that had an adverse effect on clients of the organization who were adverse to Lawyer's client, Landlord.

(C) No, because Lawyer revealed Lawyer's representation of Landlord before participating in the decision about the class action.

(D) No, because Lawyer's participation in the decision about the class action was not incompatible with Lawyer's obligations to Landlord.

150. Lawyer was a member of her State Bar's Committee on Disciplinary Rules and Procedures (the DRC). The DRC was considering reforms to the process under which lawyers in their state would be subject to discipline for violating the rules of conduct. One particular proposal was to change the burden of proof. The existing rule provided that a lawyer would be subject to discipline if the State Bar proved by a preponderance of the evidence that the lawyer had violated the rules of conduct. The DRC was considering whether to change that standard to require clear and convincing evidence of a violation of the rules of conduct before a lawyer could be subject to discipline. At the time of the debate over this proposed rule change, Lawyer represented several clients who were respondents in disciplinary proceedings and thus would be benefited by this rule change. Lawyer revealed that he represented clients who would benefit but refused to name them. Lawyer participated in the debate, and the standard was changed to clear and convincing evidence.

Did Lawyer violate the Model Rules of Professional Conduct?

(A) Yes, because Lawyer participated in the decision about a matter that benefitted his clients.

(B) Yes, because Lawyer refused to identify the clients whose interests would be benefitted.

(C) No, because Lawyer had the right to serve as a member of the DRC notwithstanding that its actions might affect the interests of his clients.

(D) No, because Lawyer revealed that he represented clients who would benefit from the rule change.

151. Lawyer wanted to make compensated service as a guardian ad litem a part of her practice. Lawyer knew that whoever served as the judge in the family court would be in a position to appoint Lawyer to serve in cases where children needed a guardian ad litem. In order to improve her chances of receiving such appointments, Lawyer worked tirelessly without compensation on the campaign of Judicial Candidate for an open seat on the Family Court. After Judicial Candidate won that election and became Family Court Judge, Lawyer received numerous lucrative appointments to serve as a guardian ad litem from Family Court Judge. Assume that, under the relevant criminal law, the provision of the uncompensated campaign services in exchange for appointment as a guardian ad litem would not constitute bribery.

Did Lawyer violate the Model Rules of Professional Conduct?

(A) Yes, because Lawyer supported a judicial candidate and then accepted benefits from that candidate after the candidate became a judge.

(B) Yes, because Lawyer made an in-kind political contribution for the purpose of obtaining court appointments.

(C) No, because lawyer only donated uncompensated services.

(D) No, because Lawyer did not commit bribery.

152. Lawyer publicly announced that she would be a candidate for election to her state's trial court in the next election and that she would file the necessary papers with the state election commission by the deadline. To fund her campaign, Lawyer wrote letters to a large number of lawyers in her community and asked them to contribute to the campaign. After a hard-fought campaign, Lawyer lost the election and never became a judge. The bar disciplinary authorities, however, sought to discipline Lawyer because she wrote letters to other lawyers asking for contributions to her judicial campaign. Did Lawyer violate the Model Rules of Professional Conduct?

Judicial Conduct

153. Judge is presiding over a complex, high-stakes commercial dispute. One of the key issues in the case involves an interpretation of an obscure provision in the Law of the Sea Treaty. Judge has no background or expertise regarding this Treaty. Judge perceives that the trial would be delayed if Judge took the time to conduct the necessary research to resolve to Judge's satisfaction the legal question that has arisen, or if Judge delegated that responsibility to Judge's law clerk. To save time, Judge consulted with a distinguished expert in the Law of the Sea Treaty and received a prompt, written response to Judge's inquiry. Judge promptly sent the expert's written response to all parties for their consideration.

Did Judge violate the Model Code of Judicial Conduct?

(A) Yes, because Judge investigated a legal question independently of the parties.

(B) Yes, because Judge did not notify the parties in advance that Judge intended to consult the expert.

(C) No, because Judge promptly reported the expert's written advice to all parties.

(D) No, because Judge's investigation was as to a matter of law rather than fact.

154. Judge formerly employed Law Student as an intern during Law Student's time in law school. Law Student was initially denied a certificate of fitness for admission to the bar and then challenged that denial in a formal proceeding before a special master. Law Student told Judge that Law Student had lined up a dozen law professors and others to testify that Law Student was a person of good character. Law Student asked Judge to join the others and testify at the hearing that Law Student was a person of good character. Judge declined to do so, even though Judge did believe that Law Student as a person of good character. Law Student asked if Judge would testify in response to a subpoena, and Judge discouraged Law Student from taking that step. To Judge's surprise, Law Student caused a subpoena to be served on Judge, summoning Judge to testify as a character witness on behalf of Law Student. Judge complied with the subpoena, appeared at the hearing, and testified that Law Student was a person of good character.

Did Judge violate the Model Rules of Judicial Conduct?

(A) Yes, because Judge testified as a character witness in an adjudicatory proceeding.

(B) Yes, because Judge discouraged a party from serving him with a subpoena.

(C) No, because Judge had personal knowledge regarding an important fact related to an adjudicatory proceeding.

(D) No, because Judge only testified as a character witness in response to the subpoena.

155. Judge served on the State Court of Appeals. Judge also served on the Board of Directors of the local chapter of the United Way, a charitable organization whose activities were not conducted for profit. Judge sent letters in which he solicited charitable contributions as part of the United Way's annual fundraising campaign. Judge sent the letters only to other judges, including justices of the State Supreme Court, other judges on the Court of Appeals, and the district (trial level) judges over whom the Court of Appeals exercised appellate jurisdiction. The text of the letters was not threatening or coercive.

Did Judge violate the Model Code of Judicial Conduct?

(A) Yes, because Judge solicited contributions for a charitable organization.

(B) Yes, because Judge solicited contributions from judges over whom Judge exercised appellate authority.

(C) No, because the text of the letters was not threatening or coercive.

(D) No, because the United Way is a charitable organization.

156. Judge presided over a lengthy, complex civil case. Judge did her best to manage the trial, particularly its length and complexity, but the nature of the case was such that it inevitably took a long time and presented issues that were hard to understand. Despite an invitation from Judge to do so, no juror took notes during the trial, and no juror submitted any written questions for Judge to consider asking the lawyers to address. During its lengthy deliberations, the jury sent questions to Judge, most of which betrayed that the jury members had no understanding of the most basic issues in the case. The jury eventually returned a verdict for the defendant. Judge entered an order and granted a new trial. In that order, Judge was highly critical of the jury's verdict because it went against the great weight of the evidence. In reaching that judgment, Judge was influenced by her knowledge and experience from her first career as an engineer.

Did Judge violate the Model Code of Judicial Conduct?

(A) Yes, because Judge criticized jurors for their verdict in a proceeding.

(B) Yes, because Judge was influenced by knowledge and experience she gained outside the record in the case.

(C) No, because Judge's criticism of the jury's verdict was justified under the circumstances.

(D) No, because Judge's criticism of the jury's verdict was in a court order.

157. Judge's Nephew was injured in an accident. Judge was appointed to serve as Nephew's guardian. As the guardian, Judge had the power to make decisions about how Nephew's money would be invested. Judge hired a broker to invest the funds, subject to Judge's supervision. Broker sent Judge monthly statements showing what stocks broker bought and sold for Nephew's guardianship estate. Judge was too busy to review the statements. If Judge had done so, Judge would have seen that broker had invested $100,000 for the benefit of Nephew

in Acme Corp. While Nephew's guardianship estate owned that stock, Judge presided over a civil case in which Acme was a defendant and faced liability that would have caused Acme to have to file bankruptcy. After a bench trial, Judge found in favor of Acme. The evidence in favor of Acme was overwhelming.

Did Judge violate the Model Code of Judicial Conduct?

(A) Yes, because Judge did not keep informed about Judge's economic interests as a fiduciary to Nephew.

(B) Yes, because Judge presided over a case in which, as a fiduciary, he had an economic interest in a party to the proceeding.

(C) No, because Judge did not know Nephew's guardianship estate had an economic interest in the proceeding.

(D) No, because the evidence in favor of Acme was overwhelming.

158. Judge has been assigned to preside over a civil case. It has come to the attention of Judge that one of the parties to the case is related to Judge by marriage. Upon investigation, Judge determines that this party is married to Judge's wife's cousin. Judge determines that there is no potential basis, other than the bare fact of this distant family relation that might disqualify Judge from presiding over the case. Must Judge disqualify himself?

159. Judge presided over a civil case in which the main issue was the credibility of the respective parties. The defendant happened to have a large nose. In opening statements, cross-examination, and closing argument, Lawyer (representing the plaintiff) made frequent references to the defendant's large nose and kept referring to the effect on Pinocchio's nose when Pinocchio would tell a lie. Lawyer asked the jurors to return a verdict for plaintiff based upon the argument that the defendant was lying, "just like Pinocchio—I mean, just look at that nose!" Over the objection of defendant's counsel, Judge permitted Lawyer to engage in this advocacy. Did Judge violate the Model Code of Judicial Conduct?

160. Judge received an inquiry from her state's Judicial Nominating Commission (JNC). The JNC informed Judge that Lawyer was under consideration for appointment as a judge to the state's court of appeals and asked Judge to comment on Lawyer's professional qualifications for appointment to judicial office. Judge responded to the inquiry and informed the JNC that, in Judge's opinion, Lawyer was fit for judicial office. The JNC nominated Lawyer for a judicial appointment, and Lawyer was eventually appointed. Did Judge violate the Model Code of Judicial Conduct?

Questions

Practice Final Exam

Suggested Completion Time: Two Hours.

There are 36 multiple-choice questions and 12 short-answer questions. Allow one hour for the multiple-choice section of the exam (about 90 seconds per question) and one hour for the short-answer section (five minutes per question).

161. Lawyer obtained her license to practice law in State A. After several years of litigating civil cases in a law firm for a number of clients, including Corporation, Lawyer received an offer to go to work as in-house counsel for Corporation. The job required Lawyer to move to State B, where Lawyer did not have a license to practice law. Lawyer accepted the job to work solely for Corporation and, among other duties, handled civil cases for Corporation in State B by admission pro hac vice for each case. Lawyer's permanent office and residence were in State B.

Did Lawyer violate the Model Rules of Professional Conduct by her work in State B?

(A) Yes, because Lawyer appeared in court in State B for Corporation.

(B) Yes, because Lawyer practiced law in State B, where she did not have a law license.

(C) No, because Lawyer only represented her employer.

(D) No, because Lawyer was duly licensed in another United States jurisdiction.

162. Lawyer represented Client in defense of criminal charges. Judge was presiding over the case. In the course of representing Client, Lawyer learned that Judge was secretly involved in a sexual relationship with Prosecutor, who represented the State in Client's case and in numerous other cases in Judge's court. By engaging in this relationship, Prosecutor violated the Model Rules of Professional Conduct. By engaging in this relationship, Judge violated the Model Code of Judicial Conduct. Lawyer consulted with Client about reporting Judge and Prosecutor to the appropriate professional authorities and strongly encouraged Client to give informed consent to the disclosures. Client feared that Prosecutor (or the successor prosecutor) and Judge (or whatever judge received Client's case, by reassignment) somehow would retaliate, to Client's detriment. Client refused to give Lawyer informed consent to reveal Prosecutor's and Judge's misconduct. Lawyer did not reveal Prosecutor's or Judge's misconduct to the appropriate professional authorities.

Did Lawyer violate the Model Rules of Professional Conduct?

(A) Yes, because Lawyer was obliged to report Prosecutor's misconduct.

(B) Yes, because Lawyer was obliged to report Judge's misconduct.

(C) No, because Lawyer did not have Client's informed consent to report Prosecutor's or Judge's misconduct.

(D) No, because Lawyer had the option but not the duty to report Prosecutor's and Judge's misconduct.

163. Lawyer committed several acts of violence on his wife and eventually was arrested and charged with domestic violence. None of the violent acts that Lawyer committed related in any way to Lawyer's practice of law. Lawyer was permitted to enter a diversion program for people accused of domestic violence. The program required Lawyer to attend counseling and to complete an anger management course. Lawyer successfully completed the diversion program, and as a result, the charges against Lawyer were dropped. Lawyer was not convicted of any crime.

Did Lawyer commit misconduct under the Model Rules of Professional Conduct?

(A) Yes, because Lawyer was arrested for violent criminal conduct.

(B) Yes, because Lawyer's violent criminal acts reflected adversely on Lawyer's fitness to practice law.

(C) No, because Lawyer's criminal acts did not occur in connection with Lawyer's practice of law.

(D) No, because Lawyer was not convicted of any crime.

164. Lawyer was licensed only in State A and had earned there an excellent national reputation for representing investors against their stockbrokers in arbitration proceedings. Most such arbitrations in Lawyer's region of the country were held in nearby State B. So many arbitrations were held in State B that Lawyer established an office there to conveniently handle the business, although Lawyer only practiced out of that office part-time. Lawyer never represented to anyone that he was licensed in State B. Client was an investor with a claim against Stockbroker. Client had signed a brokerage agreement that mandated arbitration of any claims against Stockbroker. Client's arbitration hearing was held in State B. Lawyer represented Client in the arbitration in State B. Lawyer did not engage local counsel (licensed in State B) to assist in the representation.

Did Lawyer violate the Model Rules of Professional Conduct?

(A) Yes, because Lawyer established an office in State B.

(B) Yes, because Lawyer did not engage local counsel to assist in the representation.

(C) No, because Lawyer never represented to anyone that he was licensed in State B.

(D) No, because Lawyer's activities in State B related to alternative dispute resolution proceedings and were related to his practice in State A.

165. Lawyer represented Client, an elderly woman who had been diagnosed with mild cognitive impairment. Lawyer worked closely with Client on several matters for several years. Lawyer was careful to consult with Client in the morning, and Lawyer found that Client's instructions

during that time of day were lucid and consistent with Client's long-term commitments and values. Lawyer followed those instructions. Lawyer eventually began to notice a decline in Client's mental faculties and sometimes had trouble obtaining lucid instructions, even in the morning. Lawyer was concerned and revealed to Client's doctor about what Lawyer was observing. Lawyer asked the doctor whether, in the doctor's opinion, Client was becoming so impaired that Lawyer should seek a guardian or talk to Client's children. The doctor declined to venture an opinion, because Client had not signed a waiver to permit the doctor to speak with Lawyer about her medical condition.

Did Lawyer violate the Model Rules of Professional Conduct?

(A) Yes, because Lawyer revealed confidential information to the doctor.

(B) Yes, because Lawyer acted on instructions of a client with a cognitive impairment.

(C) No, because Lawyer was impliedly authorized to reveal confidential information to the doctor.

(D) No, because Lawyer was permitted to take reasonable protective action on behalf of Client.

166. Lawyer represented Grandfather in a custody dispute involving Grandfather's Granddaughter. The judge ordered Grandfather to undergo a psychiatric evaluation. Lawyer received the report of the psychiatrist. The report stated that Grandfather was in a "precariously fragile mental state" and that granting him custody of Granddaughter would not be in the child's best interests. The report also expressed concern about Grandfather's "suicidal ideation" in discussions with the psychiatrist about what it would feel like not to obtain custody of Granddaughter. Grandfather asked Lawyer what the psychiatrist's report said, but Lawyer did not provide the information in response. Instead, Lawyer waited to reveal the substance of the report to Grandfather, pending the expected arrival of other family members who could, if necessary, safeguard Grandfather from himself. Lawyer meanwhile gave the report to Associate (who worked in the firm for Lawyer) and asked Associate to draft a motion with the court to exclude it from evidence.

Did Lawyer violate the Model Rules of Professional Conduct?

(A) Yes, because Lawyer did not promptly provide Grandfather with the information that Grandfather requested.

(B) Yes, because Lawyer gave the report, which contained confidential information, to Associate.

(C) No, because Lawyer had no duty to report the substance of the report to Grandfather.

(D) No, because Lawyer was justified in delaying the transmission of the information to Client.

167. Lawyer represented Client in a variety of transactional matters over several years. Lawyer and Client had agreed that Lawyer would bill for her time once per month and that Client would

pay the bills within thirty days. Client was habitually late paying Lawyer's bills. Lawyer and Client never anticipated that Client would pay the bills late and never discussed any consequences for doing so. The bills were a small percentage of Lawyer's income, but Lawyer found the late payments to be aggravating. Eventually, in frustration, Lawyer sent all of Client's files back to Client with a note that told Client that Lawyer was withdrawing as Client's attorney. At the time, Lawyer had no urgent pending matters for Client, but Client still owed Lawyer money for past due fees.

Did Lawyer violate the Model Rules of Professional Conduct?

(A) Yes, because Client's late payments did not result in an unreasonable financial burden on Lawyer.

(B) Yes, because Lawyer did not give reasonable warning that Lawyer would withdraw if Client did not pay the bills on time.

(C) No, because Client failed to fulfill obligations to Lawyer.

(D) No, because Client's late payments resulted in a financial burden on Lawyer.

168. Lawyer represented Client in a civil case. Lawyer and Client agreed that Client would pay Lawyer's fees within 30 days of receipt by Client of Lawyer's monthly invoice. Lawyer reasonably expended a large number of hours on behalf of Client and billed Client at the Lawyer's usual (and reasonable) hourly rate. Client did not pay that bill within 30 days. Lawyer continued to work on the case, and a month later, sent another bill with the first month's charges and an additional large amount for the second month's work. Client also paid nothing on this bill. Lawyer sought payment from Client and warned Client that Lawyer would seek to withdraw if Client did not pay the bills. Client declined to pay the bills and explained that Client was experiencing serious unexpected financial difficulties. Lawyer filed a motion to withdraw from representing Client and recited in the motion that Client had failed to fulfill the obligation to Lawyer to pay Lawyer's bills in a timely manner, that Client had been given reasonable warning, and that Lawyer would withdraw unless the obligation was fulfilled. The court granted the motion to withdraw.

Did Lawyer violate the Model Rules of Professional Conduct?

(A) Yes, because Lawyer was not entitled to seek to withdraw under these circumstances.

(B) Yes, because Lawyer revealed more confidential information of Client in the motion to withdraw than was reasonably necessary.

(C) No, because Lawyer was entitled to seek to withdraw when Client ignored Lawyer's warning that lawyer would withdraw if Client did not pay Lawyer's fees.

(D) No, because the court could not have properly considered the motion without being informed of what obligation Client had failed to fulfill.

169. Lawyer worked for Old Law Firm but was interviewing with New Law Firm to explore the possibility of changing firms. New Law Firm needed to know some information about

Lawyer's work at Old Law Firm to determine whether Lawyer would bring any conflicts of interest into New Law Firm. While he has been at Old Law Firm, Lawyer has represented Smith. New Law Firm was hesitant to hire Lawyer because of rumors that Smith might sue Jones, a major client of New Law Firm. New Law Firm did not want to hire Lawyer and then have a conflict of interest that would prevent it from representing Jones if Smith sued Jones. New Law Firm asked Lawyer, and Lawyer assured New Law Firm that Smith had told Lawyer that Smith had no intention of suing Jones. New Law Firm hired Lawyer.

Did Lawyer violate the Model Rules of Professional Conduct?

(A) Yes, because Lawyer revealed privileged information to New Law Firm in the interview.

(B) Yes, because Lawyer revealed confidential information to New Law Firm in the interview.

(C) No, because Lawyer only revealed enough information to permit New Law Firm to detect possible conflicts of interest arising from Lawyer's possible change in employment.

(D) No, because the information that Lawyer revealed did not prejudice Smith.

170. Lawyer assisted Client with the sale of a large commercial property. After the deal closed, but before the purchase funds could be wire transferred to Client, Lawyer learned that the transaction was fraudulent. Lawyer immediately contacted the counsel for the Buyer and revealed the fraudulent nature of the transaction in time for Buyer to stop the wire transfer. Client fired Lawyer and sought to have Lawyer disciplined for violation of the Model Rules of Professional Conduct.

Did Lawyer commit misconduct under the Model Rules of Professional Conduct?

(A) Yes, because Lawyer revealed confidential information without authorization.

(B) Yes, because Lawyer assisted Client in the perpetration of a fraud.

(C) No, because Lawyer was required to reveal the fraud to Buyer.

(D) No, because Lawyer's disclosure to the Buyer was permitted but not required.

171. Lawyer was a partner in Smith & Jones, a 500-person law firm that had offices all over the world. Lawyer was representing Corporation A in litigation in New York over ownership of a patent. Then Corporation B intervened as a matter of right in that litigation and claimed ownership of the patent. Because of the nature of the case, Corporation B thereby immediately became directly adverse to Corporation A. Lawyer then discovered that a lawyer in the San Diego office of Smith & Jones represented Corporation B in a wholly unrelated matter. Lawyer immediately took the necessary steps to screen the San Diego lawyer from any knowledge of or involvement in the patent litigation. Lawyer then continued his representation of Corporation A in the patent litigation.

Did Lawyer violate the Model Rules of Professional Conduct?

(A) Yes, because screening does not cure conflicts of interest.

(B) Yes, because Lawyer represented one client of Smith & Jones against another client of Smith & Jones.

(C) No, because the two matters were being handled by separate offices of Smith & Jones.

(D) No, because the two matters were unrelated.

172. Law Firm currently represents Subsidiary, Inc. Law Firm has just been asked to represent New Client as plaintiff in a suit. The defendant in the suit for New Client would be Parent, Inc. Subsidiary is a wholly owned subsidiary of Parent. Subsidiary and Parent conduct their operations out of the same office with the same people serving as general counsel, as officers, and as members of the corporations' respective boards of directors. Although Subsidiary and Parent are separate legal entities, they effectively operate as alter egos of each other. The matter for New Client would be entirely unrelated to the matter in which the firm represents Subsidiary.

Would Law Firm have a conflict of interest if it accepted the representation of New Client in its suit against Parent just because the firm already represents Subsidiary in an unrelated matter?

(A) Yes, because Parent and Subsidiary effectively operate as alter egos of each other.

(B) Yes, because Parent is part of the same corporate family as Subsidiary.

(C) No, because Parent and Subsidiary are separate legal entities.

(D) No, because the matter for New Client is unrelated to the matter that Law Firm is handling for Subsidiary.

173. Lawyer represents Client, an indigent person who wishes to appeal the denial of his social security disability benefits. Lawyer has agreed to file that appeal soon. It will be an administrative proceeding rather than a court case. To help Client and to ease Client's mind while Lawyer prepares to file the appeal, Lawyer agreed to pay all of Client's court costs and litigation expenses, without any obligation for Client ever to repay him, and to pay Client's grocery bills until the appeal is over. Lawyer has paid for two weeks of groceries so far.

Did Lawyer violate the Model Rules of Professional Conduct?

(A) Yes, because Lawyer agreed to pay the court costs and expenses without any obligation to repay them.

(B) Yes, because Lawyer gave Client money for living expenses in connection with contemplated litigation.

(C) No, because the case had not been filed yet.

(D) No, because the matter will be an administrative proceeding rather than a court case.

174. Lawyer represented Art Dealer in a lawsuit involving a former employee of Art Dealer. Client visited Art Dealer's place of business to interview witnesses. While Lawyer was on the premises, Lawyer noticed a painting that Lawyer particularly liked. Lawyer asked Art Dealer if the painting was for sale, and Art Dealer replied that it was. Art Dealer quoted a price, and Lawyer offered to pay 10% less than that asking price. Art Dealer immediately accepted Lawyer's counteroffer, and Lawyer immediately purchased the painting for what Lawyer knew to be a fair and reasonable price.

Did Lawyer violate the Model Rules of Professional Conduct?

(A) Yes, because Lawyer did not obtain informed consent to the essential terms of the transaction.

(B) Yes, because Lawyer did not advise Art Dealer in writing of the desirability of obtaining independent counsel before selling the painting to Lawyer.

(C) No, because the sale of the painting was a standard commercial transaction like the other art sales that Art Dealer routinely made.

(D) No, because the price of the painting was fair and reasonable.

175. Lawyer was a full-time salaried employee of Insurance Co. but practiced under the "firm" name of Smith & Jones, the last names of the two most senior lawyers in the "firm." Lawyer only represented policyholders of Insurance Co. Lawyer always informed clients that the lawyers in Smith & Jones were employees of Insurance Co. Lawyer was assigned by Insurance Co. to represent Policyholder in defense of a claim for damages arising from an automobile accident. Policyholder had an insurance policy with Insurance Co. under which Insurance Co. promised to provide Policyholder with a defense to such claims and indemnity from losses for such claims up to the policy limits. The claim was for less than the policy limits. Under applicable state law, Insurance Co. was not a client of Lawyer. In Lawyer's professional judgment, Lawyer believed that Policyholder would best be served by a particular legal argument. Because acceptance of that argument would hurt Insurance Co. in other cases, Insurance Co. instructed Lawyer not to make the argument. Lawyer did not make the argument.

Did Lawyer violate the Model Rules of Professional Conduct?

(A) Yes, because Lawyer represented Policyholder while Lawyer was a full-time salaried employee by Insurance Co.

(B) Yes, because Lawyer allowed Insurance Co. to regulate Lawyer's professional judgment.

(C) No, because Lawyer was an employee of Insurance Co. and thus bound to follow lawful orders of his employer.

(D) No, because Insurance Co. was paying for the defense and thus had the right to control it.

176. Lawyer formerly served as a lawyer for Government. In that capacity, Lawyer personally performed substantial work on a suit that Government brought against Airline for antitrust violations. Lawyer served as lead counsel for Government. Lawyer left Government and went to work for Law Firm. Law Firm represented Client who sued Airline for damages for the exact same violations of the antitrust laws for which Government was suing Airline in the case on which Lawyer worked. Government will not consent to Lawyer's representation of Client in this matter.

May Law Firm represent Client in this suit, consistent with the Model Rules of Professional Conduct?

(A) Yes, because Client does not have interests that are materially adverse to the interests of Government.

(B) Yes, because Law Firm may screen Lawyer from the case and thereby avoid imputation of Lawyer's conflict to the other lawyers in the firm.

(C) No, because Lawyer served as lead counsel for Government.

(D) No, because Lawyer has a conflict of interest that will be imputed to all the lawyers in Law Firm.

177. Lawyer was a partner in Law Firm. Lawyer volunteered once a month at a nonprofit legal services organization to assist members of the public pro bono with the completion of standard court-created forms necessary to obtain divorces and to seek child support. Before rendering his advice and assistance, Lawyer always obtained informed consent to a representation that was limited in scope and duration to the completion of the appropriate forms. Lawyer assisted Husband on this basis. Unbeknownst to Lawyer, Law Firm represented Wife in the divorce proceedings with which Lawyer helped Husband.

Did Lawyer violate the Model Rules of Professional Conduct?

(A) Yes, because Lawyer undertook to represent Husband when Lawyer had a concurrent conflict of interest as a result of Law Firm's representation of Wife.

(B) Yes, because Lawyer's limitation on the scope of representation of Husband was not reasonable.

(C) No, because the Model Rules of Professional Conduct do not apply to short-term pro bono representations.

(D) No, because Lawyer did not know that Law firm represented Wife.

178. Lawyer created a standard form engagement agreement for use with all of her clients. The agreement provided that the parties to the agreement agreed to arbitrate any disputes arising from the attorney-client relationship, including but not limited to any disputes regarding fees and any claims of malpractice. In Lawyer's state, the remedies available in arbitration were identical to the remedies available in civil cases for collection of fees or for legal malpractice, except that punitive damages were not available in arbitration of malpractice claims. Lawyer presented Client with the standard form agreement and gave Client a full explanation of the advantages and disadvantages of the arbitration clause, including the unavailability of punitive damages in the arbitration of malpractice claims. Lawyer advised Client to seek independent counsel about the engagement agreement and gave Client adequate opportunity to do so. Client did not obtain independent counsel. Client gave informed consent to the engagement agreement, including the arbitration clause, and signed it.

Did Lawyer violate the Model Rules of Professional Conduct?

(A) Yes, because Lawyer included an arbitration clause in the engagement agreement.

(B) Yes, because Client was not independently represented in connection with the engagement agreement.

(C) No, because Client gave informed consent to the engagement agreement, including the arbitration clause.

(D) No, because Client was advised to seek independent counsel and was given the opportunity to do so.

179. Lawyer was as an assistant public defender and carried a very heavy caseload. As a matter of routine, Judge signed an order to appoint Lawyer to represent a defendant in a murder case. As a public defender, Lawyer was not afforded the opportunity to decline this appointment. Lawyer was thrilled at the appointment, because Lawyer very much wanted to be involved in the case. After his first appearance in the murder case, when Lawyer first grasped how much effort would be required in the case, Lawyer knew that he would be unable to give appropriate attention to all of his other cases if Lawyer remained involved in the murder case. Lawyer nevertheless did not seek to withdraw from the murder case.

Did Lawyer violate the Model Rules of Professional Conduct?

(A) Yes, because Lawyer had a duty to seek to withdraw.

(B) Yes, because Lawyer had good cause to seek to avoid the appointment.

(C) No, because Lawyer was obliged to accept the court appointment.

(D) No, because Lawyer had the option but not the duty to seek to withdraw.

180. Lawyer represented Client, who was accused of a terrorist act of violence. While Client was in jail awaiting trial, Client's Sister went to clean out her storage shed, where Client also had stored a few personal items. Law enforcement had never searched the shed, perhaps because its existence and connection to Client were unknown. In the shed, Sister found a laptop computer that belonged to Client. Sister took the computer to Lawyer, who took possession of it. Lawyer examined the "browser history" on the computer to see what web sites Client had visited. The browser history showed that Client had visited several sites that gave instructions about how to build bombs like those used in the terrorist act of which Client was accused. Lawyer counseled Sister to "clear" the browser history so that any search for the web sites that Client had visited would be more difficult. Sister did so. Lawyer knew that a forensic computer specialist could still reconstruct the browser history. Lawyer then returned the computer to Sister, who returned it to the shed. The police eventually learned about the shed and executed a search warrant. The police found and took possession of the laptop before Client's trial.

Did Lawyer violate the Model Rules of Professional Conduct?

(A) Yes, because Lawyer took physical possession of tangible evidence in a criminal case.

(B) Yes, because Lawyer counseled Sister to unlawfully alter the evidence.

(C) No, because Lawyer returned the evidence to the Sister.

(D) No, because Lawyer did not alter, destroy or conceal any evidence.

181. Lawyer represented Client and attempted to secure a temporary restraining order to prevent Opposing Party from foreclosing on Client's office building. At the emergency hearing, Lawyer initially presented the Court only with the facts that were helpful to Client and not with any of the facts that were adverse to Client's position. Surprisingly, counsel for Opposing Party did not apprise the Court of all of those adverse facts, either. Lawyer still did not apprise the Court of those adverse facts. The Court nevertheless ruled against Lawyer and denied the application for a temporary restraining order. The foreclosure proceeded.

Did Lawyer commit misconduct the Model Rules of Professional Conduct?

(A) Yes, because Lawyer did not initially apprise the Court of facts that were adverse to Client.

(B) Yes, because Lawyer did not apprise the Court of facts that were adverse to Client once Opposing Counsel failed to do so.

(C) No, because the Court denied Lawyer's application for the temporary restraining order.

(D) No, because Opposing Party was represented at the hearing.

182. Lawyer represented Client in a lengthy and contentious civil case. On the eve of trial, it was clear that one issue that would be going to the jury would be whether Client was entitled to recover his attorney's fees from Defendant and, if so, what were Client's reasonable attorneys fees in the case. Only Lawyer could testify on personal knowledge to the services that were rendered. Lawyer proposed to testify to both the nature of the services rendered and their value. Lawyer also made it clear that Lawyer intended to act as an advocate for Client at trial, although other lawyers in Lawyer's firm were ready, willing and able to act as advocates for Client in the place of Lawyer. It would be a burden on Client to get another lawyer to give the testimony about fees or to act as Client's advocate. Defendant intends to contest the claim for fees, with respect to both what was done and how much it was worth. Counsel for Defendant objects to Lawyer serving as both a witness and an advocate at the trial of the case.

Under the Model Rules of Professional Conduct, may Lawyer serve as both the advocate and the witness under these circumstances?

(A) Yes, because the testimony relates to the nature and value of legal services rendered in the case.

(B) Yes, because it would be a burden on Client to get another lawyer to testify to the nature and value of legal services rendered in the case.

(C) No, because Lawyer would be testifying to disputed facts.

(D) No, because other lawyers in Lawyer's firm are ready to act as advocates at trial in the place of Lawyer.

183. Lawyer defended Client in a murder case. Client had confessed to Lawyer that Client was guilty of the charges. Lawyer nevertheless assisted Client in pleading not guilty and, at trial, vigorously attempting to secure a verdict of acquittal. In closing argument, Lawyer passion-

ately argued, based upon the facts in evidence at the trial, that Client was innocent. In closing argument, Lawyer also gave his personal opinion that Client was innocent. The jury found Client not guilty.

Did Lawyer violate the Model Rules of Professional Conduct?

(A) Yes, because Lawyer defended the case on a basis that Lawyer knew was factually frivolous and untrue.

(B) Yes, because Lawyer gave a personal opinion as to the guilt of Client.

(C) No, because Lawyer did not allude to any facts outside the record of the evidence at the trial.

(D) No, because Lawyer's conduct occurred in connection with the defense of a criminal case.

184. Lawyer represented Plaintiff in a case in which Plaintiff claimed that the defendant, Corporation, fired Plaintiff in violation of federal law. Lawyer knew that Corporation was represented by counsel in the matter. Supervisor, an employee of Corporation and the person who made the decision to fire Plaintiff, contacted Lawyer to explain why Supervisor fired Plaintiff. Lawyer did not obtain permission of Corporation's counsel to speak to Supervisor about the matter but did speak to Supervisor about the matter. Supervisor was not personally represented by counsel in the matter.

Did Lawyer violate the Model Rules of Professional Conduct?

(A) Yes, because Supervisor was an employee of Corporation and Corporation was represented by counsel in the matter.

(B) Yes, because Supervisor's actions could have been imputed to Corporation for purposes of civil liability.

(C) No, because Supervisor was not personally represented by counsel in the matter.

(D) No, because Lawyer did not initiate the contact with Supervisor.

185. Lawyer was negotiating on behalf of Client for the purchase of a private jet. Client's objective was to obtain the jet at the least cost possible. Seller of the jet was offering to sell the jet for $1.2 million. Lawyer knew that Seller in fact would accept as little as $800,000 for the jet. Lawyer knew this because Lawyer had inadvertently received an email that was sent from Seller's counsel to Seller about Seller's negotiation strategy and objectives. Lawyer also knew that Client would pay as much as $900,000 for the jet. Lawyer on behalf of Client offered $800,000 and told Seller's counsel that Client "would not pay a penny more." Lawyer did not tell Seller's counsel about Lawyer's inadvertent receipt of the email.

Did Lawyer violate the Model Rules of Professional Conduct?

(A) Yes, because Lawyer did not inform opposing counsel of Lawyer's inadvertent receipt of the email.

(B) Yes, because Lawyer lied about Client's willingness to pay more than $800,000.

(C) No, because Lawyer had the option but not the duty to reveal the inadvertent receipt of the email.

(D) No, because nothing a lawyer says in the context of a negotiation is considered to be a material fact.

186. Prosecutor used her peremptory strikes to eliminate all Caucasian men from the jury in a high-profile criminal case that had racial overtones. Defense Lawyer objected and claimed that Prosecutor had used her strikes in a discriminatory manner with respect to race. Prosecutor conceded that she had done so but argued that her conduct was legitimate advocacy. Judge decided that Prosecutor had used her peremptory challenges on a discriminatory basis and ordered that jury selection had to begin again with a new panel.

Did Prosecutor violate the Model Rules of Professional Conduct?

(A) Yes, because Judge decided that Prosecutor had used her peremptory challenges on a discriminatory basis.

(B) Yes, because Prosecutor knowingly engaged in illegitimate discrimination on the basis of race.

(C) No, because the Model Rules of Professional Conduct do not prohibit discrimination on the basis of race.

(D) No, because Prosecutor's actions were legitimate advocacy.

187. Lawyer worked as in-house counsel for Corporation. Lawyer learned that certain low-level employees of Corporation were dumping toxic chemicals into a river, in clear violation of the law. The applicable law provided for severe penalties for anyone engaging in such dumping, and Lawyer reasonably believed that the dumping was reasonably certain to cause substantial bodily harm and that the public would never know about it unless someone inside Corporation revealed it. Lawyer relayed this information to the Vice President of Environmental Compliance, who thanked Lawyer for the information. Lawyer asked whether the Vice President intended to stop the dumping, and the Vice President responded that Lawyer should not worry about that. Lawyer insisted that something should be done about the dumping to protect Corporation, but, instead of doing anything to stop the dumping, the Vice President fired Lawyer. Because Lawyer was afraid of making any more trouble for himself, Lawyer left Corporation and took no further action about the dumping. The dumping continued. Hundreds of people eventually were severely injured as a result, and Corporation was fined civilly and criminally prosecuted, with the result that Corporation eventually ceased doing business.

Did Lawyer violate the Model Rules of Professional Conduct?

(A) Yes, because Lawyer did not report his firing to Corporation's Board of Directors.

(B) Yes, because Lawyer did not publicly reveal the dumping.

(C) No, because Lawyer's obligations ended upon his discharge as a lawyer for Corporation.

(D) No, because Lawyer did not have the option to reveal the dumping publicly.

188. Lawyer was an Assistant United States Attorney who represented the United States in the prosecution of federal crimes. In one case, Prosecutor learned that the FBI had in its possession certain Evidence that tended to negate the guilt of the accused. In Prosecutor's good faith judgment, the Evidence likely would not affect the result and therefore was not "material." Defense counsel asked Lawyer to open Lawyer's file to defense counsel for the purposes of looking for exculpatory evidence. Lawyer refused to open her file to defense counsel. Lawyer did not turn over to the defense the Evidence that was in the possession of the FBI.

Did Lawyer violate the Model Rules of Professional Conduct?

(A) Yes, because the Evidence was known to Prosecutor and tended to negate the guilt of the accused.

(B) Yes, because Prosecutor did not open Prosecutor's file to defense counsel.

(C) No, because the Evidence was in the hands of the FBI and not Prosecutor.

(D) No, because Prosecutor in good faith believed that the Evidence was not material.

189. Lawyer assisted Client with the sale of Client's business. After the closing of the sale, Lawyer held the proceeds in Lawyer's trust account. Before Lawyer could disburse the proceeds to Client, Lawyer learned that Client had been divorced from Ex-Wife for several years, and that the final decree of divorce stated that Ex-Wife was entitled to one half of the proceeds should Client ever decide to sell his business. Ex-Wife had not contacted Lawyer or Client about the sale of the business and apparently did not know that the business had been sold. Client did not dispute that the divorce decree entitled Ex-Wife to one-half of the proceeds of the sale. Client instructed Lawyer nevertheless to disburse 100% of the proceeds to Client. Instead, Lawyer notified Ex-Wife that Client's business had been sold and delivered to her one-half of the proceeds from the sale.

Did Lawyer violate the Model Rules of Professional Conduct?

(A) Yes, because Lawyer disregarded the instructions of Client.

(B) Yes, because Lawyer notified Ex-Wife about the funds.

(C) No, because Ex-Wife's claim on the funds was undisputed.

(D) No, because Lawyer had the discretion to decide to whom the proceeds should be paid.

190. Lawyer opened her own law practice and decided to advertise. Lawyer placed online ads with local media outlets. The ads stated truthfully that she charged $299 for an uncontested divorce and $150 for a name change. The ad also that Lawyer had been "named the best divorce lawyer in town.*" At the bottom of the ad was the following sentence: "*Statement of a former client. The quality of a lawyer's services is a subjective judgment and any comparison of quality among lawyers cannot be objectively substantiated."

Did Lawyer violate the Model Rules of Professional Conduct?

(A) Yes, because Lawyer advertised her fees.

(B) Yes, because Lawyer advertised that Lawyer was "the best in town."

(C) No, because Lawyer included a disclaimer.

(D) No, because Lawyer had a constitutional right to advertise her services.

191. Lawyer specialized in representing victims of mass torts. Advertising Agency contacted lawyer and offered to enter into the following arrangement. Advertising Agency would produce and pay for the airing of truthful (and not misleading) television commercials asking whether viewers had taken a particular drug. Although the commercials were truthful and not misleading, they were tastelessly inflammatory in the hope that they would garner the attention of viewers. Advertising Agency would staff a call center to take in calls that were generated by the advertisements. If callers answered a standard set of questions in such a way as to indicate that the caller might have a claim against the manufacturer of the drug, Advertising Agency would recommend Lawyer and "patch in" Lawyer's office as a third party to the call. In exchange, Lawyer would pay Advertising Agency $10,000 for every caller who became a client of Lawyer, regardless of the amount of the legal fee (if any) that Lawyer earned for that client. Lawyer agreed to this proposal and accepted numerous clients through it.

Did Lawyer violate the Model Rules of Professional Conduct?

(A) Yes, because the commercials were tastelessly inflammatory.

(B) Yes, because Lawyer paid Advertising Agency to recommend her.

(C) No, because the commercials were truthful and not misleading.

(D) No, because Lawyer did not share legal fees with Advertising Agency.

192. Lawyer represented Smith only in connection with Smith's estate plan. Smith was not a lawyer. When Smith signed his will and the other documents that Lawyer prepared as part of Smith's estate plan, Lawyer advised Smith that tax laws often changed and that Lawyer would call Smith if Lawyer believed that Smith needed to change his estate plan. Smith was a curmudgeon and responded, "Don't call me, I'll call you." Years later, the estate tax laws changed, and Lawyer believed that Smith should consider whether to change Smith's estate plan to take advantage of those changes. Lawyer called Smith and offered for Lawyer's usual fee to revise Smith's estate plan to conform to the new estate tax rules.

Did Lawyer violate the Model Rules of Professional Conduct?

(A) Yes, because Smith was not a lawyer.

(B) Yes, because Smith had told Lawyer not to solicit him.

(C) No, because Smith was still Lawyer's client.

(D) No, because Smith was a former client of Lawyer.

193. Associate worked for Supervisory Lawyer and informed Supervisory Lawyer that he would be out of the office for a day because he would be working on a pro bono matter. Supervisory Lawyer informed Associate that Associate would not be subject to any discipline under the Model Rules of Professional Conduct if Associate did not render pro bono legal service. Su-

pervisory Lawyer then specifically directed Associate not to engage in any pro bono representation of anyone. Associate followed that order and did not do any pro bono work during Associate's first full calendar year working for Supervisory Lawyer.

Is Associate subject to discipline for violating the Model Rules of Professional Conduct?

(A) Yes, because Associate did not render at least fifty hours of pro bono service during his first calendar year working for the firm.

(B) Yes, because Supervisory Lawyer's order to Associate was not a reasonable resolution of an arguable question of professional duty.

(C) No, because Associate acted under the direct order of Supervisory Lawyer.

(D) No, because Supervisory Lawyer was correct that lawyers are not subject to discipline under the Model Rules of Professional Conduct if they do not render pro bono service.

194. Lawyer received a phone call from Judge, who was presiding over the penalty phase of a capital murder trial. Judge told Lawyer that defense counsel was doing a terrible job of presenting a case for mercy. It was apparent to Judge that defense counsel had done a woefully deficient job of investigating the defendant's background to try to explain to the jury what had led up to the homicide. Judge believed that this process was fundamentally unfair and might give rise later to a claim of ineffective assistance of counsel. Judge also knew that Judge eventually had the final say on whether the defendant would receive the death penalty (under state law, the judge could override the jury's recommendation), and Judge wanted all the relevant information. Without informing the parties, Judge asked Lawyer to help Judge to investigate several matters that, the Judge believed, needed to be cleared up before the Judge could render a fair decision. Lawyer determined that Lawyer had no conflict of interest in the matter and then conducted an investigation for Judge and reported back to Judge. Judge then disclosed Lawyer's involvement and the result of the investigation to all parties. On the basis of Lawyer's investigation and what Judge was able to discover through his own investigation, Judge overrode the jury's recommendation of death and imposed a life sentence, with the possibility of parole, on defendant.

Did Lawyer violate the Model Rules of Professional Conduct?

(A) Yes, because Lawyer knowingly assisted Judge in an investigation of facts relevant to the proceeding.

(B) Yes, because Lawyer knowingly assisted Judge in an investigation of facts relevant to the proceeding without prior notice to the parties that Lawyer would be assisting Judge's independent factual investigation.

(C) No, because Lawyer did not have a conflict of interest.

(D) No, because Judge disclosed Lawyer's involvement and the result of the investigation to all parties.

195. Judge formerly was associated with Law Firm. At that time, Law Firm represented Wife in a divorce case. Judge did not represent Wife in that matter and did not learn any confidential

information that was material to the matter. After Judge took the bench, Wife's divorce case was reassigned to Judge's court. Law Firm still represented Wife.

Apart from any general concern that Judge's impartiality might reasonably be questioned, does the Model Code of Judicial Conduct specifically require Judge to recuse himself in Wife's divorce case?

(A) Yes, because Law Firm represents Wife.

(B) Yes, because Law Firm represented Wife when Judge was associated with Law Firm.

(C) No, because Judge does not possess any confidential information that is material to the matter.

(D) No, because Judge did not represent Wife when Judge was at Law Firm.

196. Judge graduated from State University forty years ago. Because Judge was a prominent alum of State University, the Governor of State asked Judge to serve on the State University Historical Commission. The purpose of the Commission was to compile a comprehensive history of State University for release on the 200th anniversary of the founding of State University. Judge's work on the Commission would not take a significant amount of time. There was no reason to believe that the State University Historical Commission would be involved in litigation.

Under the Model Code of Judicial Conduct, may Judge accept appointment to the State University Historical Commission?

(A) Yes, because service on the Commission will not interfere with the proper performance of Judge's judicial duties.

(B) Yes, because service on the Commission will not lead to frequent disqualification of Judge.

(C) No, because the Commission's work does not concern the law, the legal system, or the administration of justice.

(D) No, because service on governmental commissions is a prohibited extrajudicial activity.

197. Law Firm is located in State Capitol and has decided that it would be an excellent business opportunity to offer its clients lobbying services when the state legislature is in town. The lobbyists would not be lawyers but would be employees of the law firm. The lobbyists would not have any ownership or managerial role in the firm and would be paid solely from the lobbying fees that clients pay the firm. Law Firm seeks your advice whether this business plan would violate the Model Rules of Professional Conduct.

198. Lawyer represented Client in a divorce case. Lawyer obtained a $25,000 deposit for Lawyer's hourly fees in the case. Lawyer deposited the $25,000 in Lawyer's trust account and withdrew $15,000 of it to pay Lawyer's earned fees. Lawyer had done substantial work on the case and had amassed a large file of evidentiary material. Client unjustly became disenchanted with Lawyer's representation and told Lawyer that Lawyer was fired. What are Lawyer's responsibilities?

199. You are an attorney who specializes in matters relating to legal ethics. Lawyer comes to you for advice about confidentiality and the attorney-client privilege. Lawyer has been asked to represent two business partners in a new venture. Lawyer is concerned about conflicts of interest and is concerned in particular about what, if anything, Lawyer should say to these prospective joint clients about confidentiality and privilege if Lawyer represents them both. Has Lawyer already breached confidentiality by seeking your advice, and what advice would you give Lawyer about what to say to the prospective joint clients about confidentiality and privilege?

200. Lawyer Smith represented Client several years ago in connection with a business transaction. Lawyer Smith helped Client to obtain a business loan from Bank based upon Client's assets, all of which Lawyer disclosed to Bank. The deal closed, and Lawyer Smith no longer represents Client. Lawyer Smith leaves her firm and joins Jones & Brown. Soon after Lawyer Smith joins Jones & Brown, the firm is asked to represent Bank in an attempt to collect on the business loan that Lawyer Smith helped Client to negotiate. Explain what Jones & Brown may do to make it possible for the firm to undertake this new representation.

201. Lawyer was representing Client, a wealthy individual who put together venture capital deals. Lawyer assisted Client with a series of such deals. Then, only after the deals closed, Lawyer learned that several of the deals had been fraudulent. Client confessed to Lawyer that Client had in the past used Lawyer's services to perpetrate frauds. Client assured Lawyer that Client would never do so again, and Client asked Lawyer to assist with a new transaction. Lawyer agreed to do so and helped Client with a legitimate (not criminal or fraudulent) transaction. Did Lawyer violate the Model Rules of Professional Conduct?

202. Client was interested in purchasing a piece of real property. Client hired Lawyer to perform a title search on the property for Client. Lawyer concluded in writing that the title was clear. Client decided for other reasons not to purchase the property. Unbeknownst to Lawyer, Client gave Lawyer's title opinion to Plaintiff, who relied on it in purchasing the property from Seller. The title in fact was not clear, and Lawyer's failure to discover the encumbrance did not meet the standard of care of a reasonable lawyer in similar circumstances. After the sale closed, Plaintiff learned for the first time of the encumbrance on the land, but Seller had absconded with Plaintiff's funds. Plaintiff sued Lawyer for malpractice. What would be Lawyer's best defense to the malpractice action?

203. Defense Lawyer filed a notice of appearance to represent Defendant in a criminal conspiracy case. Part of the evidence in the case was a set of wiretaps. On those recordings, Defense Lawyer had several conversations with Witness. At trial, Defense Lawyer would need to cross-examine Witness about those conversations and what the true meaning of and intent behind their conversations were. There is no indication that Defense Lawyer will testify under oath at the trial. As Prosecutor, what would be the best argument you could make to disqualify Defense Counsel?

204. Lawyer represented Client in a suit about injuries that Client allegedly suffered in a collision with a truck driven by Driver, who was employed by Corporation and working within the scope of his employment at the time of the accident. Lawyer had filed suit against Corporation

and had been in settlement negotiations with Corporation's lawyer. Driver called Lawyer and told Lawyer that Corporation had fired Driver and that Driver wanted to "come clean" about what happened. May Lawyer interview Driver without the knowledge of Corporation's lawyer, consistent with the Model Rules of Professional Conduct?

205. Lawyer worked as in-house counsel to Corporation and was investigating whether a particular division of Corporation had been violating laws related to international trade. Lawyer interviewed Employee about what the division had been doing. Employee was not individually represented by counsel. When Lawyer indicated to Employee that some of the division's practices—including particularly activities in which Employee personally engaged—might be violations of the law, Employee responded, "Am I in trouble? What should I do? Should I try to make a deal with the authorities?" What duties, if any, does Lawyer owe to Employee at that moment?

206. Lawyer represented Client on a contingent fee basis in a personal injury case. With Client's permission, Lawyer settled the case and received a check for $100,000 from the defendant's insurance company. Lawyer's written contract with Client provided that Lawyer would receive a fee of 25% of the gross recovery for Client. Lawyer incurred no expenses for Client. Lawyer deposited the settlement check to Lawyer's operating account, where Lawyer kept personal funds, and immediately sent Client a check for $75,000. Explain to Lawyer how Lawyer has violated the Model Rules of Professional Conduct and what Lawyer should have done.

207. Lawyer Brown has come to you for advice about her firm name. The name of the firm has been Smith, Jones & Brown for many years. The firm had three partners—Smith, Jones and Brown—and several associates. Smith just died, and Jones has just been elected as attorney general of Lawyer's state. Jones intends to return to the firm when his term in public office ends. Lawyer Brown shares office space with Lawyer White. Lawyer Brown suggests that the name she would like to use for her firm is Smith, Jones, Brown & White. Advise Lawyer Brown whether that name, or any parts of it, would comply with the Model Rules of Professional Conduct.

208. Judge served on the United States District Court. On a part-time basis, Judge taught a course on federal court jurisdiction at Law School. Judge received a stipend for teaching the course. The stipend was the same as every other adjunct professor at Law School received for teaching a similar course. Teaching the course took no more than a few hours per week of the judge's time, all in the evenings. Did Judge violate the Model Code of Judicial Conduct?

Answers

Regulation of the Legal Profession

1. **The correct answer is (A).** Opposing Counsel violated Rule 1.16(a)(2), which requires a lawyer to withdraw from representing a client "if the lawyer's physical or mental condition materially impairs the lawyer's ability to represent the client." Here, it was evident that Opposing Counsel had a mental condition that had impaired his ability to represent his clients. Under Rule 8.3, Lawyer was required to report Opposing Counsel, because Opposing Counsel had committed a violation of the rules that raised a substantial question as to Opposing Counsel's fitness as a lawyer. Although Lawyer's obligation to reveal the violation to the professional authority was subject to Lawyer's duty of confidentiality to his clients under Rule 8.3(c), here, the clients had given informed consent to the necessary disclosure. Answer **(B)** is wrong because Lawyer was not obliged to report all violations of the rules but rather only to report (subject to confidentiality) those violations that raised a substantial question as to Opposing Counsel's honesty, trustworthiness or fitness as a lawyer. *See* Comment 3 to Rule 8.3. Answer **(C)** is incorrect because the report under Rule 8.3(a) is mandatory. Answer **(D)** is wrong because Lawyer did know from personal observation that Opposing Counsel was continuing to represent clients despite a physical condition that made withdrawal mandatory. ABA Formal Opinion 03-341 recognizes that a lawyer's unfitness in most cases will manifest itself in a pattern of conduct, which is the situation presented in the question. The right answer is **(A)**.

2. **The correct answer is (D).** By giving legal advice in State B, Lawyer was practicing law in a state where Lawyer was not licensed. Such activity is generally not permitted, under Rule 5.5(a). Rule 5.5, however, contains a number of exceptions, one of which applies here. Under Rule 5.5(c)(2), Lawyer may practice law on a temporary basis in State B if Lawyer's activities "are in or reasonably related to a pending or potential proceeding before a tribunal in this or another jurisdiction, if the lawyer, or a person the lawyer is assisting, is authorized by law or order to appear in such proceeding or reasonably expects to be so authorized...." Here, Lawyer's temporary activities related to a pending proceeding in the state where the activities occurred, and Lawyer's Supervisor reasonably expected to be authorized by order to appear in the proceeding. Answer **(A)** is incorrect because one of the exceptions to the general rule, that a lawyer may not practice in a state where the lawyer is not licensed, applies. Answer **(B)** is wrong because it is enough that Lawyer's Supervisor expected to be authorized by order. Lawyer herself need not have any such expectation under Rule 5.5(c)(2). Answer **(C)** is incorrect because the practice of law does not consist only of appearing in court. Entering into another state to give legal advice is the practice of law in that state, and a lawyer needs to have a license to do so or be able to satisfy one of the exceptions in Rule 5.5. Answer **(D)** is correct.

3. **The correct answer is (A).** Under Rule 5.2(b), a subordinate lawyer does not violate the rules if the lawyer "acts in accordance with a supervisory lawyer's reasonable resolution of an ar-

guable question of professional duty." Here, however, the Supervisory Lawyer's resolution was not reasonable or arguably correct. Junior Associate knew that Older Lawyer had taken money from his trust account in violation of Rule 1.15. Junior Associate was therefore obliged to report Older Lawyer, because stealing client money was a violation of the rules that raised a "a substantial question as to that lawyer's honesty, trustworthiness or fitness as a lawyer." Supervisory Lawyer's advice that there was no duty to report was not, therefore, a reasonable resolution of an arguable question of professional duty. Answer (B) is incorrect because subordinate lawyers are allowed to rely on the advice of their supervisors, as long as the advice is a reasonable resolution of an arguable question of professional duty. Junior Lawyer owed a duty of independent professional judgment to clients, under Rule 2.1, but Junior Lawyer certainly may follow reasonable advice from a supervisor. Answer (C) is wrong because Rule 8.3 is not limited to requiring reports of lawyers in the same firm. Rule 8.3(a) requires much more generally that "[a] lawyer who knows that another lawyer has committed a violation of the Rules of Professional Conduct that raises a substantial question as to that lawyer's honesty, trustworthiness or fitness as a lawyer in other respects, shall inform the appropriate professional authority." Answer (D) is incorrect because subordinate lawyers can rely on a supervisor's instructions under Rule 5.2(b) only if they reflect a reasonable resolution of an arguable question of professional duty. Here, the supervisor's instructions were clearly wrong. The right answer is (A).

4. **The correct answer is (C).** Lawyer practiced law in a state where he was not licensed, but he did so on a temporary basis, and his work for Player arose from Lawyer's practice of representing baseball players in State A. Under Rule 5.5(c)(4), a lawyer is permitted to represent a transactional client in a state where the lawyer is not licensed if these conditions are met. Answer (A) is incorrect because Lawyer was authorized by the exception of Rule 5.5(c)(4) to practice law temporarily in State B, despite the general rule in Rule 5.5(a) against practicing law in a state where a lawyer is not licensed. Answer (B) is wrong because it is not possible to obtain pro hac vice admission for a transaction. Rule 5.5(c)(4) authorized what the Lawyer did, without the need for judicial permission. Answer (D) is incorrect because informed consent is not a solution to a problem of multijurisdictional practice. Regardless of Player's informed consent, Lawyer could not have represented Player in a state where lawyer was not licensed unless one of the exceptions of Rule 5.5 had applied. Answer (C) is right.

5. **The correct answer is (A).** Under Rule 5.4(d)(1), "[a] lawyer shall not practice with or in the form of a professional corporation or association authorized to practice law for a profit, if: (1) a nonlawyer owns any interest therein...," with one inapplicable exception. Here, the brother owned stock in the law firm through which Lawyer was practicing law. Answer (B) is incorrect because law firms can offer non-legal services under certain conditions. See Comment 9 to Rule 5.7 for a list of some of the law-related services that lawyers may offer. Answer (C) is wrong because it is not enough that the brother could not control or direct Lawyer's professional judgment. That step is essential under Rule 5.4(d)(3), but even with that proviso Lawyer may not practice in a firm in which a nonlawyer owns an equity stake. Answer (D) is incorrect because the strict segregation of legal fees away from the nonlawyer is a necessary but not sufficient condition to make the arrangement permissible. Rule 5.4(a) requires that lawyers not

share legal fees with nonlawyers, but this arrangement separately runs afoul of Rule 5.4(d)(1)'s prohibition on nonlawyer ownership. The right answer is (A).

6. **The correct answer is (B).** Under Rule 8.1(a), an applicant for admission to the bar shall not knowingly make a false statement of material fact, and an applicant who does so is subject to discipline as a lawyer if the lawyer is admitted and the deception is detected. *See* Comment 1 to Rule 8.1(a). The arrest was a material fact about which the bar was entitled to know. Bar Applicant did not reveal it, because he thought he would not get caught. Regardless of whether there was ever an adjudication of guilt or some kind of "expungement," the fact remained that Bar Applicant was arrested, and he gave a false answer to that question. Answer (A) is incorrect because Bar Applicant was not a member of the bar at the time of the commission of the criminal act. Bar Applicant was under a duty to reveal the arrest so that the bar could consider it, but he would not be subject to discipline after admission for a criminal act that he committed before admission. Answer (C) is wrong because a lawyer can be disciplined for a violation of Rule 8.1(a) that occurred before admission. *See* Comment 1 to Rule 8.1. Answer (D) is incorrect because the violation is the false statement on the bar questionnaire. The disposition of the criminal charge is irrelevant to that. Answer (B) is correct.

7. **The correct answer is (B).** Under Rule 5.6(b), a lawyer may not participate in offering or making "an agreement in which a restriction on the lawyer's right to practice is part of the settlement of a client controversy." Here Lawyer offered to do exactly that. Answer (A) is incorrect because the Model Rules of Professional Conduct do not take a position on whether settlements can be confidential. There are public policy arguments about why they should be confidential (facilitating settlement) and should not be confidential (protecting the public), but this is not a matter governed by the rules. Answer (C) is wrong because, although making the agreement confidential was permissible, there was another problem with what Lawyer did: he offered to restrict his right to practice as part of the settlement of Client's case. Answer (D) is incorrect because Rule 5.6(b) forbids not just the making of such an agreement but also the offering. Here, Lawyer made the forbidden offer. Answer (B) is the right answer.

8. **The correct answer is (B).** Under Rule 5.4(a), a lawyer may not share legal fees with a nonlawyer, with certain exceptions that do not apply here. Lawyer received fees for representing clients who came from Podiatrist, and Lawyer shared a percentage of those fees with Podiatrist. That is a violation of Rule 5.4(a). (Note also that paying someone for referrals is a separate violation, with some exceptions, under Rule 7.2(d).) Answer (A) is incorrect because reciprocal referral arrangements are permitted under Rule 7.2(b)(4), as long as they meet certain conditions. Answer (C) is wrong because lawyers may not share fees with nonlawyers, even if clients give informed consent to the arrangement and the amount. Those are conditions for the sharing of fees among lawyers not in the same firm, but they do not affect the prohibition of sharing fees with nonlawyers. Answer (D) is incorrect because the violation of Rule 5.4(b)'s ban on sharing fees with nonlawyers is separate from the question of the propriety of the referral arrangement. A reciprocal fee arrangement can be permissible (see Rule 7.2(b)(4)), but sharing of the fees with Podiatrist was not allowed. The right answer is (B).

9. **The correct answer is (A).** Rule 5.3(a) requires the partners in a firm to "make reasonable efforts to ensure that the firm has in effect measures giving reasonable assurance that the person's conduct is compatible with the professional obligations of the lawyer." Lawyer, as a sole practitioner, was obliged to engage in sufficient training and/or supervision to make sure that Office Manager did not bill for unreasonable expenses in violation of Rule 1.5(a). *See* ABA Formal Op. 93-379 ("in the absence of disclosure to the contrary, it would be improper if the lawyer assessed a surcharge on these disbursements over and above the amount actually incurred"). Answer **(B)** is wrong because Lawyer did not order the conduct, did not (with specific knowledge of it) ratify it, and did not fail to take remedial action at a time when Lawyer knew about it and its consequences could be avoided. *See* Rule 5.3(c). Lawyer is subject to discipline for his own violation of the rules, the failure to train and/or supervise, not for the overbilling itself. Answer **(C)** is incorrect because the secret "mark up" of expenses violated Rule 1.5(a)'s requirement that clients shall not be charged unreasonable amounts for expenses. *See* ABA Formal Op. 93-379. Answer **(D)** is wrong because Lawyer had a duty to train and/or supervise Office Manager regarding Lawyer's professional responsibilities, regardless of Lawyer's lack of knowledge that Office Manager was doing anything wrong. Answer **(A)** is correct.

10. **The correct answer is (B).** If Associate had deleted the email, Associate would have committed misconduct by unlawfully destroying evidence in violation of Rule 3.4(a). Rule 5.3(c)(2) governs Associate's vicarious responsibility for the actions of Law Clerk and provides for vicarious liability when "the lawyer is a partner or has comparable managerial authority in the law firm in which the person is employed, or has direct supervisory authority over the person, and knows of the conduct at a time when its consequences can be avoided or mitigated but fails to take reasonable remedial action." Associate had direct supervisory authority over Law Clerk and had four days to remedy Law Clerk's wrongdoing but did not do so. Associate is therefore vicariously liable, as a matter of discipline, for Law Clerk's actions. Answer **(A)** is incorrect because vicarious liability is not automatic. Just being the supervisor is not enough. As the supervisor, Associate could be disciplined for violating Rule 5.3(b) and 5.3(c), but those rules require more than mere proof of status as a supervisor of another. Answer **(C)** is wrong because the duty to take remedial action in Rule 5.3(b)(2) applies to supervisory lawyers as well as to partners and managers. Associate was Law Clerk's direct supervisor and thus had the duty to take remedial action. Answer **(D)** is incorrect because Rule 5.3 provides several ways for a lawyer to be responsible for the acts of another. Of course, a lawyer will be responsible if the lawyer orders it under Rule 5.3(c)(1) (see also Rule 8.4(a)), but vicarious liability also attaches if the lawyer ratifies the conduct or, as a partner, manager or supervisor, fails to take remedial action after learning about the misconduct in time to do something about it. A direct order is not necessary. Answer **(B)** is the right answer.

11. The proposed arrangement is permitted. The general rule in Rule 5.4(a) seeks to safeguard lawyer independence by providing that a lawyer may not share legal fees with a nonlawyer, but Rule 5.4 contains several exceptions. One of those exceptions is in Rule 5.4(a), which states that "an agreement by a lawyer with the lawyer's firm, partner, or associate may provide for the payment of money, over a reasonable period of time after the lawyer's death, to the lawyer's estate or to one or more specified persons." Such an arrangement presents little or no threat to the independence of a lawyer.

12. Lawyer must not agree to this part of the plan. Lawyer may employ the suspended Classmate, just like Lawyer may employ other assistants who are not licensed to practice law, but under Rule 5.5(a), Lawyer must not assist Classmate in the unauthorized practice of law. Although the "practice of law" is defined in various ways in different states, giving "preliminary basic advice" will almost certainly qualify. Especially when the employee had been a licensed attorney who presumably was accustomed to giving advice, the danger of Lawyer being found to have assisted Classmate in the unauthorized practice of law is very high.

13. Lawyer must refuse to go to work for Law Firm on this basis. Rule 5.6(a) provides that a "lawyer shall not participate in offering or making: (a) a partnership, shareholders, operating, employment, or other similar type of agreement that restricts the right of a lawyer to practice after termination of the relationship, except an agreement concerning benefits upon retirement...." The purposes of Rule 5.6(a), as explained in Comment 1 to Rule 5.6, are to protect the lawyer's autonomy and the freedom of clients to choose their lawyer. Law Firm has already violated Rule 5.6(a) by offering an agreement with a covenant not to compete. Lawyer must not violate the rule by accepting the offer.

14. Lawyer needs to be careful to comply with Rule 5.3 and Rule 5.5(a). Under Rule 5.3(a), Lawyer must make reasonable efforts to put in place policies and procedures that will give a reasonable assurance that the paralegals will understand and act in conformity with Lawyer's professional responsibilities. Under Rule 5.3(b), Lawyer must make reasonable efforts to supervise the paralegals as they perform their duties to make sure that they are acting in ways that are compatible with Lawyer's professional responsibilities. A particular concern will be to train and supervise the paralegals to ensure that they do not give clients legal advice or otherwise engage in the unauthorized practice of law. Lawyer must ensure that she is not "assisting" the paralegals in the unauthorized practice of law, in violation of Rule 5.5(a). As Comment 2 to Rule 5.5 notes, "[t]his Rule does not prohibit a lawyer from employing the services of paraprofessionals and delegating functions to them, so long as the lawyer supervises the delegated work and retains responsibility for their work."

The Client-Lawyer Relationship

15. **The correct answer is (B).** What depositions to take is a question of the means of achieving Client's objective. Under Rule 1.2(a), Lawyer and Client shared responsibility for questions of means, and Lawyer's general obligation under Rule 1.2(a) as to means was to consult with Client. A client may authorize a lawyer to take specific actions without further consultation, but a client may revoke that authority at any time. Comment 3 to Rule 1.2. That is what happened here. Once Client revoked the authority to proceed with the depositions without further consultation, Lawyer's obligation to consult with Client came back into effect. Answer (A) is incorrect because Client gave Lawyer initially the authority to take the depositions without further consultation. Answer (C) is wrong because Client had the right to revoke such authorization and did so. Answer (D) is incorrect because questions of means are not left to the "professional discretion" of Lawyer. Questions of means are shared responsibilities between lawyers and clients. The correct answer is (B).

16. **The correct answer is (A).** Rule 1.2(a) provides guidance about the division of authority between a lawyer and a client. One of the decisions that the rule explicitly gives to the client is the criminal defendant's decision about whether to testify. Furthermore, Rule 3.3(a)(3) gives the lawyer some authority over the decision whether to present evidence that the lawyer reasonably believes will be false, but that authority does not extend to such testimony by a criminal defendant. Answer (B) is incorrect because it is overbroad, for two reasons. First, whether to have a client testify, other than a defendant in a criminal matter, is a question of means, and Rule 1.2(a) provides generally that decisions about means are a shared responsibility. Second, the lawyer is empowered by Rule 3.3(a)(3) to refuse to present evidence that the lawyer reasonably believes is false, even if it is the client who wants to present the evidence, except when the client is a criminal defendant. Answer (C) is wrong because a lawyer's power under Rule 3.3(a)(3) to refuse to offer evidence that the lawyer reasonably believes to be false extends to all evidence except what is at stake here: the testimony of a criminal defendant. Answer (D) is incorrect because the decision whether to present the testimony of a criminal defendant is not simply a matter of the lawyer's professional judgment. The decision belongs to the client alone, under Rule 1.2(a). Answer (A) is correct.

17. **The correct answer is (D).** Rule 1.5(d)(1) forbids a lawyer from entering into an agreement for a contingent fee in a divorce case. That is what Lawyer did here with Father. Answer (A) is incorrect because no agreement for a contingent fee in a divorce case, including one that complies with Rule 1.8(f) (regarding acceptance of payment from a third-party), is permissible under Rule 1.5(d)(1). Answer (B) is incorrect because Rule 1.5(d)(1) forbids such agreements outright, with or without consent. Although the underlying reason for the ban is a concern

about a conflict of interest (for example, the lawyer who gets paid only upon divorce will not give independent advice about reconciliation), this is not a conflict of interest that is consentable. Answer (**C**) is incorrect because it is not the source of the payment but rather its contingent nature that is the problem. Under appropriate circumstances, lawyers may accept payment of their fees from third parties. *See* Rule 1.8(f). The right answer is (**D**).

18. **The correct answer is (A).** A lawyer may accept payment of a fee in property but must comply with Rule 1.8(a). See Comment 4 to Rule 1.5. Rule 1.8(a)(2) requires that "the client is advised in writing of the desirability of seeking and is given a reasonable opportunity to seek the advice of independent legal counsel on the transaction." That did not happen here. Answer (**B**) is incorrect because lawyers may accept property as payment of a fee under the right conditions. See Comment 4 to Rule 1.5. Answer (**C**) is incorrect because the reasonableness of the underlying trade is only one of the conditions that must be satisfied under Rule 1.8(a). The client also must be "advised in writing of the desirability of seeking and [be] given a reasonable opportunity to seek the advice of independent legal counsel on the transaction." Answer (**D**) is incorrect because the Model Rules of Professional Conduct in several respects, including this one, protect clients from their lawyers. The point of having restrictions such as those imposed in Rule 1.8(a) is to keep lawyers from taking advantage of the trust that clients place in them. Client agreement is not enough. The right answer is (**A**).

19. **The correct answer is (C).** The assertion of a claim for custody as a "bargaining chip" is a question of means to achieving the objective of a favorable financial settlement. Under Rule 1.2(a), Lawyer's obligation was to consult with Father about means. Lawyer fulfilled that responsibility. Answer (**A**) is incorrect because this is a circumstance in which withdrawal would have been permissive rather than mandatory. Under Rule 1.16(b)(4), Lawyer could have sought to withdraw because Father's strategy was repugnant or was something with which Lawyer had a fundamental disagreement. However, none of the mandatory withdrawal provisions of Rule 1.16(a) applied. Answer (**B**) is incorrect because Lawyer was permitted to help Father do a legal but repugnant thing. Under Rule 1.2(d), the lawyer cannot assist with a crime or a fraud, but there is nothing criminal or fraudulent about helping a father try to get custody of his children, even if the prospects are slim and the underlying motive is despicable. Answer (**D**) is incorrect because the Model Rules of Professional Conduct do not assign final authority over questions of means to either the lawyer or the client. Comment 2 to Rule 1.2 states that "lawyers usually defer to the client regarding such questions as ... concern for third persons who might be adversely affected," but it also states that, in the case of disagreement, "this Rule does not prescribe how such disagreements are to be resolved." The right answer is (**C**).

20. **The correct answer is (D).** Rule 1.5(e) imposes conditions on fee-sharing arrangements between lawyers who are not in the same firm. One of the conditions is that the client must agree to the share that each lawyer will receive. Rule 1.5(e)(2). That condition was not met here. Answer (**A**) is incorrect because the agreement to be jointly responsible is a way of satisfying one of the conditions (Rule 1.5(e)(1)), rather than the only condition, that must be satisfied. The client also must agree to the share that each lawyer will receive. Answer (**B**) is incorrect because, although client consent is required to a fee-sharing arrangement, that consent must include agreement to the share that each lawyer will receive. Answer (**C**) is incorrect because

it is not necessary that the lawyers share the fee only in proportion to the work performed. The arrangement must comply with Rule 1.5(e)(1), but that can be accomplished either by sharing in proportion to the work performed or by agreeing to be jointly responsible for the case. The right answer is **(D)**.

21. **The correct answer is (A).** Under Rule 1.2(a), the lawyer must reasonably consult with the client about the means that will be used to achieve the client's objectives. Hiring the expert was such a means. Answer **(B)** is incorrect because it is not improper to make repayment of expenses contingent upon the outcome of the case. *See* Rule 1.8(e)(1) ("a lawyer may advance court costs and expenses of litigation, the repayment of which may be contingent on the outcome of the matter"). Answer **(C)** is incorrect because the decision about means is a shared responsibility under Rule 1.2(a) and not something that "belongs" to the lawyer. *See* Comment 2 to Rule 1.2. Answer **(D)** is wrong because the lawyer was required to consult even though the repayment of the expenses was contingent upon the outcome of the case. In fact, Comment 2 to Rule 1.2 states that "lawyers usually defer to the client regarding such questions as the expense to be incurred...." The right answer is **(A)**.

22. **The correct answer is (B).** Lawyer had a duty under Rule 1.4(a)(2) to "reasonably consult with the client about the means by which the client's objectives are to be accomplished." Client's objective was to maximize the financial recovery, and Lawyer failed to inform Client about a way of doing that. Answer **(A)** is wrong because Lawyer and Client were able to limit the scope of the representation under Rule 1.2(c). The limit was reasonable, and Client gave informed consent. Answer **(C)** is incorrect because, as between Lawyer and Client, Lawyer is in a better position to recognize ways of achieving Client's objectives, even if the action that would be required was outside the limited scope of the representation. The limit on the scope does not circumscribe Lawyer's duty to communicate ways of achieving Client's objectives, even if Lawyer would not be the one to take the necessary steps. Answer **(D)** is wrong because, even though the limit on the scope of the representation satisfied Rule 1.2(c), in that it was reasonable and Client gave informed consent, that limit did not nullify Lawyer's duty to communicate information relevant to achievement of Client's known objective. Answer **(B)** is right.

23. **The correct answer is (D).** According to ABA Informal Opinion 86-1518, under these circumstances (often described as the "scrivener's error"), Lawyer "should contact the lawyer for [Opposing Party] to correct the error and need not consult [Client] about the error." This result follows from the fact that "a meeting of the minds has occurred." Answer **(A)** is incorrect because, according to Informal Opinion 86-1518, Client has already made the decision about the Clause and therefore there is no decision about which Client needs to be informed. Answer **(B)** is wrong because, again according to the ABA Informal Opinion, Client "does not have a right to take unfair advantage of the error." Lawyer, therefore, owed no duty of loyalty to help Client achieve something that Client had no right to do. Answer **(C)** is incorrect because there are no duties of "civility and cooperation" as such in the Model Rules of Professional Conduct. Although many states and local bar associations have aspirational codes of civility, and some states have begun to incorporate civility into their rules of conduct, the Model Rules do not explicitly contain a duty of "civility and cooperation." Answer **(D)** is correct.

24. **The correct answer is (A)**. Lawyer violated Rule 1.5(a) by charging unreasonable fees. If Lawyer had been obliged to attend three different calendar calls of four hours each on behalf of these three clients, then Lawyer would have actually spent 12 hours and could reasonably bill for that time. Here, however, there was a fortunate coincidence that the Lawyer's waiting time was in connection with the matters for three clients simultaneously. ABA Formal Opinion 93-379 addresses this exact scenario and concludes that, in these circumstances, a lawyer may not charge for more than four hours. Here, Lawyer has not earned more than four hours of compensation because Lawyer only spent four hours at the courthouse. Answer (B) is wrong because lawyers and clients in personal injury cases are free to agree to hourly billing rather than the more customary contingent fee. Answer (C) is incorrect because Rule 1.5(a) prohibits charging or collecting unreasonable fees. Lawyer did not collect unreasonable fees, but Lawyer nevertheless violated Rule 1.5 by charging them. Answer (D) is incorrect because, according to ABA Formal Opinion 93-379, the economies associated with simultaneous appearances on behalf of multiple clients must inure to the benefit of the clients and not Lawyer. Answer (A) is right.

25. **The correct answer is (D)**. Lawyer had a duty of confidentiality to Client Two under Rule 1.6(a) but had a simultaneous and conflicting duty of communication with Client One under Rule 1.4(b). Client Two refused to give informed consent for Lawyer to comply with the duty of communication to Client One. Therefore, if Lawyer had continued representing Client One, Lawyer would have been obliged to violate either the duty of confidentiality to Client Two (by fulfilling the duty of communication with Client One) or to violate the duty of communication to Client One (by fulfilling the duty of confidentiality to Client Two). When a lawyer faces a situation in which continued representation of a client would require the lawyer to violate the rules of conduct, then under Rule 1.16(a)(1), the lawyer must withdraw. Answer (A) is incorrect because the continued representation of Client Two did not require Lawyer to violate the rules of conduct. Lawyer's duty of communication to Client One terminated upon withdrawal as counsel for Client One, and Lawyer could continue to represent Client Two and fulfill Lawyer's duty of confidentiality. Answer (B) is wrong because Lawyer could not comply with Lawyer's duty of communication to Client One without violating Lawyer's duty of confidentiality to Client Two. Lawyer's only option was to withdraw from representing Client One. Answer (C) is incorrect because Lawyer had no choice but to withdraw. This is a situation of mandatory withdrawal under Rule 1.16(a)(1) rather than permissive withdrawal under Rule 1.16(b). Answer (D) is correct.

26. **The correct answer is (C)**. Under Rule 1.6(a)(2), Lawyer had the option to reveal the fraud to buyer because disclosure was reasonably necessary to prevent Client from perpetrating a fraud, in furtherance of which Client used Lawyer's services, that would cause substantial financial harm to Buyer. Lawyer was not required, however, to reveal the fraud. Rule 1.6(b)(2) is optional, and this situation did not fulfill all of the criteria for mandatory disclosure under Rule 4.1(b). Under that rule, Lawyer had a duty to reveal the fraud if doing so was necessary to avoid assisting in the fraud. Disclosure became unnecessary as soon as Lawyer's "noisy withdrawal" dissuaded the Buyer from being the next victim. Answer (A) is incorrect because Lawyer was under no duty to reveal the fraud to Buyer. Rule 4.1(b)'s mandate did not apply.

Answer (B) is wrong because Lawyer was entitled to give notice of withdrawal and to disaffirm the documents as part of a "noisy withdrawal" that had its intended effect: to prevent the fraud that the Lawyer had unwittingly assisted. *See* Comment 10 to Rule 1.2 and Comment 3 to Rule 4.1. Answer (D) is incorrect because Rule 1.16(b)(3) gives Lawyer the option to withdraw because Client had used Lawyer's services in the past to perpetrate frauds, but past fraud by itself does not require withdrawal. Answer (C) is right.

27. **The correct answer is (B).** Under Rule 1.2(a), a lawyer in a criminal case is obliged to abide by a client's decision with respect to the plea to be entered, but only "after consultation with the lawyer." Lawyer did not fulfill this specific duty to consult with Client before Client made the decision to accept the offer. More generally, the plea is a means of achieving Client's objective (presumably minimizing the punishment), and under Rule 1.2(a), Lawyer had a duty to consult about means. *See also* Rule 2.1 ("In representing a client, a lawyer shall exercise independent professional judgment and render candid advice."). Answer (A) is incorrect because Lawyer did not have the authority to accept a plea offer on behalf of Client. The decision whether to accept a plea offer belonged solely to Client, after consultation with Lawyer. Answer (C) is wrong because conveying the offer was only one of Lawyer's duties. *See* Comment 2 to Rule 1.4 (" … a lawyer who receives from opposing counsel an offer of settlement in a civil controversy or a proffered plea bargain in a criminal case must promptly inform the client of its substance …"). Lawyer also had the duty to consult with Client about the offer. Answer (D) is incorrect because, although the final decision about the plea rested with Client, Lawyer was obliged to consult with Client as Client made this important decision. Answer (B) is right.

28. **The correct answer is (D).** Lawyer proposed the revised fee agreement for Lawyer's benefit, to eliminate the risk of receiving no fee for years of work. Although generally lawyers and clients are free to change fee agreements, agreements in the middle of the representation that are to the lawyer's advantage are subject to special scrutiny. Here, Lawyer's threat to withdraw as counsel after years of litigation on the eve of trial essentially left Client no choice but to agree. An agreement made under these circumstances is not enforceable. *See* ABA Formal Op. 11-485. Answer (A) is incorrect because contracts between lawyers and clients are different from regular commercial contracts, given the fiduciary nature of the lawyer's relationship with the client. It is never enough simply to say that a contract between a lawyer and a client is enforceable because the client agreed. For example, a lawyer-client fee contract is always subject to the requirement that the fee is reasonable under Rule 1.5(a). Answer (B) is wrong because Client had the right to reject the settlement offer. That right belonged exclusively to Client under Rule 1.2(a). Lawyer was not permitted to change the deal to Lawyer's advantage, and use duress to do it, just because Client did something Client had the absolute right to do. Answer (C) is incorrect because the Model Rules of Professional Conduct contemplate that lawyers and clients may agree under some circumstances to change fee arrangements. *See* Rule 1.5(b) ("Any changes in the basis or rate of the fee or expenses shall also be communicated to the client."). Answer (D) is right.

29. **The correct answer is (D).** Under Rule 1.2(a), Client had the right to decide whether or not to waive jury trial, and Lawyer normally would have been obliged to consult with Client about that under Rule 1.4(a)(1) and 1.4(b). But Client had already told Lawyer not to waive jury

trial, and therefore no consultation was necessary. See Comment 2 to Rule 1.4 ("If these Rules require that a particular decision about the representation be made by the client, paragraph (a)(1) requires that the lawyer promptly consult with and secure the client's consent prior to taking action unless prior discussions with the client have resolved what action the client wants the lawyer to take."). Lawyer was under no obligation to consult or communicate with Client. Answer (**A**) is incorrect because, although the decision to waive a jury trial belongs to the client, this Client had already made the decision and instructed Lawyer. Answer (**B**) is wrong because Lawyer was not obligated to communicate with Client about the matter once Client had made the decision and instructed Lawyer. Answer (**C**) is incorrect because this decision belonged exclusively to Client and not Lawyer under Rule 1.2(a). Answer (**D**) is correct.

30. **The correct answer is (C).** Lawyer had no duty under Rule 1.16(a)(1) to withdraw because Lawyer did not know that Client was using Lawyer's services to perpetrate a fraud. If Lawyer had that knowledge, the Lawyer would have had to withdraw to avoid violating Rule 1.2(d), which prohibits such knowing assistance. But Lawyer did have the option to withdraw under Rule 1.16(b)(2) when Client persisted in a course of conduct that Lawyer reasonably believed was fraudulent. Answer (**A**) is incorrect because Lawyer did not know that the transactions were fraudulent. Rule 1.2(d) only prohibits assistance with transactions that a lawyer knows to be criminal or fraudulent. Answer (**B**) is wrong because Lawyer did have the option under Rule 1.16(b)(2) to withdraw because Lawyer reasonably believed that Client was persisting in a course of conduct that was fraudulent. Answer (**D**) is incorrect because Lawyer did not have the duty to withdraw under Rule 1.16(b)(1)(a) because Lawyer did not know the transactions were fraudulent. Answer (**C**) is right.

31. Yes, Lawyer violated Model Rule of Professional Conduct 1.8(e), which forbids lawyers from providing most types of financial assistance to clients in connection with pending litigation. According to comment 5 to Rule 1.8, a guaranty of a loan to the client is an example of the type of financial assistance that is forbidden. Even though Lawyer's motives were pure, and Client was well served, Lawyer violated Rule 1.8(e).

32. Estate Lawyer may not do as Husband instructs. Wife is making a will in which she leaves her estate to Husband, presumably in reliance upon Husband's intentional misrepresentation that he is leaving his estate to her. Husband is attempting to perpetrate a fraud on Wife, and under Rule 1.2(d), Lawyer may not assist a client in the perpetration of a crime or a fraud. Furthermore, Lawyer owes a duty of communication under Rule 1.4(b) to Wife, who presumably would find it relevant to Lawyer's work to know that Husband was a liar and a philanderer. Wife probably would have different instructions for Lawyer regarding her will if she knew all the relevant facts of which Lawyer is now aware.

33. Lawyer complied with the Model Rules of Professional Conduct. Under Rule 1.2(d), Lawyer was permitted to "discuss the legal consequences of any proposed course of conduct with a client," which Lawyer did by explaining that the proposed venture was a crime. By further explaining that he could not help with a crime, Lawyer complied with Rule 1.4(a)(5). That rule required Lawyer to "consult with the client about any relevant limitation on the lawyer's conduct when the lawyer knows that the client expects assistance not permitted by the Rules of

Professional Conduct or other law." Finally, Lawyer complied with Rule 1.2(d) by refusing to assist Client with a crime. Rule 1.2(d) provides that "[a] lawyer shall not counsel a client to engage, or assist a client, in conduct that the lawyer knows is criminal or fraudulent."

34. Client is right. This is a classic example of an "episodic client," one who from time to time needs a lawyer and repeatedly obtains the services of a particular lawyer. The Client believes that Lawyer is still her lawyer, and the only question is whether that is a reasonable belief. Here, it would be, because Lawyer has represented Client in a number of matters over a long period of time and has done nothing to disclaim the continuity of an ongoing attorney-client relationship. Because Client has a reasonable belief in the existence of the attorney-client relationship, that relationship exists, regardless of what Lawyer thinks. It was up to Lawyer to clarify. *See* Comment 4 to Rule 1.3 ("If a lawyer has served a client over a substantial period in a variety of matters, the client sometimes may assume that the lawyer will continue to serve on a continuing basis unless the lawyer gives notice of withdrawal. Doubt about whether a client-lawyer relationship still exists should be clarified by the lawyer, preferably in writing, so that the client will not mistakenly suppose the lawyer is looking after the client's affairs when the lawyer has ceased to do so.").

35. The contract between Lawyer and Client did not violate the Model Rules of Professional Conduct just because it called for a "reverse" contingent fee. Rule 1.5(d) prohibits contingent fees in only two circumstances, in domestic relations cases and in criminal cases. ABA Formal Opinion 93-379 concludes that reverse contingent fees in other kinds of cases are permissible, subject to the usual constraints on all fees, that the fee is reasonable under all the circumstances and the client gives informed consent to it. This "reverse contingent fee" contract is not a per se violation of the Model Rules of Professional Conduct.

Client Confidentiality

36. **The correct answer is (C).** Lawyer learned information about Client in the course of investigating the matter for which Lawyer represented Client. That was "information relating to the representation" and therefore confidential under Rule 1.6(a). That rule, however, contains exceptions to the general duty of confidentiality, including permission under Rule 1.6(b)(1) to reveal confidential information if a lawyer reasonably believes it is necessary in order "to prevent reasonably certain death or substantial bodily harm." Here, the death sentence was about to be carried out on the wrong person. Lawyer had the option to reveal the client's confidential information to save a life. Answer **(A)** is incorrect because Lawyer did not learn the information from the client. The attorney-client privilege and confidentiality are related but not co-extensive concepts. Answer **(B)** is wrong because an exception to confidentiality did exist—Lawyer's reasonable belief that revealing the confidential information was reasonably necessary to save a life. Answer **(D)** is incorrect because Lawyer's duty of confidentiality survived the termination of the attorney-client relationship. *See* Comment 20 to Rule 1.6 ("The duty of confidentiality continues after the client-lawyer relationship has terminated.") and Rule 1.9(c)(2) ("A lawyer who has formerly represented a client in a matter ... shall not thereafter: ... reveal information relating to the representation except as these Rules would permit or require with respect to a client."). Answer **(C)** is correct.

37. **The correct answer is (D).** Lawyer reasonably believed that Client had diminished capacity, was at substantial risk of financial harm, and could not protect himself. Under those circumstances, Lawyer was authorized under Rule 1.14(b) to take protective action, and under Rule 1.14(c), Lawyer was impliedly authorized to reveal confidential information to the extent reasonably necessary to protect Client's interests. Under Comment 5 to Rule 1.14, one type of protective action is to consult with family members, which is what Lawyer did. Answer **(A)** is wrong because one exception to the general duty of confidentiality is implied authorization. Rule 1.14(c) provides that this is a situation in which Lawyer was impliedly authorized to reveal confidential information. Answer **(B)** is incorrect because the Model Rules of Professional Conduct do not contain rules about privilege. Privilege and confidentiality are related but separate concepts, and it is not a violation of the Model Rules of Professional Conduct to compromise the attorney-client privilege. The same act might violate the rules of conduct with respect to confidentiality, but that is different from saying that a lawyer violated the rules by violating the privilege. Answer **(C)** is wrong because it is not enough that Lawyer determined that revelation of the information was in Client's best interest. The client normally gets to decide that. In this particular circumstance, however, Lawyer had an option to reveal despite Client's wishes, because Client was at risk and unable to protect himself. The right answer is **(D)**.

38. **The correct answer is (D).** Here, Lawyer has only one Client, the policyholder. However, Client was using Lawyer's services to perpetrate insurance fraud, to see that the Acme Insurance Company paid a claim for catastrophic damages when in fact the accident was not within the coverage of the policy. Under Rule 1.2(d), Lawyer could not assist in the perpetration of a fraud and was obliged under Rule 1.16(a)(1) to seek to withdraw when continuing the representation would require the lawyer to violate Rule 1.2(d). Under Rule 1.6(b)(2), Lawyer had the option to reveal Client's confidential information to prevent the financial injury to the insurance company. That option was triggered by Client's fraud, in connection with which Client was using Lawyer's services. Answer (A) is wrong because Lawyer had the option under Rule 1.6(b)(2) to reveal the confidential information. Answer (B) is incorrect because Lawyer was obliged to seek to withdraw when it became apparent that continuing the representation would require Lawyer to violate a rule of conduct. Answer (C) is wrong because the payment of a fee for someone else to receive legal services does not entitle the payor to receive confidential information. To the contrary, under Rule 1.8(f), a lawyer is forbidden from accepting payment from a third party if the client's confidential information is not going to be protected. The right answer is (D).

39. **The correct answer is (D).** Under Rule 1.6(a), a lawyer may share a client's confidential information if the lawyer is "impliedly authorized" to do so. Comment 5 uses this exact situation as an example: "Lawyers in a firm may, in the course of the firm's practice, disclose to each other information relating to a client of the firm, unless the client has instructed that particular information be confined to specified lawyers." Answers (A) and (C) are both wrong because they concern the attorney-client privilege rather than what the question asks about: the duty of confidentiality under the Model Rules of Professional Conduct. Privilege is a matter of evidence, whereas confidentiality is governed by the Model Rules of Professional Conduct. Answer (B) is incorrect because informed consent is one of but not the only circumstance under which a lawyer may share a client's confidential information. "Implied authorization" is another. The right answer is (D).

40. **The correct answer is (C).** Under Rule 1.6(b)(1), Lawyer at all times had the option but not the duty to reveal the confidential information to prevent the husband's death. Answer (A) is incorrect because Rule 1.6(b) is permissive rather than mandatory. The two places where revelation of confidential information is mandatory are in Rules 3.3 and 4.1(b). Answer (B) is incorrect because the duty of confidentiality continues even when the attorney-client relationship ends. *See* Comment 20 to Rule 1.6. Answer (D) is incorrect because Lawyer did have a choice. The conditions for permissive disclosure under Rule 1.6(b)(1) were present. The right answer is (C).

41. **The correct answer is (B).** Lawyer learned about the past fraud as part of the Lawyer's work for the client. The information therefore was related to the representation and confidential under Rule 1.6. Lawyer did not have the option to reveal the past fraud under Rule 1.6(b)(3), because Lawyer's services were not used in the perpetration of the fraud. Answer (A) is incorrect because the problem is not the nature of the harm. In fact, under the right circumstances, lawyers are permitted to reveal confidential information to prevent financial harm. *See* Rule 1.6(b)(2) and (3). The problem here is that this is not one of those circumstances. Answer (C)

is incorrect because Lawyer learned the information "in the course of preparing the necessary documents" for the client, and therefore the information related to the representation of the client, regardless of the time period to which the information related. The information was confidential under Rule 1.6(a). Answer (**D**) is incorrect because it states only one of the necessary conditions for disclosure under Rule 1.6(b)(3). Another is that the lawyer's services must have been used in furtherance of the fraud, and that is not the case here. The right answer is (**B**).

42. **The correct answer is (B).** Lawyer learned about the mall project while representing Client. That was information relating to the representation of Client and therefore was confidential under Rule 1.6(a). Lawyer then used Client's confidential information to the disadvantage of Client by acquiring the land for the parking lot and forcing Client to pay a higher price for it. This was a violation of Rule 1.9(c)(1), which provides that a lawyer who has formerly represented a client shall not "use information relating to the representation to the disadvantage of the former client except as these Rules would permit or require with respect to a client, or when the information has become generally known." Here, there would be no authority to use client confidential information such as this with respect to a client, nor had the information become generally known. Answer (**A**) is incorrect because the Model Rules of Professional Conduct do not generally prohibit entering into business transactions with former clients. Indeed, a lawyer may enter into a business transaction even with a current client if the lawyer satisfies the requirements of Rule 1.8(a). Answer (**C**) is wrong because Lawyer's duty of confidentiality continued after the termination of Lawyer's attorney-client relationship with Client. *See* Comment 20 to Rule 1.6. Answer (**D**) is incorrect because it does not matter whether the mall project was within the scope of Lawyer's attorney-client relationship with Client. The crucial fact is that the plan for the mall project was information relating to the representation with respect to the planned community, because Lawyer learned that information in the course of obtaining financing for Client for that project. The information was, therefore, confidential under Rule 1.6(a), and Rule 1.9(c)(1) forbade lawyer from using it to the disadvantage of Client later. Answer (**B**) is right.

43. **The correct answer is (A).** The attorney-client privilege protects conversations among "privileged persons." Usually, the two "privileged persons" are the lawyer and the client. Sometimes, however, a lawyer's agent and/or a client's agent will participate in the communications, and if an agent is necessary to facilitate the communication, then the agent is a "privileged person." Son was present as an agent of his father to help his father communicate with Lawyer. Son was therefore a "privileged person," and the privilege protected the conversation. Answer (**B**) is incorrect because Elderly Client's permission is not enough to make Son a "privileged person." The Son had that status not merely because his father permitted him to be present but rather because he had a role, to facilitate the communications between Lawyer and Elderly Client. Answer (**C**) is wrong, even though the presence of a third party can sometimes mean that the communications between a lawyer and client are not made in confidence and therefore are not within the privilege. Here, the communications are still deemed to be in confidence, because Son was there to facilitate the communications on behalf of Elderly Client. Answer (**D**) is incorrect because Son was a privileged person due to his role in facilitating the attorney-client communications. Answer (**A**) is right.

44. **The correct answer is (C).** The photos are tangible things that were prepared in anticipation of litigation. They are, therefore, work product and presumptively immune from discovery. However, there is an exception to the work product doctrine if the party seeking the work product has substantial need for the materials and cannot without undue hardship obtain the substantial equivalent by other means. The photos are crucial evidence of Plaintiff's sight line, and they cannot be replicated, because the stand of trees is no longer there. Plaintiff should have been allowed to obtain the photos. Answer (A) is incorrect because it is not enough to establish that the photos were prepared in anticipation of litigation. Unlike privilege, there is a way to overcome work product immunity, and this is such a case. Answer (B) is wrong because photos do not contain any mental impressions or opinions of the lawyer. They are merely truthful depictions of how the scene looked at the time of the accident. If the work product did contain mental impressions or opinions, then the court would be obliged to protect those aspects of the work product from discovery. Answer (D) is incorrect because items can acquire work product status if they are prepared in anticipation of litigation or for trial by the lawyer or the lawyer's agents. Here, Lawyer's agent prepared the photos. Answer (C) is correct.

45. **The correct answer is (B).** Rule 1.6(c) imposes an affirmative obligation on lawyers to "make reasonable efforts to prevent the inadvertent or unauthorized disclosure of, or unauthorized access to, information relating to the representation of a client." In the particular circumstances here, where an employee has a claim against an employer and uses company email to communicate with a lawyer about the claim, the risk of the employer accessing the emails is high and may not be evident to the client. According to ABA Formal Opinion 11-459, "as soon as practical after a client-lawyer relationship is established, a lawyer typically should instruct the employee-client to avoid using a workplace device or system for sensitive or substantive communications, and perhaps for any attorney-client communications, because even seemingly ministerial communications involving matters such as scheduling can have substantive ramifications." Answer (A) is incorrect because, as a general rule, lawyers may use unencrypted email for communication with clients. *See* ABA Formal Op. 99-413. In this special situation, however, Lawyer must recognize that there is no reasonable expectation of privacy and must advise Client of the risk. Answer (C) is wrong because Rule 1.6(c) imposes an affirmative duty to make reasonable efforts to protect confidential information. This duty goes beyond the duty merely not to reveal such information without authorization. Answer (D) is incorrect because Lawyer and Client did not have a reasonable expectation of privacy in these circumstances. In fact, according to ABA Formal Op. 11-459, "[u]nless a lawyer has reason to believe otherwise, a lawyer ordinarily should assume that an employer's internal policy allows for access to the employee's e-mails sent to or from a workplace device or system." Answer (B) is correct.

46. **The correct answer is (D).** Under Rule 1.6(b)(5), Lawyer had the option to reveal confidential information "to establish a claim or defense on behalf of the lawyer in a controversy between the lawyer and the client, ... or to respond to allegations in any proceeding concerning the lawyer's representation of the client...." Lawyer had the right to use the confidential information to defend against Client's charges of misconduct. Answer (A) is wrong because informed consent is not always required before a lawyer may reveal confidential information. Such con-

sent is a sufficient condition for revealing confidential information, but it is not a necessary one. Lawyers may also reveal confidential information if doing so is impliedly authorized or if one of the exceptions in 1.6(b) is available. Here, Rule 1.6(b)(5) gave Lawyer the option to reveal confidential information. Answer (B) is incorrect because Lawyer need not have waited until the disciplinary proceeding formally commenced. *See* Comment 10 to Rule 1.6. Answer (C) is wrong because disclosure under implied authorization is always for the benefit of the client. Here, Lawyer was not carrying out the representation of Client but was rather defending himself against Client. There was no implied authorization to reveal this confidential information. The right answer is (D).

47. Lawyer did not violate the Model Rules of Professional Conduct. The information that Lawyer obtained was "information relating to the representation" and was therefore confidential under Rule 1.6(a). Lawyer was not permitted to reveal it unless Client gave informed consent, the revelation was impliedly authorized, or an exception applied. Here, the exception in Rule 1.6(b)(4) applied, because Lawyer revealed the information to Ethics Professor in order "to secure legal advice about [Lawyer's] compliance with these Rules." Ethics Professor presumably would have given Lawyer advice about the applicability of the last sentence of Rule 3.3(a)(3) to this particular situation.

48. No, Lawyer did not violate his duty of confidentiality when he shared what he had learned from General Counsel with the employees. What Lawyer learned from the General Counsel about the OSHA investigation was information related to the representation and was therefore protected by Rule 1.6. Remember that the client was Corporation, not the employees of Corporation. Therefore, Lawyer's revelation of confidential information to the employees was improper unless it was somehow authorized. In this case, it was impliedly authorized. Lawyer needed to tell employees what OSHA's concerns were in order to conduct the investigation requested by General Counsel. Under Rule 1.6(a), a lawyer may reveal confidential information when, as here, doing so is impliedly authorized to carry out the representation. *See also* Comment 2 to Rule 1.13.

49. The discussions between Lawyer and Client are not covered by the attorney-client privilege. Lawyer and Client consulted for the purpose of committing the future crime of obstruction of justice. Such communications, even though they were confidential and between Lawyer and Client for the purpose of obtaining or receiving advice, fell within the crime-fraud exception to the privilege. Discussions of past crimes in these circumstances would be privileged. Discussions to plan the next crime were not, because of the crime-fraud exception.

Conflicts of Interest

50. **The correct answer is (A).** There was a significant risk of a material limitation under Rule 1.7(a)(2) in Lawyer's representation of Paralegal. Lawyer had a personal interest in the continuance of the sexual relationship with her client. Lawyer's advice might have been compromised by the interest. For example, a lawyer without that conflict might advise a client to cease an extramarital affair during the pendency of divorce proceedings, or might even counsel a client to consider reconciliation with his wife. Lawyer should have considered whether the conflict was consentable under Rule 1.7(b)(1) and, if so, should have sought informed consent under Rule 1.7(b)(4). Answer **(B)** is wrong because a preexisting sexual relationship is an exception to the general rule that a lawyer may not be in a sexual relationship with a client. Rule 1.8(j) states that a "lawyer shall not have sexual relations with a client unless a consensual sexual relationship existed between them when the client-lawyer relationship commenced." Answer **(C)** is incorrect because the timing of the commencement of the sexual relationship is not the only issue with respect to conflicts of interest. Although the preexistence of the sexual relationship means that Rule 1.8(j) does not apply, the more general conflict provisions of Rule 1.7(a) do apply. Answer **(D)** is wrong because it is consent to the conflict rather than consent to the sexual relationship that matters. The lawyer had a conflict of interest under Rule 1.7(a)(2) and should have at least sought informed consent to undertaking the representation (if the lawyer determined that the conflict was consentable under Rule 1.7(b)(1)). The right answer is **(A)**.

51. **The correct answer is (A).** Under Rule 1.9(b), a lawyer who moves from one law firm to another does not have a conflict of interest in representing a client in the new firm against a client of the lawyer's former firm, even in the same or a substantially related matter, unless the lawyer acquired confidential information that is material to the matter. Here, the associate did not participate in the case or acquire any confidential information. Therefore, the associate does not have a conflict of interest, and there is no conflict to impute to other members of the law firm. Answer **(B)** is wrong because it is not necessary to screen the associate in these circumstances. The associate does not have a conflict of interest. If the associate did bring a conflict into the firm, Law Firm could remain as counsel for the defendant if it complied with the screening and other requirements of Rule 1.10(a)(2), but those steps are unnecessary when the incoming lawyer does not have a conflict of interest. Answer **(C)** is incorrect because the associate did not acquire any confidential information that would be material to the matter and therefore under Rule 1.9(b) does not have a conflict of interest. Answer **(D)** is wrong because, even though the associate is in a sense "switching sides," the associate never was involved in the case for the plaintiff. Without the acquisition of confidential information that is material

to the matter, the associate does not have a conflict of interest in moving to the "other side" of the case. The right answer is (**A**).

52. **The correct answer is (C).** Client A became a former client upon the termination of the attorney-client relationship in the personal injury matter. Lawyer was thereafter free under Rule 1.9(a) to represent a new client, such as Client B, against Client A in any matter, as long as it was not the same matter as the one on which Lawyer had represented Client A or was not substantially related to that matter. Matters are "substantially related," according to Comment 3 to Rule 1.9, "if they involve the same transaction or legal dispute or if there otherwise is a substantial risk that confidential factual information as would normally have been obtained in the prior representation would materially advance the client's position in the subsequent matter." There would not appear to be any such risk in a will contest when the prior representation was about an accident. Answer (**A**) is wrong because a lawyer can possess confidential information of a former client and still not have a conflict, as long as the confidential information is not material to the new matter—in other words, as long as the two matters are not substantially related. Answer (**B**) is incorrect because lawyers are permitted to sue their former clients (but not their current clients) without informed consent, as long as the new matter is not substantially related to the old one. Answer (**D**) is wrong because it is too broad. It would permit a lawyer to sue his former client in any matter, but Rule 1.9(a) places the representation of new clients in some matters—those that are the same or are substantially related to the first matter—off limits. The right answer is (**C**).

53. **The correct answer is (D).** The attorney would have a conflict of interest under Rule 1.7(a)(2) because the lawyer would be materially limited in seeking the best arrangements for any one client because of Lawyer's obligation to also seek the best arrangements for the other clients. That conflict would not be consentable under Rule 1.7(b)(1), which requires a lawyer to reasonably believe that the lawyer can provide competent and diligent representation to each client despite the conflict. Here, the issues to be negotiated are zero sum—every time Lawyer helps one client, he hurts another. As Comment 8 to Rule 1.7 puts it, "a lawyer asked to represent several individuals seeking to form a joint venture is likely to be materially limited in the lawyer's ability to recommend or advocate all possible positions that each might take because of the lawyer's duty of loyalty to the others." The solution would be to limit the scope of the representation under Rule 1.2(c) to eliminate any role for Lawyer in negotiating matters that benefit one client to the detriment of another, but here, the scope of the representation would include such matters. Answer (**A**) is wrong because Lawyer cannot ask for informed consent to a nonconsentable conflict. Answer (**B**) is incorrect because the Model Rules of Professional Conduct do not make a distinction between a "potential conflict" and an "actual conflict" (although the courts do make such a distinction in connection with claims of ineffective assistance of counsel). Under the rules, a conflict exists if there is a significant risk of a material limitation, regardless of whether a lawyer has actually helped one client to the detriment of the others. Answer (**C**) is wrong because the problem is an immediate one, not the prospect of future conflicts. The conflicts already exist, because the clients have different interests in connection with the structure of the joint venture. The right answer is (**D**).

54. **The correct answer is (D).** The lawyer who purports to represent two defendants in a criminal case when there are big differences in culpability (and therefore significant opportunities to

negotiate a deal for one to the detriment of the other) has a conflict of interest under Rule 1.7. Under <u>Wheat v. US</u>, 486 U.S. 153 (1988), the judge can disqualify defense counsel in such circumstances, when the serious potential for conflict rebuts the presumption that the defendants get to choose their own counsel. Answer **(A)** is incorrect because the prosecutor has standing under <u>Wheat</u>. Answer **(B)** is incorrect because consent does not always cure the problem that Wheat is designed to solve: namely, the possibility that the case will proceed to judgment but then, afterwards, a defendant will seek to set aside the consent as not knowing and voluntary and thereby obtain a new trial for ineffective assistance of counsel. Answer **(C)** is wrong because it is an overstatement. Comment 23 to Rule 1.7 states that, ordinarily, the conflict is so grave as to preclude dual representation, but Rule 1.7 does not impose a categorical ban. The right answer is **(D)**.

55. **The correct answer is (D).** Under Rule 1.8(d), "[p]rior to the conclusion of representation of a client, a lawyer shall not make or negotiate an agreement giving the lawyer literary or media rights to a portrayal or account based in substantial part on information relating to the representation." This prohibition exists because of the fear that the lawyer's representation of the client will be undermined by the lawyer's personal interest in maximizing the value of the literary rights rather than protecting the client's interests. Answer **(A)** is wrong because the problem is not the amount of the fee but rather the skewing of the lawyer's interest toward making sure that the literary rights are enough to cover the fee, perhaps at the cost of representing the client's interests. Answer **(B)** is wrong because the lawyer's acquisition of an interest in the literary rights before the conclusion of the representation is absolutely prohibited, regardless of whether the client is independently represented. Answer **(C)** is incorrect because a lawyer may under the right circumstances contract for a lien on the client's home as security for the fee. The lawyer will need to be careful to comply with the provisions of Rule 1.8(a), but the acquisition of a security interest in the client's home, when the home is not the subject of the litigation, is not prohibited (unlike acquisition of an interest in the client's literary rights). *See* Comment 4 to Rule 1.5. Answer **(D)** is right.

56. **The correct answer is (B).** Lawyer has a conflict of interest, but it is a conflict that arises from her personal interest in remaining faithful to her religious beliefs. There is nothing about her religious beliefs that creates a conflict of interest for other members of her firm. Rule 1.10(a)(1) contains an exception to the general rule that conflicts of interest are imputed among members of a law firm. That exception applies here, because "the prohibition is based on a personal interest of the disqualified lawyer and does not present a significant risk of materially limiting the representation of the client by the remaining lawyers in the firm." Answer **(A)** is wrong because personal beliefs, religious or otherwise, can create conflicts. Here, there would be a significant risk that Lawyer's representation of Client would be materially limited by her personal interest in remaining true to her religious beliefs. That is a conflict of interest. Answer **(C)** is wrong because the conflict will not be imputed. The exception in Rule 1.10(a)(1) applies. Answer **(D)** is incorrect; the issue is not whether Lawyer could seek consent under these circumstances—she could not, because of Rule 1.7(b)(1)—but rather whether the firm can undertake the representation despite Lawyer's nonconsentable conflict. It can, because of Rule 1.10(a)(1). Answer **(B)** is right.

57. **The correct answer is (A).** When Husband came to see Lawyer, Husband was a prospective client. Under Rule 1.18(d)(1), the only way Lawyer personally could represent Wife against Husband, once Lawyer was in possession of information that would be significantly harmful to Husband, would be to obtain informed consent of both parties. Husband refused to consent, and therefore, Lawyer could not represent Wife against Husband. Answer **(B)** is incorrect because it is overly broad. Lawyers sometimes are permitted to represent clients against former prospective clients. The lawyer is disqualified under Rule 1.18(c) from doing so only when, as here, the lawyer "received information from the prospective client that could be significantly harmful to that person in the matter." Answer **(C)** is wrong because Lawyer's precautions were potentially important only to the possible imputation of Lawyer's conflict and not to Lawyer's personal disqualification. If Lawyer had been in a firm, then under Rule 1.18(d)(2), the firm could have undertaken representation of Wife if the firm screened Lawyer, apportioned Lawyer no part of the fee, and gave Husband written notice. This option would have been available, because Lawyer took reasonable precautions to avoid being exposed to more information than would have been necessary to decide whether to accept the representation. Those precautions do not, however, allow Lawyer personally to represent Wife against Husband in the absence of consent of Husband. Answer **(D)** is incorrect because Lawyer did owe certain duties to Husband as a prospective client, including the duty as spelled out in Rule 1.18(c) not to represent a new client against the prospective client under certain circumstances, even though Husband never became a client. Answer **(A)** is correct.

58. **The correct answer is (B).** Rule 1.7(b)(3) lists among the conflicts that are not consentable "the assertion of a claim by one client against another client represented by the lawyer in the same litigation or other proceeding before a tribunal." That is exactly what was happening in this case. As Comment 17 to Rule 1.7 explains, this is a conflict that is "nonconsentable because of the institutional interest in vigorous development of each client's position when the clients are aligned directly against each other in the same litigation or other proceeding before a tribunal." Answer **(A)** is incorrect because there are times when a lawyer may be an advocate for one client against a current client, when both clients give informed consent. *See* Comment 6 to Rule 1.7. Answer **(C)** is wrong because this is a nonconsentable conflict, under Rule 1.7(b)(3). Answer **(D)** is incorrect because there was a conflict of interest. Undivided loyalty to Plaintiff Two would mean that Lawyer would try to defeat the cross-claim, if for no other reason than to prevent Plaintiff Two's insurance rates from rising. Undivided loyalty to Plaintiff One would mean that Lawyer would seek recovery from Plaintiff Two regardless of any consequences for Plaintiff Two. The right answer is **(B)**.

59. **The correct answer is (B).** Lawyer's representation of Big Client will fall victim to the "hot potato" doctrine, which prevents a lawyer from dropping one client "like a hot potato" in order to eliminate a conflict that would prevent the lawyer from representing a new, more lucrative client. Even though a lawyer may be able to implement this strategy without violating the rules of conduct, disqualification law will prevent it, because it is considered disreputable for a lawyer to act in such a self-interested way. Answer **(A)** is incorrect because generally a lawyer may sue a former client, as long as the new matter is not the same matter in which the lawyer represented the former client or substantially related to it. Answer **(C)** is wrong because this

is not just a question of compliance with the rules. Under Rule 1.9(a), a lawyer may sue a former client in this entirely unrelated matter. What subjects Lawyer to disqualification, however, is the fact that Lawyer dropped Small Client for the purpose of being able to undertake a new, more lucrative matter for Big Client against Small Client. The "hot potato" doctrine applies even if there is no violation of Rule 1.9(a). Answer (D) is incorrect because the issue is not just the propriety under the rules of the withdrawal. It is true that, under Rule 1.16(b)(1), Lawyer had the option to withdraw from representing Small Client when the withdrawal would have no material adverse effect on Small Client. But the "hot potato" doctrine would still apply and disqualify Lawyer from participating in the new matter for which Lawyer forsook Small Client. Answer (B) is right.

60. **The correct answer is (B).** Under Rule 1.8(f), a lawyer may accept payment from a third party if three conditions are met. Here, two of them were met: Lawyer protected Client's confidential information, and Lawyer did not permit anyone to interfere in the attorney-client relationship. But Rule 1.8(f) also requires that clients give informed consent to the payment of a lawyer's fee by a third party. That did not happen here. Answer (A) is incorrect because lawyers are permitted to accept payment from third parties, if all of the conditions of Rule 1.8(f) are satisfied. Answer (C) is wrong because it recites only two of the three conditions that must be satisfied before a lawyer may accept payment from a third party. Informed consent is also necessary. Answer (D) is wrong because the issue is the source of the payment, not the amount. No matter how reasonable the fee, a lawyer may not accept payment from a third party unless all three requirements of Rule 1.8(f) are satisfied. Answer (B) is correct.

61. **The correct answer is (A).** Rule 1.11 governs conflicts for government lawyers who move to private practice. Absent government consent, such a lawyer may not "represent a client in connection with a matter in which the lawyer participated personally and substantially as a public officer or employee." A "matter" is a defined term. Rule 1.11(e) defines "matter" to include "any judicial or other proceeding, application, request for a ruling or other determination, contract, claim, controversy, investigation, charge, accusation, arrest or other particular matter involving a specific party or parties." The drafting of legislation does not involve specific parties, and therefore Lawyer does not have a conflict of interest. There is no conflict of interest that might be imputed to the firm, and there is no impediment to the firm undertaking the representation. Answer (B) is incorrect because it does not matter which "side" Lawyer is on for the government and then in private practice. If a lawyer was involved personally and substantially in a matter for the government, then absent consent, the lawyer may not represent a client in that matter in private practice, regardless of which "side" the client is on. Answer (C) is wrong because Lawyer's personal and substantial involvement came in connection with the drafting of legislation and not a "matter" as defined in Rule 1.11. Answer (D) is wrong because no screening is necessary. Rule 1.11 does allow for screening if a former government lawyer was involved personally and substantially in a matter while the lawyer worked for the government, but here, no screening is necessary because drafting the legislation was not a "matter." Answer (A) is the right one.

62. **The correct answer is (C).** Under Comment 6 to Rule 1.7, it is clear that Lawyer did not have a conflict of interest, because "simultaneous representation in unrelated matters of clients

whose interests are only economically adverse, such as representation of competing economic enterprises in unrelated litigation, does not ordinarily constitute a conflict of interest and thus may not require consent of the respective clients." Answer (A) is incorrect because no consent is necessary when there is no conflict of interest. Lawyer obtained informed consent from his existing client, but even that was unnecessary. Answer (B) is wrong because there is no conflict at all, much less a conflict that is so severe as to be nonconsentable under rule 1.7(b). Answer (D) is incorrect because no consent is necessary where there is no conflict. Furthermore, if there had been a conflict, both clients would have had to give informed consent. *See* Rule 1.7(b)(4) (consent to a conflict effective only if "each affected client gives informed consent"). Answer (C) is correct.

63. **The correct answer is (C).** Comment 24 to Rule 1.7 provides that "[o]rdinarily a lawyer may take inconsistent legal positions in different tribunals at different times on behalf of different clients." Here, the cases are pending in different counties before trial courts. There is no indication that one client or one client's matter is more important to the lawyer than the other one. There is no significant risk that the lawyer would feel materially limited under these circumstances and "pull a punch" for one client in order to help the other. There is no conflict. Answer (A) is incorrect because consent would only matter if there were a conflict. There is no conflict, and therefore no consent is necessary. Answer (B) is wrong because there is no conflict, much less a nonconsentable one. Comment 24 to Rule 1.7 states, "[t]he mere fact that advocating a legal position on behalf of one client might create precedent adverse to the interests of a client represented by the lawyer in an unrelated matter does not create a conflict of interest." Answer (D) is incorrect because there could be a conflict of interest under special circumstances, even though the conflict is merely "positional." If, for example, the lawyer were representing two clients simultaneously before a court of last resort, so that one client would lose and the other would win the issue, then there could be a conflict of interest. Answer (C) is right.

64. **The correct answer is (B).** Under Rule 1.8(i), Lawyer was not allowed "to acquire a proprietary interest in the cause of action or subject matter of litigation the lawyer is conducting for a client" (with some exceptions that do not apply here). That is what Lawyer did by taking a contingent interest in a one-third undivided share of the skybox. Answer (A) is incorrect because lawyers may enter into contingent fee contracts in any type of case except domestic relations and criminal defense. *See* Rule 1.5(d). Answer (C) is wrong because Lawyer did more than contract for a contingent fee in an estate case. Lawyer acquired a contingent interest in the very property that was the subject matter of the case. Answer (D) is incorrect because this is a prohibited transaction under Rule 1.8(i) rather than a transaction that would be permitted under Rule 1.8(a) if these (and other) conditions were satisfied. Answer (B) is correct.

65. **The correct answer is (C).** Law Firm would be subject to disqualification if the lawyers working on the case had conflicts of interest. Under these facts, the only way they could have a conflict of interest would be if Law Clerk had a conflict that was imputed to them. Under Rule 1.12(a), Law Clerk personally had a conflict of interest because of her service as law clerk to the federal judge who was participating personally and substantially in the antitrust case. Rule 1.12(c), however, allowed Law Firm to avoid imputation of that conflict to its other lawyers by under-

taking the screening and notice steps that it took. Answer (**A**) is incorrect because Law Firm was permitted to pay Law Clerk even while Law Firm received revenue from the antitrust case, as long as Law Clerk did not receive any compensation directly related to the case. *See* Comment 4 to Rule 1.12. Answer (**B**) is wrong because Law Clerk's conflict would not be imputed, due to the screening and notice that Law Firm undertook pursuant to Rule 1.12(c). Answer (**D**) is incorrect because Rule 1.12(a) applies to those who participate in a matter "personally and substantially as a judge or other adjudicative officer or law clerk to such a person...." Law Clerk was not an adjudicative officer, but she was nevertheless subject to Rule 1.12(a). Answer (**C**) is right.

66. **The correct answer is (C).** Rule 1.8(j) prohibited Associate from starting a sexual relationship with Client while Associate represented Client. Rule 1.8(k), however, provides that "[w]hile lawyers are associated in a firm, a prohibition in the foregoing paragraphs (a) through (i) that applies to any one of them shall apply to all of them." Note the omission of Rule 1.8(j) from that imputation rule. The prohibition on what Associate could do was not imputed to Lawyer. Answer (**A**) is incorrect because Rule 1.8(k) excludes the prohibition in Rule 1.8(j) from being imputed to other members of Associate's firm. Answer (**B**) is wrong because there was nothing for Lawyer to report to the bar. Associate withdrew from representing Client before commencing the sexual relationship and thus did not violate Rule 1.8(j). Answer (**D**) is incorrect because Rule 1.8(j) did prohibit Associate from representing Client. Answer (**C**) is the correct answer.

67. **The correct answer is (B).** Rule 1.8(c) forbade Lawyer from preparing the will under these circumstances. The educational trust was certainly a substantial gift, and Grandson was sufficiently closely related to trigger the prohibition in the rule. Lawyer did not solicit the gift, and Lawyer need not have prevented it, but Lawyer could not prepare the instrument himself. Answer (**A**) is incorrect because Rule 1.8(c) is an absolute prohibition on a lawyer drafting an instrument under these circumstances. There is no provision for informed consent taking care of the conflict. Answer (**C**) is wrong because, although Lawyer's advice to seek independent counsel and the grant of sufficient time to do so were prudent, those steps still did not allow Lawyer to prepare the will. Someone else had to do that, regardless of whether Client was advised to seek independent counsel and had time to do so. Answer (**D**) is incorrect because the gift went to someone who was "related to" Lawyer. Rule 1.8(c) defines "related persons" for purposes of the rule to include a grandchild. Answer (**B**) is right.

68. Law Firm may not undertake this representation without informed consent of Corporation and New Client. Corporation is still a client (in the slip and fall case) and therefore under Rule 1.7(a), Law Firm may not represent New Client against Corporation, a current client, even in an unrelated matter, without informed consent of both clients. *See* Comment 6 to Rule 1.7. If Law Firm no longer represented Corporation, then under Rule 1.10(b) Law Firm could represent New Client against Corporation, unless two things were true: "(1) the matter is the same or substantially related to that in which the formerly associated lawyer represented the client; and (2) any lawyer remaining in the firm has [confidential] information ... that is material to the matter."

69. It will not be necessary to screen Lawyer. Rule 1.11(b) would require the firm to screen Lawyer if the firm wished to continue involvement in the case, but only if Lawyer herself were dis-

qualified under Rule 1.11(a) from participating in it. Lawyer would be disqualified only if she had had "personal and substantial" involvement in the case for the government agency. Lawyer was just a supervisor of other lawyers who were handling the case. Because Lawyer had no personal and substantial involvement in the case, she may leave the government and join the firm, without the necessity of the firm screening her from participation in the case.

70. Law Firm will need informed consent under Rule 1.10(c) to this conflict. Rule 1.10(b) provides that a firm may represent a new client against a former client who had been represented by a lawyer who left the firm, unless two things are true: the matter for the new client is the same or is substantially related to the matter in which the departed lawyer represented the former client, and there is a lawyer remaining in the firm with confidential information about the matter. Unfortunately for Law Firm, both of those conditions are met in the question. New Client wants to raise the same allegations as were made in Class Action, the case in which the departed lawyer represented Corporation while Corporation was a client of Law Firm. Also, a lawyer with confidential information is left behind. Rule 1.10 makes no provision for screening the lawyer in this situation, and therefore the firm's only option is to seek informed consent, as allowed by Rule 1.10(c).

71. Yes, Lawyer has a conflict of interest. Even though the transactions are unrelated, Client A is a current client rather than a former client. As Comment 7 to Rule 1.7 explains, "if a lawyer is asked to represent the seller of a business in negotiations with a buyer represented by the lawyer, not in the same transaction but in another, unrelated matter, the lawyer could not undertake the representation without the informed consent of each client."

72. Lawyer must conform her conduct to Rule 1.8(g). Each client must give written, signed, informed consent to the settlement after Lawyer has disclosed the total amount of the settlement, the nature of all the claims and the participation of each client in the settlement. The disclosure must also include the fees and costs that Lawyer will receive as part of the settlement and the method by which costs are to be apportioned among the clients. *See* ABA Formal Op. 06-438.

73. Lawyer must be sure to comply with all of the requirements of Rule 1.8(a). Because clients tend to trust their lawyers, and because trust is something that the rules of conduct should promote, Rule 1.8(a) contains protections for a trusting client from being taken advantage of by his or her lawyer. Here, Lawyer must make sure that the terms of the sale are fair and reasonable and are given to Client in writing in a way that Client can understand them. Lawyer must also advise Client in writing of the desirability of seeking independent legal advice about the transaction and must give Client the opportunity to do so. Finally, Client must give written informed consent to the essential terms of the deal, including whether or not Lawyer will represent Client in it.

Competence, Legal Malpractice, and Other Civil Liability

74. **The correct answer is (D).** Rule 1.1 requires lawyers to provide competent representation. Initially, Lawyer did not have the legal knowledge or skill to represent Client. But, as Comment 2 to Rule 1.1 provides, "[a] lawyer can provide adequate representation in a wholly novel field through necessary study." That is exactly what Lawyer did. Answer (A) is wrong because Lawyer became competent for each stage of the case before Lawyer had to act for Client. If a lawyer could not accept a representation and then become competent in a timely way, then Comment 2's assurance that a lawyer can become competent through necessary study would be a Catch-22. The lawyer could not accept the representation until the lawyer performed the necessary study, but the lawyer would have no incentive to perform the necessary study if the lawyer did not have a client. As long as Lawyer was competent at each stage as it came, Lawyer did not violate Rule 1.1. Answer (B) is incorrect because Lawyer did not have to associate an experienced lawyer. That was one option for dealing with Lawyer's lack of competence (*see* Comment 3 to Rule 1.1), but it was not the only one. Studying hard to become competent was another option, and that is what Lawyer did. Answer (C) is incorrect because having a law license does not make a lawyer competent to undertake all kinds of representation. Graduation from law school and passing the bar are intended to give the public some assurance of the basic competence of all lawyers, but Rule 1.1 exists to ensure that lawyers personally undertake only those matters for which they are actually competent or can become competent through necessary study. Answer (D) is correct.

75. **The correct answer is (B).** Lawyers owe fiduciary duties to their clients, including the duties to act with utmost good faith and loyalty and not to take advantage of confidential information learned in the course of representing a client. That is what Lawyer did here. He learned that his married Client had an impairment that might make it easier for Lawyer to benefit himself by initiating and maintaining a sexual relationship with Client. That was an abuse of the relationship, was disloyal, and was an improper use of confidential information. *See, e.g.,* Tante v. Herring, 211 Ga. App. 322 (1993). Answer (A) is incorrect because the term "legal malpractice" customarily refers to cases of professional negligence. Here, Lawyer did a fine job in representing Client in the worker's compensation case, all while Lawyer was breaching the fiduciary duty of loyalty, among others. Those actions were reprehensible, but they did not constitute what is generally known as legal malpractice. Answer (C) is wrong because it was not enough for Lawyer to conduct the case competently and successfully. He had simultaneous fiduciary duties (which he breached) not to act disloyally or to misuse confidential information of Client, regardless of the outcome of the case. Answer (D) is incorrect because Client's con-

sent was not enough (even if it might be legally effective such that Lawyer did not commit sexual assault). Lawyer was not just another person to Client. Lawyer was Client's fiduciary and would be held to a higher standard. Answer (**B**) is the right answer.

76. **The correct answer is (A).** Rule 1.1 requires lawyers to be competent, and that includes the duty to maintain competence. Comment 8 to Rule 1.1 particularly mentions competence with respect to changing technology: "To maintain the requisite knowledge and skill, a lawyer should keep abreast of changes in the law and its practice, including the benefits and risks associated with relevant technology...." Lawyer breached his duty to maintain competence by not keeping abreast of cloud computing and how he could conform his professional responsibilities to this technology. Answer (**B**) is wrong because lawyers are generally permitted to use cloud computing, as long as they exercise reasonable care that they do not violate their professional responsibilities through its use. Answer (**C**) is incorrect because it is not enough for Lawyer to be permitted to use cloud computing. Lawyer must inform himself—maintain his competence—about how he can use the technology and still keep his duty of confidentiality to his clients. Answer (**D**) is wrong because Lawyer had duties beyond simply not revealing or using client confidential information. Under Rule 1.6(c), Lawyer was obliged to "make reasonable efforts to prevent the inadvertent or unauthorized disclosure of, or unauthorized access to, information relating to the representation of a client." He did not do so here, because he violated Rule 1.1's requirement that he maintain his competence, including with respect to changing technology. Answer (**A**) is right.

77. **The correct answer is (B).** When a lawyer settles a claim for malpractice liability with a former client, Rule 1.8(h)(2) requires the lawyer to advise the former client in writing of the desirability of seeking independent counsel in connection with the settlement. Here, Lawyer gave the right advice but did not put it in writing. Answer (**A**) is incorrect because it is not necessary that a former client be represented in connection with the settlement of a malpractice claim. Such representation is required under Rule 1.8(h)(1) if a lawyer seeks a prospective agreement limiting the lawyer's malpractice liability, but this agreement is for a representation that is over. Answer (**C**) is wrong because, although Client received the right advice, the advice about the desirability of seeking the advice of independent counsel had to be in writing. Answer (**D**) is incorrect because Rule 1.8(h)(2) puts conditions on a lawyer's settlement of a malpractice claim after the fact, albeit fewer restrictions than on a prospective agreement that limits malpractice liability for future action. Answer (**B**) is right.

78. **The correct answer is (A).** Prospective Client never became a client, but Lawyer gave negligent advice that harmed Prospective Client. This is one of the rare circumstances when a nonclient, here a prospective client, may sue a lawyer even thought there was no attorney-client relationship. If Lawyer wanted to avoid malpractice liability in these circumstances, Lawyer should not have rendered any advice or assistance. *See* Restatement (Third) of the Law Governing Lawyers § 51(1). The advice was negligent because Lawyer did not undertake an adequate investigation before giving it. A reasonable lawyer who does not understand a set of medical records would not give advice about a medical malpractice claim without doing more, such as consulting a specialist. Answer (**B**) is incorrect because Lawyer was under no duty to file the claim. Lawyer never represented Prospective Client. Answer (**C**) is wrong because a

lawyer who gives advice or assistance to a prospective client, even if the prospective client never becomes a client, is subject to a suit for malpractice. Answer (D) is wrong because Lawyer's "judgment" that there was no claim was based upon a deficient investigation. Lawyer's lack of diligence, rather than Lawyer's lack of good judgment, is what caused the harm and is what constituted the malpractice for which Prospective Client may recover. Answer (A) is the correct answer.

79. **The correct answer is (D).** Professor was not competent to represent a criminal defendant and did not undertake the necessary study or associate a lawyer with competence. Ordinarily, therefore, Professor would have been in violation of Rule 1.1's duty of competence. However, Professor was asked to render service on short notice on an emergency basis. Comment 3 to Rule 1.1 provides that "[i]n an emergency, a lawyer may give advice or assistance in a matter in which the lawyer does not have the skill ordinarily required where referral to or consultation or association with another lawyer would be impractical." That was the situation that Professor faced. Answer (A) is incorrect because of the emergency exception to the general rule against representing clients without the competence to do so. Answer (B) is wrong because there was no time to associate anyone, and in such emergency circumstances, a lawyer may proceed to render assistance. Answer (C) is incorrect because it is not enough merely to have a license. Law is complex and specialized, and not every licensed lawyer is competent to do everything that a lawyer might do. Answer (D) is correct.

80. **The correct answer is (C).** Lawyer owed Client a duty of diligence under Rule 1.3. That duty is to "act with reasonable diligence and promptness in representing a client." However, Comment 3 to Rule 1.3 provides specifically that "[a] lawyer's duty to act with reasonable promptness, however, does not preclude the lawyer from agreeing to a reasonable request for a postponement that will not prejudice the lawyer's client." That is all that Lawyer did in this situation. Answer (A) is incorrect because this slight delay that did not harm Client is not a violation of Rule 1.3, as Comment 3 to Rule 1.3 explains. The 15-day delay did not affect any other deadlines or scheduled events in the case. It did not prejudice Client. Answer (B) is wrong because Lawyer's general duty of consultation about means under Rule 1.2(a) is not implicated by something as routine and harmless as this extension. Rule 1.2(a) itself provides that Lawyer "may take such action on behalf of the client as is impliedly authorized to carry out the representation." This routine extension falls into that category. Note also that the duty of communication about means in Rule 1.4(a)(2) is a duty to *reasonably* consult. Consultation is not required for every tiny step that a lawyer chooses to take for a client. Answer (D) is incorrect because questions of means do not belong exclusively to Client. They are generally a shared responsibility between Lawyer and Client under Rule 1.2(a), but here, Lawyer had the unilateral option to grant a routine extension of time that did not prejudice Client. Answer (C) is right.

81. **The correct answer is (D).** The general rule regarding malpractice in criminal defense is that the client must either show actual innocence of the charges, or exoneration from the conviction, or both. Otherwise, the client is deemed to have caused the client's own injuries by committing the criminal acts that led to the conviction. Here, Client has not been exonerated and will be unable to prove actual innocence. Client's guilt has already been adjudicated finally

through all appeals. Without proof of damage that flowed from Lawyer's malpractice, Client's malpractice claim must fail. Answer (A) is incorrect because, although the failure to deliver the plea offer would be a breach of Lawyer's standard of care, Client must prove not only the breach but also damage. In one sense, of course, Client may have been damaged, because presumably Client would testify that Client would have accepted the plea and saved nine years in prison. In criminal cases, however, the "cause" of the incarceration for those nine years is deemed to be the criminal activity rather than Lawyer's breach of the standard of care. Answer (B) is wrong because an incorrect assessment of the likelihood of conviction under conditions of uncertainty would not be a breach of the standard of care but rather would be covered by the doctrine of judgmental immunity. Answer (C) is incorrect. Client had not previously indicated that this particular offer would be acceptable, and the decision to accept or reject the offer belonged exclusively to Client under Rule 1.2(a). Lawyer was therefore obliged by Rule 1.4(a)(1) to convey the plea offer. *See also* Comment 2 to Rule 1.2. Failure to do so was a breach of the standard of care. Answer (D) is correct.

82. **The correct answer is (A).** Lawyer did not represent Ward but nevertheless owed some duties to Ward as the lawyer for Ward's fiduciary. One of those duties was to act to prevent Trustee from defrauding Ward when Lawyer knew about the fraud before the harm was done. *See* Restatement (Third) of the Law Governing Lawyers § 51(4). Lawyer had this special duty to a nonclient, because Lawyer was in a position to detect the fraud, and Lawyer was representing Trustee in Trustee's capacity as a fiduciary to Ward. Answer (B) is incorrect because Ward was never Lawyer's client. Lawyer owed duties to Ward because Lawyer was helping Trustee act to benefit Ward, but there was never an attorney-client relationship between them. Answer (C) is wrong because the key is that Lawyer knew about the fraud at a time when it could still be prevented. Whether Lawyer knowingly assisted in the fraud is not relevant. Lawyer had a duty to protect Ward from Trustee's fraud even if Lawyer had provided no assistance. Restatement (Third) of the Law Governing Lawyers § 51(4)(b). Answer (D) is incorrect because this is a special case in which Lawyer is liable for professional negligence even though the usually required attorney-client relationship was not present. Sometimes, in rare cases, lawyers are liable to nonclients for professional negligence. This is one of those times. Answer (A) is the right answer.

83. **The correct answer is (C).** Lawyer breached the standard of care by reaching a legal conclusion that was wrong and then failing to introduce the value of the tax credits into the negotiation. The problem for Client, however, is that it is speculative what would have happened next. In a transactional context, Client must prove that Client would have gotten a better deal or would have declined to make a deal at all. It is a given in the question that Client would not have walked away. Therefore, Client's only path to recovery is the "better deal" scenario, which depends upon proof that Buyer would have agreed to pay more for the business if Lawyer had introduced the tax credits into the negotiations. But Buyer has refused to cooperate, and so what Buyer's reaction would have been—whether it would have been willing to pay any more for the business with the tax credits—is pure speculation. Client will not be able to prove damages. Answer (A) is incorrect because Lawyer's lack of diligence may have been a breach of the standard of care, but Client cannot recover because Client cannot prove damages. An-

swer (**B**) is wrong for the same reason. Lawyer's advice was a breach of the standard of care, but there can be no recovery without proof of damage. Answer (**D**) is incorrect because it is too broad. It is hard but not impossible to recover for malpractice in a transactional context. If a plaintiff can produce evidence that the plaintiff would not have entered into a transaction, and would have been better off that way, then that plaintiff can show damage. Similarly, if a plaintiff can show that, but for the lawyer's breach of the standard of care, the plaintiff would have been able to make a better deal, then the plaintiff may recover. This Client cannot do either of those things, but that does not mean that there can never be a malpractice recovery when the underlying work was transactional. Answer (**C**) is right.

84. **Yes, Lawyer violated the Model Rules of Professional Conduct.** Under Rule 1.8(h)(1), "[a] lawyer shall not: … make an agreement prospectively limiting the lawyer's liability to a client for malpractice unless the client is independently represented in making the agreement.…" Here, Client was advised to get independent counsel and had the chance to do so but did not obtain it. The advice and the opportunity were not enough (in contrast to the situation where the lawyer and former client settle claims for malpractice after the fact, under Rule 1.8(h)(2)). Lawyer committed misconduct by entering into an agreement limiting his liability to the client for malpractice without the client having independent representation in connection with that agreement.

85. **Lawyer would not be liable to Client for malpractice under these circumstances** under the doctrine of "judgmental immunity." Lawyer gave advice based upon exhaustive research under conditions of irreducible uncertainty about how the courts would decide the question. It turned out that Lawyer's judgment was incorrect, but Lawyer is not a guarantor for Client. If lawyers could be sued by clients every time lawyers turned out to be wrong in their considered judgment, then lawyers would be reluctant to give such judgments. Yet the considered judgments of diligent lawyers are what clients need most. "Judgmental immunity" will insulate Lawyer from liability in this case.

86. **Lawyer violated Rule 4.1 by making a false statement of material fact** to the client who asked whether Lawyer was insured. Comment 1 to Rule 4.1 makes it clear that a lawyer can violate Rule 4.1(a) by making a misleading statement. Lawyer's statement that she was "insured" was misleading, because one would normally assume that this meant she had an insurance policy. Lawyer did not violate the rules by not having a malpractice insurance policy or by not affirmatively revealing to all clients and prospective clients that she did not have such a policy. The rules impose no duty to carry insurance or to tell clients about the lack of insurance.

87. **Yes, Lawyer is liable to Girlfriend** even though Girlfriend was never in an attorney-client relationship with Lawyer. Lawyer committed malpractice. Usually, one element of a claim for legal malpractice is the existence of an attorney-client relationship between the plaintiff and the lawyer. This situation presents an exception to that general rule. Lawyer knew that Client's objective was to benefit Girlfriend. In the absence of a duty to Girlfriend, it is unlikely that Lawyer's obligation of competence to Client could be enforced. By the time the damage occurred, Client was dead. Client's estate was not diminished by the malpractice and so could not sue. In these circumstances, as long as there is nothing about imposing a duty on lawyer

to protect Girlfriend that would interfere with Lawyer's representation of Client (in this situation there would not be), Lawyer owed duties to the non-client Girlfriend and would be liable. *See* Restatement (Third) of the Law Governing Lawyers § 51.

Litigation and Other Forms of Advocacy

88. **The correct answer is (D).** Under Rule 3.6(c), "a lawyer may make a statement that a reasonable lawyer would believe is required to protect a client from the substantial undue prejudicial effect of recent publicity not initiated by the lawyer or the lawyer's client." Here, the false report of the results of the DNA test had an obvious potential to prejudice Client in the eyes of the public. Lawyer had the right to counteract that publicity by sharing the real report. Answer (A) is incorrect because the source of the substantial undue adverse publicity is irrelevant. Regardless of the source, Lawyer had the right under Rule 3.6(c) to speak publicly to counteract the effect of such publicity. Answer (B) is wrong because 3.6(c) is an exception to the general rules about what lawyers may not say about a pending case. Answer (C) is incorrect because, generally, a lawyer may not reveal the results of any test related to the case, regardless of its admissibility (*see* Comment 5(3) to Rule 3.6). This case is an exception to that general rule, but the exception arises not from the report's admissibility but rather from the substantial undue prejudicial effect of the release of the false report. Answer (D) is right.

89. **The correct answer is (A).** Rule 3.3(a)(3) states that "[i]f a lawyer, the lawyer's client, or a witness called by the lawyer, has offered material evidence and the lawyer comes to know of its falsity, the lawyer shall take reasonable remedial measures, including, if necessary, disclosure to the tribunal." "Reasonable remedial measures" are described in Comment 10 to Rule 3.3, and they consist of three steps, the first two of which Lawyer took. Lawyer tried to get Client to correct the record, and when that failed, Lawyer sought to withdraw. When the court denied that motion, Lawyer's obligation was to "make such disclosure to the tribunal as is reasonably necessary to remedy the situation, even if doing so requires the lawyer to reveal information that otherwise would be protected by Rule 1.6." This is one of the very rare circumstances where revelation of client confidential information is mandatory. Answer (B) is incorrect because, although Lawyer presented false evidence, Lawyer did not do so knowingly. Rule 3.3(a)(3) prohibits a lawyer from offering evidence that the lawyer knows to be false. Answer (C) is wrong because Lawyer was required upon learning that false evidence had been presented to institute the reasonable remedial measures, and disclosure as a reasonable remedial measure became mandatory when remonstrating with Client and seeking to withdraw did not cure the situation. Answer (D) is incorrect because the privileged nature of the conversation is irrelevant to Lawyer's duties under the Model Rules of Professional Conduct. The only way to comply with Lawyer's duty to inform the court is to report the privileged conversation. Answer (A) is correct.

90. **The correct answer is (C).** Under Rule 3.3(a)(3), Lawyer had the power to "refuse to offer evidence, other than the testimony of a defendant in a criminal matter, that the lawyer reasonably

believes is false." Here, the testimony in question was that of the friend, not the defendant, and Lawyer reasonably believed the testimony would be false. The rules give this discretion to the lawyer for a reason. As Comment 9 to Rule 3.3 explains, it is intended to protect the client by protecting the lawyer's credibility: "Offering such proof may reflect adversely on the lawyer's ability to discriminate in the quality of evidence and thus impair the lawyer's effectiveness as an advocate." Answer (A) is incorrect because Rule 3.3(a)(3) specifically gives this decision to Lawyer and because it also misstates the general rule on the allocation of authority between a lawyer and a client. A lawyer generally must abide by a client's decisions about objectives of the representation, not decisions about means. Answer (B) is wrong because this is not one of the special rules about criminal defendants. Even in a criminal case, a lawyer has the discretion not to offer evidence that the lawyer reasonably believes to be false, except for the testimony of the defendant. Here, the evidence would have been coming from someone else. Answer (D) is wrong because a lawyer may offer evidence that the lawyer reasonably believes is false. Rule 3.3(a)(3) prohibits the offering of evidence that the lawyer knows to be false, but a reasonable belief is not the same as knowledge. Answer (C) is the right answer.

91. **The correct answer is (A).** Under Rule 3.3(b), Lawyer had an affirmative duty to take reasonable remedial measures, including if necessary disclosure to the tribunal, once Lawyer knew that someone intended to engage in criminal conduct related to the proceeding. Answer (B) is incorrect because the Rules do not place any duty on lawyers to report to law enforcement. The duty is to take "reasonable remedial measures," which certainly could include a report to the court without a report directly to law enforcement. Answer (C) is wrong because the duty under Rule 3.3(b) to protect the integrity of the proceeding overrides the Lawyer's general duty of confidentiality. Rule 3.3(c) states that "The duties stated in paragraphs (a) and (b) … apply even if compliance requires disclosure of information otherwise protected by Rule 1.6." Answer (D) is incorrect because Lawyer violated Rule 3.3(b) when he failed to take reasonable remedial measures once he knew that someone planned to engage in criminal activity related to the proceeding. The fact that the bribery either did not take place or was somehow otherwise ineffective is irrelevant. Lawyer had a duty to act as soon as he knew about the plans. Answer (A) is right.

92. **The correct answer is (C).** Rule 3.1 provides that a lawyer may not bring a proceeding or assert an issue unless there is a non-frivolous basis in law and fact for doing so, but the Rule also provides specifically that it is not frivolous to make "a good faith argument for an extension, modification or reversal of existing law." The law changes and grows because lawyers are free to challenge the status quo, and Rule 3.1 is not an impediment to that process. Answer (A) is incorrect because Lawyer did not need to have all of the evidence right away. Comment 2 to Rule 3.1 provides that "action taken for a client is not frivolous merely because the facts have not first been fully substantiated or because the lawyer expects to develop vital evidence only by discovery." Answer (B) is wrong because Lawyer was free to take a legal position that was inconsistent with existing law, as long as Lawyer had a good faith argument to change the law. Answer (D) is incorrect because Lawyer's personal belief is irrelevant. Even if Lawyer believed that the argument would fail, Lawyer may make it. As Comment 2 to Rule 3.1 states, "action is not frivolous even though the lawyer believes that the client's position ultimately will not prevail." Answer (C) is correct.

93. **The correct answer is (A).** Rule 3.4(f) specifically governs the circumstances under which a lawyer may ask someone other than a client not to voluntarily give relevant information to another party. For such a request to be permissible, the person must be a relative, employee or agent of the lawyer's client, *and* the lawyer must reasonably believe that the person's interests will not be adversely affected. Here, the first requirement was not met, and therefore Lawyer was prohibited by Rule 3.4(f) from making this request. Answer **(B)** is incorrect because it is not always improper to ask a witness not to cooperate voluntarily. Answer **(C)** is wrong because it states only one of the two requirements that must be satisfied before a lawyer may ask someone not to voluntarily give information to another party. Answer **(D)** is incorrect because there are limits on when a lawyer may ask a witness not to cooperate. Rule 3.4(f) states specific limitations on a lawyer's ability to do so. Answer **(A)** is the right answer.

94. **The correct answer is (C).** Rule 3.3(a)(2) imposes the obligation to cite harmful legal authority, but that duty exists only for "legal authority in the controlling jurisdiction." <u>Smith v. Jones</u> is persuasive authority from another state, but it is not from a controlling legal authority. Answer **(A)** is incorrect because lawyers are not obliged to cite every legal authority that is directly adverse to their clients' positions. Under Rule 3.3(a)(2), lawyers must cite such authority only if it comes from a controlling jurisdiction and only when opposing counsel does not cite it. Here, the case did not come from a controlling jurisdiction. Answer **(B)** is wrong because there is never a duty to cite adverse authority that is merely persuasive rather than controlling. Answer **(D)** is incorrect because sometimes a lawyer must cite authority even if doing so hurts the client. Rule 3.3(a)(2) sets forth those circumstances. Answer **(C)** is correct.

95. **The correct answer is (D).** Rule 3.6 prohibits some public statements by lawyers about pending cases, but it only regulates the speech of lawyers who are participating or have participated in the investigation or litigation of the matter. Because Lawyer did neither, Rule 3.6 does not prohibit his statements. Answer **(A)** is incorrect because Lawyer has not been involved in the case. Comment 5(4) to Rule 3.6 provides that any public statement of an opinion about the guilt of a defendant in a criminal proceeding is more likely than not to be prohibited, but only for lawyers who are participating or have participated in the matter. Answer **(B)** is wrong because not all press conferences by lawyers about pending cases are prohibited by Rule 3.6. In fact, Rule 3.6(b) specifically sets forth a number of things that a lawyer involved in a matter may say at such a conference. Answer **(C)** is incorrect because Lawyer did not make those statements to protect a client from the publicity. Lawyer had no client in the matter. Rule 3.6(c) does provide for a limited right of reply for lawyers whose clients have been the subject of certain prejudicial publicity, but it does not apply to Lawyer. Answer **(D)** is the right answer.

96. **The correct answer is (B).** Lawyer was implementing reasonable remedial measures in accordance with Rule 3.3(a)(3) and Comment 10 to Rule 3.3, but Lawyer was not entitled to reveal confidential information. Lawyer only *reasonably believed* that the testimony was false. In order to have the right to reveal confidential information under 3.3(a)(3), a lawyer must *know*, and not just reasonably believe, that a witness has presented false evidence. Answer **(A)** is incorrect because Lawyer had the right under Rule 1.16(b)(2) to seek to withdraw because Lawyer reasonably believed that Client was persisting in a criminal course of conduct. Perjury is a crime, and Client would not retract testimony that Lawyer reasonably believed was perjurious. An-

swer (C) is wrong because Rule 3.3 applies to testimony in ancillary proceedings such as depositions and not just to testimony in open court. Comment 1 to Rule 3.3. Answer (D) is incorrect because appointed counsel owes exactly the same duties as retained counsel, including the duty to maintain confidences. Comment 3 to Rule 6.2. Answer (B) is right.

97. **The correct answer is (A).** Under Rule 3.4(e), Lawyer was not permitted to allude in trial to any matter that she did not reasonably believe would be supported by admissible evidence. A lawyer's opening statement and closing argument are not evidence, and the jury's decision should be based on the evidence in the record and not anything outside the record that a lawyer mentions. Answer (B) is incorrect because Rule 3.4(e) is not a rule of strict liability. Lawyers can be surprised by a court's rulings about the admissibility of evidence. Any rule that made it misconduct to mention something that later, surprisingly, was excluded would be too much of a constraint on advocacy. Answer (C) is wrong because Lawyer violated a different part of Rule 3.4(e). Personal opinion is not permitted, but neither are references to matters that a lawyer does not reasonably believe will be supported by admissible evidence. Answer (D) is incorrect because the standard for alluding to matters in front of the jury is not whether the argument is frivolous. The standard is higher. The lawyer must reasonably believe that the matter will be supported by admissible evidence. Answer (A) is the right answer.

98. **The correct answer is (D).** Rule 3.5(b) forbids lawyers from communicating ex parte with judges, jurors, prospective jurors and other officials. The issue is whether an automatic message sent from the web site because a lawyer viewed the profile is a communication from the lawyer. ABA Formal Opinion 466 examined this question and concluded that "[t]he fact that a juror or a potential juror may become aware that a lawyer is reviewing his Internet presence when a network setting notifies the juror of such does not constitute a communication from the lawyer in violation of Rule 3.5(b)." Answer (A) is incorrect because, under the Model Rules of Professional Conduct, the message from the web site to Juror Smith was not a communication from Lawyer. Answer (B) is wrong because the passive review of a juror's Internet presence is not a communication. *See* ABA Formal Op. 466. Answer (C) is incorrect because Rule 3.5(b) does not have a state of mind requirement. Many of the Model Rules of Professional Conduct forbid lawyers from doing things "knowingly." That limitation is not present in Rule 3.5(b). Answer (D) is right.

99. **The correct answer is (C).** Rule 3.3(b) provides that "[a] lawyer who represents a client in an adjudicative proceeding and who knows that a person intends to engage, is engaging or has engaged in criminal or fraudulent conduct related to the proceeding shall take reasonable remedial measures...." Lawyer knew that the police officer had committed perjury, a criminal act, but Lawyer did not represent anyone in the proceeding and thus was not bound to take reasonable remedial measures under Rule 3.3(b). Answer (A) is incorrect because Lawyer was under no obligation to report Prosecutor, even though Lawyer knew that Prosecutor had violated rule 3.3(a)(3) by knowingly presenting false evidence. Rule 8.3(c) provides in relevant part that "[t]his Rule does not require disclosure of information ... gained by a lawyer ... while participating in an approved lawyers assistance program." Answer (B) is wrong because Rule 3.3(b)'s mandate to take reasonable remedial measures does not apply to a lawyer who does not represent anyone in the proceeding. Answer (D) is incorrect because the obligations of

Rule 3.3(b) continue to the conclusion of the proceeding. Rule 3.3(c). The proceeding is not concluded until "a final judgment in the proceeding has been affirmed on appeal or the time for review has passed." Comment 13 to Rule 3.3. Prosecutor's case was still on appeal. Answer (C) is correct.

100. **The correct answer is (C).** Lawyer knew that Client intended to testify falsely. "Knowledge" means actual knowledge, but knowledge can be inferred from the circumstances. Rule 1.0(f). The surveillance video and the ATM receipt are circumstances from which one could only conclude that Lawyer knew Client would lie on the stand about his whereabouts. When Client insisted, Lawyer's only option was to refuse to offer the evidence. *See* Comment 6 to Rule 3.3. Once Judge ordered Lawyer to present the evidence, however, Lawyer's obligation to follow Judge's order superseded Lawyer's obligation under the rules of conduct. *See* Comment 7 to Rule 3.3. Answer (A) is incorrect because Lawyer did "know" that Client's testimony would be false. Lawyer's knowledge of the falsity of the evidence would be inferred from the circumstances. Answer (B) is wrong because Lawyer's obligation under Rule 3.3(a)(3) not to present the false evidence was subordinate to Lawyer's obligation to do as Judge ordered. Comment 7 to Rule 3.3. Answer (D) is incorrect because the prohibition on offering evidence that the lawyer knows to be false applies to criminal defendants just as it applies to everyone else. Id. Answer (C) is right.

101. **The correct answer is (B).** Rule 3.4(c) provides that a lawyer shall not "knowingly disobey an obligation under the rules of a tribunal except for an open refusal based on an assertion that no valid obligation exists." An open refusal would have permitted the parties and the court to address the propriety of the rule. Lawyer's secret refusal did not. Answer (A) is incorrect because lawyers are permitted to refuse to follow a rule of a tribunal as long as the refusal is open and is based on the assertion that the rule is invalid. Answer (C) is wrong because Lawyer's consultation with Client, although required by Rule 1.2(a), did not excuse Lawyer's duty to the Supreme Court under Rule 3.4(c) to reveal that Lawyer was refusing to follow the rule. Answer (D) is incorrect because lawyers may not secretly refuse to honor rules that they determine to be unconstitutional or otherwise invalid. Their arguments to that effect must see the light of day so that the claim can be properly adjudicated. Answer (B) is correct.

102. **The correct answer is (D).** Because Prosecutor had been involved in the investigation of Defendant's case, Prosecutor was bound to observe the limits in Rule 3.6 on what Prosecutor could say about the matter publicly. However, Rule 3.6(b)(6) contains explicit authorization for Prosecutor to issue "a warning of danger concerning the behavior of a person involved, when there is reason to believe that there exists the likelihood of substantial harm to an individual or to the public interest...." Prosecutor was within this "safe harbor" when speaking to protect the public. Answer (A) is incorrect because, even if the remarks had a substantial likelihood of heightening public condemnation of Defendant, the remarks served a legitimate law enforcement purpose and thus were permitted by Rule 3.8(f). Answer (B) is wrong because of the safe harbor in Rule 3.6(b)(6). Statements within the safe harbor of Rule 3.6(b) may be made, notwithstanding the possibility that they will materially prejudice the proceeding. Answer (C) is incorrect because Prosecutor's earlier involvement in the investigation of Defendant was enough to trigger the obligations of Rule 3.6. "Personal and substantial in-

volvement" is relevant for government lawyers who are analyzing whether they have conflicts of interest once they have left government service, but Rule 3.6(a) applies to any lawyer who "is participating or has participated in the investigation or litigation of a matter." Answer (**D**) is correct.

103. **The correct answer is (B)**. Rule 3.3(a) provides that a lawyer shall not knowingly "make a false statement of fact or law to a tribunal or fail to correct a false statement of material fact or law previously made to the tribunal by the lawyer." A binding arbitration is a "tribunal" as defined in Rule 1.0(m). Lawyer did not knowingly make the false statement, but Lawyer did knowingly fail to correct it and thereby violated rule 3.3(a). Answer (**A**) is incorrect because the initial misstatement was not made knowingly. Answer (**C**) is wrong because the initial statement, the one that Lawyer believed to be true, is not the violation. Rather, Lawyer violated Rule 3.3(a) by his knowing failure to correct the earlier misstatement. Answer (**D**) is incorrect because a binding arbitration is a tribunal under Rule 1.0(m). Answer (**B**) is right.

104. Lawyer violated Rule 3.4(b), which forbids a lawyer to "unlawfully obstruct another party's access to evidence or unlawfully alter, destroy or conceal a document or other material having potential evidentiary value." The significance of the box was its location. Client was being investigated for possession of child pornography. The evidence was hidden on Client's property. A natural inference would be the truth: the box and its contents hidden on Client's property belonged to Client. By removing the box from the client's property, it is as if Lawyer removed a tag on it that would tie the evidence to Client (*see* <u>People v. Meredith</u>, 29 Cal. 3d 682 (1981)).

105. Yes, Lawyer will be committing misconduct. By asking, Lawyer would be attempting to violate Rule 3.2's requirement that "[a] lawyer shall make reasonable efforts to expedite litigation consistent with the interests of the client." Regardless of whether opposing counsel agrees to the delay, an attempt to violate Rule 3.2 (or any other rule) is misconduct under Rule 8.4(a). This delay has no purpose other than to enable Client to obtain a benefit. The delay would be in the interests of the client, but the Comment to Rule 3.2 makes it clear that "[r]ealizing financial or other benefit from otherwise improper delay in litigation is not a legitimate interest of the client."

106. Lawyer has no obligation with respect to the obstruction of justice. If Lawyer had learned of the threat before the conclusion of the proceeding, then Lawyer would have known that someone had engaged in criminal conduct related to an adjudicative proceeding in which Lawyer represented a client. Lawyer would have been obliged under Rule 3.3(b) to take reasonable remedial measure that, if necessary, would have included disclosure to the tribunal. However, Lawyer does not have an affirmative obligation to take these steps now, because the proceeding has concluded. *See* Rule 3.3(c). The case concluded for purposes of Rule 3.3 when the final judgment was affirmed on appeal. *See* Comment 13 to Rule 3.3.

107. Yes, Lawyer violated Rule 3.5(c)(2), which forbids lawyers from contacting a juror after discharge of the jury if "the juror has made known to the lawyer a desire not to communicate." Otherwise, a lawyer may contact jurors after the trial as long as the communication is not prohibited by law or court order and as long as the communication does not involve misrep-

resentation, coercion, duress or harassment. Here, there is no law or court order to stop Lawyer, and there is no indication that Lawyer intends to engage in misrepresentation, coercion, duress or harassment. But Lawyer was obliged to stop trying to contact Juror Ten once Lawyer received the voicemail and learned that Juror Ten had made known a desire not to communicate with Lawyer.

108. Yes, Lawyer's law firm may represent Client in the fraud case. Lawyer is a necessary witness and thus is disqualified under Rule 3.7(a) from acting as Client's advocate and testifying. None of the exceptions in Rule 3.7(a) apply. The testimony will not be about an uncontested issue or the nature and amount of legal services rendered in the case. Nor could Lawyer try personally to remain as an advocate in the case based upon substantial hardship, because the need for Lawyer to testify was apparent as soon as the case was filed. However, under Rule 3.7(b), Lawyer's personal disqualification from acting as both a necessary witness and an advocate will not be imputed to the other lawyers in the firm. Note particularly that Lawyer's testimony will be favorable to Client and consistent with what Client would have testified to, and therefore there is no conflict of interest under Rule 1.7(a) between Lawyer and Client. Other lawyers in the firm may act as advocates even though Lawyer is a necessary witness.

Transactions and Communications with Persons Other Than Clients

109. **The correct answer is (A).** Lawyer knew that the emails were between counsel and senior management and were therefore privileged even under the restrictive "control group" test. Lawyer nevertheless chose to obtain the privileged documents. That is a violation of Model Rule of Professional Conduct 4.4(a), which states in relevant part that a lawyer "shall not … use methods of obtaining evidence that violate the legal rights of such a [third] person." Answer (B) is incorrect because Lawyer was permitted to communicate with a former employee of a represented organization. *See* Comment 7 to Model Rule of Professional Conduct 4.2. Answer (C) is incorrect because the emails were between counsel and the senior management that guided and controlled Acme's operations. That is the definition of the "control group." *See* Upjohn v. U.S., 449 U.S. 383 (1981). Answer (D) is incorrect because, although Lawyer had the right to talk with the former employee, Lawyer had no right to use that permissible contact under Rule 4.2 to gather privileged information in violation of Rule 4.4(a). The right answer is (A).

110. **The correct answer is (C).** Under Model Rule of Professional Conduct 4.4(b), a lawyer who receives a document inadvertently must promptly notify the sender so that the sender can decide what, if anything, to do. Comment 2 to Rule 4.4 makes it clear that this is the only obligation imposed by the rules, although other law may require the lawyer to take other steps. Answer (A) is wrong because Rule 4.4(b) only requires notification of the receipt of an inadvertent communication. It may be that by agreement or court order, the receiving lawyer eventually will delete the memorandum, but the rules of conduct do not dictate that result. Answer (B) is incorrect because the discoverability of the document is beyond the scope of the rules of conduct. Once the lawyer complies with the duty under Rule 4.4(b) to inform the sending lawyer about what happened, the matter may go before the court. The status of the document as opinion work product may ultimately be important to the judge, but the receiving lawyer's duty under the rules of conduct is simply to notify the sender promptly regardless of the nature of the document. Answer (D) is wrong because the rules of conduct do not purport to resolve the effect of inadvertently sending a privileged or otherwise protected document. Comment 2 to Rule 4.2 makes it clear that the "question of whether the privileged status of a document or electronically stored information has been waived" is beyond the scope of the rules of conduct. All Rule 4.4(b) requires is that the receiving lawyer notify the sender. The right answer is (C).

111. **The correct answer is (B).** Under Rule 4.1(b), a lawyer shall not knowingly "fail to disclose a material fact to a third person when disclosure is necessary to avoid assisting a criminal or

fraudulent act by a client, unless disclosure is prohibited by Rule 1.6." Here, Lawyer assisted in the upcoming fraud by preparing the paperwork. Lawyer tried to prevent the fraud through a "noisy withdrawal," but Next Buyer intended to go forward with the deal. Disclosure of Client's confidential information was not prohibited by Rule 1.6, because Rule 1.6(b)(2) permits Lawyer to reveal confidential information to the extent that Lawyer believes doing so is reasonably necessary "to prevent the client from committing a crime or fraud that is reasonably certain to result in substantial injury to the financial interests or property of another and in furtherance of which the client has used or is using the lawyer's services. . . ." It became necessary to reveal the fraud in order to avoid assisting in it once Next Buyer did not get the hint of the noisy withdrawal. This was one of the rare circumstances when disclosure of client confidential information was mandatory. Answer (**A**) is incorrect because it states the circumstances under which disclosure of confidential information is an option under Rule 1.6(b)(2) rather than when doing so is a mandate under Rule 4.1(b). Answer (**C**) is wrong because there are times when revelation of client confidences to prevent fraud are optional (Rule 1.6(b)(2)), and there are times when doing so is mandatory (Rule 1.4(b)). This time it was required. Answer (**D**) is wrong for two reasons. First, the concept of "reasonable remedial measures" establishes what lawyers sometimes have to do in litigation to satisfy their duty of candor to a tribunal. That concept has no applicability here, in a transactional context. Furthermore, the noisy withdrawal was not enough. It would have been, if Next Buyer had taken the hint and backed out of the transaction. Then disclosure of Client's confidential information would not have been necessary to avoid assisting in Client's fraud. Once Next Buyer said that the deal would be going forward, it was clear that the noisy withdrawal had not had its intended effect, and disclosure became required. Answer (**B**) is right.

112. **The correct answer is (A).** Lawyer violated the criminal law of the state by secretly recording the conversation. Rule 8.4(b) defines misconduct to include the commission of "a criminal act that reflects adversely on the lawyer's honesty, trustworthiness or fitness as a lawyer in other respects." *See also* ABA Formal Op. 01-422 ("A lawyer may not, however, record conversations in violation of the law in a jurisdiction that forbids such conduct without the consent of all parties. . . ."). Answer (**B**) is wrong because Lawyer did not know that Slumlord was represented by counsel. Rule 4.2 requires that a lawyer know that the other party is represented before its limitations come into effect. Answer (**C**) is wrong because Lawyer committed misconduct in the recording of the conversation. It does not matter, therefore, that Lawyer did not also commit misconduct by violating Rule 4.2. Answer (**D**) is wrong because, even if using a "tester" is "authorized by law" in some jurisdictions (and therefore not a violation of Rule 4.2), Lawyer still must abide by the criminal law of the state with respect to the recording of the conversation. The right answer is (**A**).

113. **The correct answer is (B).** Rule 4.3 governs Lawyer's interactions on behalf of a client with an unrepresented person. Part of a lawyer's responsibility to an unrepresented person is to "make reasonable efforts to correct" a misunderstanding if "the lawyer knows or reasonably should know that the unrepresented person misunderstands the lawyer's role in the matter. . . ." Here, Wife's expression of gratitude for "helping us" betrays a fundamental misunderstanding of Lawyer's role, which is to help Husband and not to help Wife. Lawyer simply replied,

"You're welcome" when Lawyer instead should have taken reasonable efforts to correct Wife's misunderstanding. Answer (A) is wrong because a party's willingness to settle a matter for a particular amount is not a "material fact" for purposes of Rule 4.1. *See* Comment 2 to Rule 4.1. Answer (C) is wrong because Lawyer had an affirmative duty to correct a misunderstanding about Lawyer's role. It is not enough simply to refrain from deception. Answer (D) is wrong because, although Lawyer is entitled under Comment 2 to Rule 4.1 to "bluff" regarding Husband's willingness to settle, Lawyer is required by Rule 4.3 to make sure that Wife understands Lawyer's role and does not place unfounded trust in Lawyer in the mistaken belief that Lawyer is "helping" her. Answer (B) is right.

114. **The correct answer is (D).** Although Rule 4.2 prohibits Lawyer from having direct contact with Husband because Husband has a lawyer, represented parties may speak directly to each other. *See* Comment 4 to Rule 4.2. Answer (A) is incorrect because this is a special case. Generally, it is true that a lawyer may not violate the rules through the acts of another (*see* Rule 8.4(a)), but a lawyer may send a client to have direct contact with the opposing party, even if the opposing party is represented. *See* ABA Formal Opinion 11-461. Answer (B) is wrong because the lawyer may initiate the idea and coach the client as long as the lawyer does not "overreach." Id. Here, Lawyer took an important step to prevent overreaching by instructing Wife to tell Husband to speak with his counsel before signing anything. Answer (C) is incorrect because it is not the lack of response that permits the communication but rather the fact that the communication is party-to-party. Such a communication between represented parties would have been proper even if there had never been a settlement proposal. The right answer is (D).

115. Lawyer violated Rule 4.1, which forbids a lawyer from "making a false statement of material fact or law to a third person." Lawyer knowingly made a false statement of law concerning the statute of limitations to opposing counsel. Lawyer did not violate the rules with his bluff about what his client would be willing to accept in settlement. Statement about "a party's intentions as to an acceptable settlement of a claim" generally are not considered to be statements of material fact because, under generally accepted conventions in negotiation, everyone knows not to treat them as such. See Comment 2 to Rule 4.1.

116. Lawyer must first explain that he represents Client and not Husband. Then Lawyer is free to do all the things he wants to do. He may prepare the settlement agreement, present the settlement offer to Husband, explain his view of the meaning of the documents to Husband, and articulate his view of the underlying legal obligations to Husband. *See* Comment 2 to Rule 4.3. Any other result would make settlement with an unrepresented party difficult. Lawyer simply needs to make sure first that there is no misunderstanding about Lawyer's role.

Different Roles of the Lawyer

117. **The correct answer is (D).** Under Model Rule of Professional Conduct 1.13(a), Lawyer's client was the corporation. Lawyer discovered serious wrongdoing by corporate constituents and was required to "report up" within the corporation's hierarchy, per Rule 1.13(b). In some circumstances, a lawyer who reports up all the way to a corporation's board of directors has the option to "report out" under Rule 1.13(c) what the lawyer has learned, in order to protect the corporate client from a board that refuses to act regarding a serious matter. Here, however, Lawyer learned the damaging information as part of an investigation into the matter, and under Rule 1.13(c) and (d), Lawyer therefore did not have the option to "report out." Answer (A) is wrong for two reasons. First, "reporting out" under Rule 1.13(c) is never required. It is, at most, an option. Second, in this situation, Lawyer did not even have the option to report out, because Lawyer learned the information as part of an investigation of the wrongdoing. Answer (B) is incorrect because Lawyer did not owe a duty of confidentiality to the Vice President. The corporation, and not the Vice President, was the client. Answer (C) is wrong because Lawyer did not even have the option to "report out" under Rule 1.13(c), because Lawyer learned the information while investigating the matter for the corporation. Answer (D) is right.

118. **The correct answer is (C).** Under Rule 1.6(b)(1), Lawyer had the option but not the mandate to reveal the client's confidential information, because disclosure was reasonably necessary to prevent reasonable certain substantial bodily harm. Under Rule 1.13(c), Lawyer had the option to reveal the information because: (1) Lawyer did not gather the information while he was defending Corporation or investigating for Corporation with respect to the pollution, and (2) Lawyer reasonably believed that disclosure was necessary to prevent substantial injury to Corporation. Rule 1.6(b)(1) and Rule 1.13(c), however, only provide options to disclose. Neither imposes a mandate of disclosure. Answer (A) is incorrect because a lawyer for an entity has an option but not a duty to disclose confidential information to protect the entity under the conditions set forth in Rule 1.13(c). Answer (B) is wrong because Rule 1.6(b)(1), like all of the exceptions in Rule 1.6(b) to the general rule of confidentiality, creates an option but not a mandate for the lawyer to disclose confidential client information. Answer (D) is wrong because Lawyer had the option to reveal the information regardless of the orders of the Board of Directors. The entity, and not the Board, was Lawyer's client, and Rule 1.13(c) provides a means for a lawyer sometimes to protect an entity client even from those individuals who are in charge of the entity's affairs. Answer (C) is correct.

119. **The correct answer is (B).** Rule 3.8(g) requires a prosecutor to promptly disclose evidence to an appropriate court or authority if the prosecutor "knows of new, credible and material evidence creating a reasonable likelihood that a convicted defendant did not commit an offense of

which the defendant was convicted." Those conditions were met here. Rule 3.8(g) imposes additional duties when the conviction was obtained in the prosecutor's jurisdiction, but here, the case had been tried in another jurisdiction. Answer (**A**) is incorrect because the duty to share information with the defendant only arises if the conviction was obtained in the prosecutor's jurisdiction (*see* Rule 3.8(g)(2)(i)). Answer (**C**) is wrong because Prosecutor had the limited duty to inform the court or other appropriate authority even if the conviction was obtained in another jurisdiction. Doing nothing is not an option. Answer (**D**) is incorrect because Prosecutor's belief in Killer's guilt is irrelevant. Once Prosecutor determined that the evidence was new, credible and material, and that it created a reasonable likelihood that Killer was innocent, the duty to share it with the court or other appropriate authority arose. The right answer is (**B**).

120. **The correct answer is (A).** Rule 1.13(g) provides that a lawyer representing an organization may, subject to Rule 1.7, represent both the organization and a constituent of the organization, but any necessary consent from the organization must come from someone other than the constituent whom the lawyer would also be representing. Here, Lawyer determined that there was a consentable conflict and obtained informed consent from both clients, but the consent for Corporation had to come from someone other than the individual co-client, the General Counsel. Lawyer represented both clients despite an unresolved conflict of interest. Answer (**B**) is incorrect because lawyers sometimes may represent organizations and constituents in the same matter, subject to Rule 1.7. *See* Rule 1.13(g). Answer (**C**) is wrong because the informed consent from Corporation is ineffective because of its source: it came from the same individual who was becoming a co-client with the company. Answer (**D**) is incorrect because lawyers do not "automatically" represent any constituent by virtue of representing the entity. Under Rule 1.13(a), it is a fundamental principle of entity representation that "[a] lawyer employed or retained by an organization represents the organization acting through its duly authorized constituents." Answer (**A**) is right.

121. **The correct answer is (B).** Under Rule 3.8(f), a prosecutor has special responsibilities with respect to pretrial publicity. Prosecutors are of course personally bound by Rule 3.6, and Lawyer would have violated Rule 3.6(a) by personally publicizing the DNA test result. *See* Comment [5](3) (the list of things that should not be publicized includes "the performance or results of any examination or test"). In addition, however, prosecutors have the special responsibility under Rule 3.8(f) to "exercise reasonable care to prevent investigators, law enforcement personnel, employees or other persons assisting or associated with the prosecutor in a criminal case from making an extrajudicial statement that the prosecutor would be prohibited from making under Rule 3.6 or this Rule." Here, Lawyer knew of Police Commissioner's plan but did nothing to try to stop it. That is not reasonable care. Answer (**A**) is incorrect because Police Commissioner was not acting at the request or instruction of Lawyer and thus was not Lawyer's agent. *See* Comment 1 to Rule 8.4. Answer (**C**) is wrong because Lawyer owed a duty under Rule 3.8(f) that went beyond the duty from Rule 3.6 not to publish the test results personally. Lawyer had to exercise reasonable care to prevent law enforcement from doing so, and Lawyer did nothing. Answer (**D**) is incorrect because the limited right of reply in Rule 3.6(c) would have permitted release of otherwise prohibited information to pro-

tect a client from the substantial undue prejudicial effect of recent publicity generated by others. The Police Department, however, was not Lawyer's client. The right answer is (**B**).

122. **The correct answer is (D)**. Usually a lawyer is not expected to offer advice that the client does not seek. However, according to Comment 5 to Rule 2.1, "when a lawyer knows that a client proposes a course of action that is likely to result in substantial adverse legal consequences to the client, the lawyer's duty to the client under Rule 1.4 may require that the lawyer offer advice if the client's course of action is related to the representation." That is the situation Lawyer found herself in. Especially when a client like this one is inexperienced in legal matters, purely technical legal advice ("just drawing up the papers") would not serve Client well. *See* Comment 3 to Rule 2.1. Answer (**A**) is incorrect because sometimes lawyers must or at least should offer advice beyond that which a client requests. Here, where Client is about to close a deal and not be able to develop the property as he wishes, Lawyer had a duty to volunteer advice about nuisance law. Answer (**B**) is wrong because under Rule 2.1 Lawyer had the option to give moral advice that developing the halfway house next to the school might not be the "right thing to do." Answer (**C**) is incorrect because giving moral advice is permissible but not required. Answer (**D**) is right.

123. **The correct answer is (C)**. Lawyer Jones made a threat, but it was a threat to call the police about the exact same act for which Lawyer Jones represented Client civilly. That threat, therefore, was not a crime, and it was permitted under the Model Rules. ABA Formal Op. 92-363. Answer (**A**) is incorrect because the Model Rules of Professional Conduct, unlike the earlier Code of Professional Responsibility, do not contain a specific prohibition on threatening criminal prosecution in order to advance a client's civil claim. Lawyers may not make threats relating to the prosecution of unrelated matters, because such a threat would constitute the crime of extortion, and Rule 8.4(b) provides that a lawyer commits misconduct if the lawyer commits "a criminal act that reflects adversely on the lawyer's honesty, trustworthiness or fitness as a lawyer in other respects." Here, however, the threat arises from the same facts and is therefore not extortion. Answer (**B**) is incorrect. Generally, under Rule 8.3(a) lawyers must report other lawyers if the lawyer "knows that another lawyer has committed a violation of the Rules of Professional Conduct that raises a substantial question as to that lawyer's honesty, trustworthiness or fitness as a lawyer in other respects." However, that duty is nullified if the report would require the lawyer to reveal confidential information and the client will not give informed consent to its release. Rule 8.3(c) and Comment 2 to Rule 8.3. Here, Client has refused consent. Answer (**D**) is wrong because Rule 8.3(a) makes reporting a fellow lawyer's serious misconduct mandatory rather than optional (subject to the necessity of client consent). Answer (**C**) is right.

124. **The correct answer is (D)**. Rule 3.9 governs Lawyer's obligations in connection with a non-adjudicative proceeding such as a legislative hearing. Rule 3.9 imposes on lawyers who represent clients in such proceedings the duty to conform their conduct to certain rules that, by their own terms, only apply to adjudicative proceedings. One of those is Rule 3.3, and Rule 3.3(a)(3) required Lawyer to take reasonable remedial measures once Lawyer knew that Client had presented false evidence. Comment 10 to Rule 3.3 describes reasonable remedial measures to include trying to persuade the client to correct the record, withdrawing from the represen-

tation, and (if withdrawal does not correct the problem) informing the tribunal. Here, Lawyer unsuccessfully tied to get Client to correct the problem and then withdrew. Withdrawal, however, did nothing to undo the effect of the false evidence, and so disclosure of the falsity of the evidence to the Committee was required. Answer (**A**) is incorrect because Lawyer was required to reveal the false evidence as part of Lawyer's reasonable remedial measures under Rule 3.3(a)(3), as incorporated into Rule 3.9. Answer (**B**) is wrong because Lawyer had the option to withdraw under Rule 1.16(b)(3), because Client was persisting in a criminal course of conduct involving Lawyer's services. Answer (**C**) is incorrect because Lawyer had duties that extended beyond merely making sure not to present or assist in the presentation of false evidence. Lawyer had a duty to take reasonable remedial measures even if Lawyer had nothing to do with the preparation or presentation of the false evidence. Answer (**D**) is correct.

125. Lawyer's obligation is, in the language of Rule 2.4(b), to "explain the difference between the lawyer's role as a third-party neutral and a lawyer's role as one who represents a client." Mother's question seeks legal advice, and from that question, Lawyer reasonably should have known that Mother did not understand Lawyer's role in the matter. That confusion triggered Lawyer's duty to clarify that, as a mediator, Lawyer was present to assist Father and Mother, neither of whom were clients of Lawyer, to settle their dispute over child custody.

126. Yes, Lawyer violated the Model Rules of Professional Conduct. Under Rule 2.3, Lawyer was permitted to evaluate the title to Clients' properties for Bank, because Lawyer could have reasonably believed that the evaluation was compatible with other aspects of Lawyer's relationship with Client. The information that Lawyer gathered about the liens was confidential, because it was information relating to the representation. Where information that is gathered for a third party poses no significant risk to the client, a lawyer is impliedly authorized to share that information. *See* Comment 5 to Rule 2.3. Here, however, the information about the liens was likely to affect Client's interests materially and adversely, and therefore Lawyer needed informed consent of Client to share that information with Bank. Id.

127. Lawyer must first communicate the offer to Client. *See* Comment 2 to Rule 1.4. Then Lawyer must provide independent professional judgment and candid advice under Rule 2.1. In this particular situation, that means giving Client news that Client does not want to hear, that Client is better off to agree to go to prison under the deal than to risk a longer sentence on the slight chance of an acquittal. It is part of Lawyer's duty to give this bad news. Lawyer should deliver the advice as kindly as possible, consistent with honesty, but as Comment 1 to Rule 2.1 states, "a lawyer should not be deterred from giving candid advice by the prospect that the advice will be unpalatable to the client."

Safekeeping Funds and Other Property

128. **The correct answer is (A).** Under Rule 1.15(e), Lawyer was obliged to hold the property in dispute (the amount of the expert's fees), but he was required to "promptly distribute all portions of the property as to which the interests are not in dispute." Answer (B) is incorrect because Lawyer was permitted by Rule 1.5(c) to charge a contingent fee in a personal injury case and by Rule 1.8(e)(1) to advance the expenses with repayment contingent upon the outcome of the case. Answer (C) is wrong because Lawyer was required to withhold only the funds in dispute, not the entire amount. Lawyer should have paid himself his contingent fee and paid Client the rest, minus the amount of the expert's fee. Answer (D) is incorrect because notification is only one of Lawyer's responsibilities. Lawyer must notify Client of the receipt of the settlement funds but must also deliver the funds not in dispute. *See* Rule 1.15(d) and (e). Answer (A) is right.

129. **The correct answer is (B).** ABA Formal Opinion 475 provides that "if two or more lawyers have an agreement that satisfies Rule 1.5 regarding a division of fees, and one lawyer receives a payment that must be divided with the other lawyer pursuant to their agreement, the other lawyer is a 'third person' for purposes of Rule 1.15." Because Lawyer Jones is a 'third person,'" Lawyer Smith must place the check in the trust account, promptly notify Lawyer Jones and promptly pay Lawyer Jones her share. Rule 1.5(a), (d). Lawyer Smith may not bypass this process by depositing the check into the operating account and disbursing the shared funds from there. Answer (A) is wrong because the fee sharing arrangement between Lawyer Smith and Lawyer Jones conforms to the requirements of Rule 1.5(e). It is therefore permissible to enter into the agreement, even if it provides compensation for the referral. Answer (C) is incorrect because it does not matter whether the fees have been earned or not. Part of that check was the property of Lawyer Jones, and when Lawyer Smith came into possession or property that belonged to a third party, Lawyer Smith was obliged by Rule 1.5(a) to place that property into a trust account. Answer (D) is incorrect because the prompt notice and prompt payment fulfilled only two of Lawyer Smith's obligations. Another was to place the check into, and disburse the funds from, the trust account rather than the operating account. *See* ABA Formal Op. 475. The correct answer is (B).

130. **The correct answer is (A).** Lawyer's obligation was to deliver to Client the Client's property promptly once Client was "entitled to receive" it. Rule 1.15(c). Upon termination of the attorney-client relationship, Lawyer was obliged under Rule 1.16(d) to surrender possession of Client's property. Client was, therefore, at that point entitled to receive it, and Lawyer should not have awaited a request years later. *See* ABA Formal Op. 471. Answer (B) is incorrect because Rule 1.15(a) requires that all personal property of clients must be kept separate from

the personal property of the lawyer, but no provision of the Model Rules requires that Lawyer segregate personal property of every client. A lawyer who does wills, for example, might keep dozens of original wills together in one fireproof safe without violating the rules. Comment 1 to Rule 1.15 requires that each client's property must be identified as such, but Lawyer did that in this case. Answer (C) is wrong because Lawyer should have delivered the note promptly once the attorney-client relationship ended rather than wait for a request. Answer (D) is wrong because Rule 1.15 governs how lawyers must deal with the property of others, including money, but certainly not limited to money. Answer (A) is right.

131. **The correct answer is (B).** Rule 1.15(b) provides that "[a] lawyer may deposit the lawyer's own funds in a client trust account for the sole purpose of paying bank service charges on that account, but only in an amount necessary for that purpose." Lawyer placed much more than was necessary for that purpose in the account. Answer (A) is wrong because Lawyer was permitted by Rule 1.15(b) to place some personal funds in the trust account to cover the bank charges. Answer (C) is wrong because it is not enough to keep good records of what personal money is in the trust account. That amount of personal money should not have been in the trust account at all. Answer (D) is incorrect because Lawyer's good intentions do not matter. His option under Rule 1.15(b) to put personal funds into the trust account is limited to the amount necessary for that purpose. Lawyer put way too much in there, and that is a violation regardless of intent. Answer (B) is correct.

132. **The correct answer is (A).** Rule 1.15(e) required Lawyer to keep the disputed funds separate until the dispute was resolved. Comment 4 provides that a lawyer is not to "unilaterally arbitrate" the matter. It is not up to Lawyer to decide who gets the funds. Lawyer's job was to hold them until an appropriate authority decided. Answer (B) is incorrect because, although Lawyer had the option to resolve the dispute by interpleader, that step was not required. *See* Comment 4 to Rule 1.15. Answer (C) is wrong because Lawyer had to hold the funds until a proper authority decided who was entitled to them, not just until Lawyer unilaterally decided who was entitled to them. Answer (D) is incorrect because Rule 1.15(d) places no such obligation on Lawyer. To the contrary, Rule 1.15(d) required Lawyer to wait for a resolution, no matter what Lawyer's personal opinion about the merits of the dispute may be. Answer (A) is the right answer.

133. Lawyer must safeguard the property appropriately given its value and its uniqueness. As Comment 1 to Rule 1.15 provides, "[a] lawyer should hold property of others with the care required of a professional fiduciary." The Comment gives as an example: "Securities should be kept in a safe deposit box, except when some other form of safekeeping is warranted by special circumstances." Lawyer will be expected to take reasonable measures to protect the negatives from loss, fire, damage, or theft. Those measures will require at least a fireproof safe deposit box and perhaps even more stringent protections.

134. Lawyer must deposit the funds into Lawyer's trust account and promptly notify Brother and Sister. Lawyer must then promptly deliver the funds to which Brother and Sister are entitled. Presumably, there will be fees and expenses associated with the closing, and therefore Brother and Sister probably will be receiving less that $200,000 each. If either Brother or Sister requests

an accounting, Lawyer is obliged to promptly render a full accounting of the funds. *See* Rule 1.15(d).

135. Lawyer must establish a trust account and deposit the $10,000 to keep it separate from Lawyer's property. Lawyer must not place any portion of the deposit in Lawyer's Operating Account, because that would commingle Client's funds with Lawyer's personal funds, in violation of the requirement of Rule 1.15(a) that such funds be kept separate. Rule 1.15(a) also requires Lawyer to keep complete records with respect to the money for five years after termination of the representation. As fees are earned and expenses are incurred, Lawyer must withdraw the funds from the trust account and presumably will deposit them in the Operating Account. *See* Rule 1.15(c).

Communications about Legal Services

136. **The correct answer is (B).** Rule 7.4(d)(2) requires that any advertisement as a certified specialist must include the name of the certifying organization. Lawyer did not do that. Answer (A) is wrong because, under Rule 7.4(d)(1), the certifying organization need not be accredited by the American Bar Association, as long as it has been "approved by an appropriate state authority." Here, the State Supreme Court had approved the Institute. Answer (C) is incorrect because it was not enough that the Institute had been approved; Lawyer needed to identity the organization in her advertisements. Answer (D) is wrong because experience alone would not give Lawyer the right to advertise herself as a "certified specialist." Under Rule 7.4(a), Lawyer could advertise the type of work that she does or does not do (e.g., "practice limited to tractor-trailer accidents"), and even call herself a "specialist," but that is different from claiming to be a "certified specialist." The right answer is (B).

137. **The correct answer is (A).** Under Rule 7.3(c), Lawyer was permitted to solicit professional employment through a recorded communication, but the rule requires that the words "Advertising Material" be included "at the beginning and ending of any recorded … communication." Here, those words only appear at the end of the recording. Answer (B) is incorrect because Lawyer's solicitation by telephone was not "live telephone." Under Rule 7.3(a), a lawyer may not solicit a potential client "by in-person, live telephone or real-time electronic contact" if a significant motive is pecuniary gain. Lawyer's solicitation was presumably for pecuniary gain, but Rule 7.3(a) does not apply to an auto-dialed recorded phone call. Answer (C) is wrong because it is possible to violate Rule 7.3 without a face-to-face solicitation by soliciting potential clients by live telephone or real-time electronic contact. Answer (D) is incorrect because the words "advertising material" need to be present at both the beginning and end of a recorded solicitation. Answer (A) is right.

138. **The correct answer is (D).** Rule 7.3(d) contains a specific exception to the general rule against in-person or live telephone solicitation. Lawyers are permitted to participate in such plans, even if the plan "uses in-person or telephone contact to solicit memberships or subscriptions for the plan from persons who are not known to need legal services in a particular matter covered by the plan." Answer (A) is incorrect because the rules contain no general prohibition on lawyers participating in prepaid group legal services plans and in fact explicitly recognize that lawyers may do so (*see* Rule 7.2(b)(1)). Lawyers must, of course, be careful to safeguard their independence of judgment (*see* Rule 5.4(c)), but there is no blanket prohibition. Answer (B) is wrong because this is one type of solicitation that is expressly permitted by Rule 7.3. Although it is generally true that a lawyer commits misconduct when he or she violates a rule through the acts of another (Rule 8.4(a)), here the underlying act—the cold calling—is not

a violation of the rules. Answer (C) is incorrect because, as just noted, lawyers need not personally commit an act that violates the rules in order to commit misconduct. The right answer is (D).

139. **The correct answer is (B).** LGI falsely advertised that it matched potential clients with lawyers, and it did not reveal that the lawyers who received the leads had paid for that privilege. That is false and misleading. *See* Comment 5 to Rule 7.2. Lawyer is responsible under Rule 8.4(a) for these violations of Rule 7.1, because Lawyer is violating Rule 7.1 through the acts of LGI. Answer (A) is incorrect because Lawyer is permitted to pay lead generators, just as lawyers are permitted to pay the usual costs of advertising. *See* Comment 5 to Rule 7.2. Answer (C) is wrong because, although Lawyer did not personally engage in any false advertising, Lawyer did so indirectly by subscribing to LGI and benefiting from LGI's false and misleading advertising. Answer (D) is incorrect because, although Lawyer may generally pay the fees associated with lead generation, Lawyer violated Rule 7.1 by paying the fees of this particular dishonest lead generator. The correct answer is (B).

140. **The correct answer is (A).** Rule 7.5 permits lawyers to use trade names, but the trade name must not be misleading and must not "imply a connection with a government agency or with a public or charitable legal services organization...." The name "U.S. Copyright Law Office" implies a connection to the United States Government and therefore is improper. Answer (B) is incorrect because trade names are permitted as long as they meet the conditions of Rule 7.5. Answer (C) is wrong because it is not enough for a trade name to be technically "true." Perhaps it is true that Lawyer's firm is a "U.S. Copyright Law Office" in the sense that Lawyer's practice is limited to such work, but even a truthful name, like any truthful advertising, can violate the rules if it is misleading. The implication of a connection to the United States Government is misleading, and therefore, Lawyer committed misconduct by violating Rule 7.5. Answer (D) is wrong because the permission in Rule 7.5 does not include the use of a trade name that implies a connection to the United States Government. Answer (A) is correct.

141. **The correct answer is (C).** Rule 7.3(a) generally prohibits solicitation of employment as a lawyer through face-to-face, live telephone, or real-time electronic communication, with certain exceptions, but only where a significant motive for doing so is the lawyer's pecuniary gain. Here, Lawyer sought to represent Prospective Client pro bono, as a political statement, and sought no financial gain. It was not, therefore, a violation of Rule 7.3 for Lawyer to solicit Prospective Client. Answer (A) is incorrect because not every solicitation face-to-face violates Rule 7.3. If the solicitation is not for the lawyer's pecuniary gain, or if the person solicited is a lawyer, a former client, a close personal friend, or a family member, face-to-face solicitation is permitted (with some exceptions in Rule 7.3(b)). Answer (B) is incorrect because, even if a lawyer solicits someone who is not a family member, a former client, or a close personal friend, solicitation is not improper if the lawyer does not have a significant motive of financial gain. Answer (D) is wrong because the potential misconduct was the solicitation. Seeking to become someone's lawyer in violation of Rule 7.3(a) is misconduct, whether or not the potential client succumbs to the pressure of being solicited. Answer (C) is right.

142. **The correct answer is (D).** Generally, lawyers may only enter into reciprocal referral arrangements if the arrangement is not exclusive and the client is informed. *See* Rule 7.2(b)(4). These restrictions do not, however, apply to referrals within one firm. Comment 8 to Rule 7.2. Answer **(A)** is incorrect because the compensation is permitted in this particular intra-firm circumstance, even though generally under Rule 7.2(b) lawyers may not pay anyone for referrals (with exceptions as noted in Rule 7.2). Answer **(B)** is wrong because informing the client is not necessary. If a lawyer enters into a reciprocal referral arrangement with someone outside the firm, the client must be informed under Rule 7.2(b)(4)(ii), but Rule 7.2 does not apply to referrals within firms. Answer **(C)** is incorrect because there is no general exception for reciprocal referrals between lawyers. Reciprocal referral arrangements, whether they are between lawyers in different firms or between a lawyer and a nonlawyer, are subject to the restrictions of 7.2(b)(4). Answer **(D)** is correct.

143. **The correct answer is (B).** Comment 1 to Rule 7.4 provides that lawyers generally may call themselves "specialists" but that any such claim is subject to Rule 7.1's standard that advertising must not be false or misleading. The advertisement would be misleading, because the use of the word "specialist" would lead a reasonable person to believe that lawyer had experience in worker's compensation matters when in fact she had none. *See* Comment 2 to Rule 7.1 ("A truthful statement is also misleading if there is a substantial likelihood that it will lead a reasonable person to formulate a specific conclusion about the lawyer or the lawyer's services for which there is no reasonable factual foundation."). Answer **(A)** is incorrect because lawyers who limit their practice to certain areas may generally describe themselves as "specialists" (unless that word would, as here, be misleading) and need not be certified as such. If Lawyer claimed to be a "certified specialist," then the special requirements of Rule 7.4(d) would apply. Answer **(C)** is wrong because the use of the word "specialist" is misleading. Under Rule 7.4(a), Lawyer is specifically permitted to communicate that she practices only in one area of law, but she is not allowed by Rule 7.1 to use the word "specialist" and mislead potential clients into thinking that Lawyer knows what she is doing. Answer **(D)** is wrong because the term "specialist" is misleading even though Lawyer did not claim to be "certified" as one. Answer **(B)** is right.

144. By advertising her big verdicts, Lawyer would be risking a violation of Rule 7.1's prohibition on making statements that are false or misleading. Comment 3 provides that "[a]n advertisement that truthfully reports a lawyer's achievements on behalf of clients or former clients may be misleading if presented so as to lead a reasonable person to form an unjustified expectation that the same results could be obtained for other clients in similar matters without reference to the specific factual and legal circumstances of each client's case." The Twitter posts of the results achieved for Lawyer's clients could run afoul of this provision. One thing Lawyer could do would be to take the suggestion of Comment 3 and tweet a disclaimer, because the "inclusion of an appropriate disclaimer or qualifying language may preclude a finding that a statement is likely to create unjustified expectations or otherwise mislead the public."

145. Yes, Lawyer committed misconduct. It is misconduct under Rule 8.4(a) to attempt to violate a rule of conduct, even if the plan does not go into effect. Here, Lawyer sought to solicit professional employment for pecuniary gain from his sister's patients. Lawyer attempted to have

his sister do the improper solicitation for him, but it is misconduct to violate the rules of conduct through the acts of another. Lawyer committed misconduct because he attempted to violate Rule 7.3(a) through the acts of another.

146. Yes, Lawyer committed misconduct. Lawyer's advertisement did not violate Rule 7.1, because the ad was truthful. Lawyer actually *was* able to achieve results for clients outside the bounds of the law. The problem for Lawyer is not Rule 7.1, but rather Rule 8.4(e), which provides that it is misconduct for a lawyer to "state or imply an ability to influence improperly a government agency or official or to achieve results by means that violate the Rules of Professional Conduct or other law." That is exactly what Lawyer truthfully advertised. That is misconduct.

Lawyers' Duties to the Public and the Legal System

147. **The correct answer is (C).** Although Rule 6.1 provides that "[e]very lawyer has a professional responsibility to provide legal services to those unable to pay," the rule does not require any such service. Instead, Rule 6.1 is purely aspirational: "A lawyer should aspire to render at least (50) hours of pro bono publico legal services per year." Answer **(A)** is incorrect because there is no requirement of good cause to avoid pro bono work. The "good cause" standard applies under Rule 6.2 to court appointments, but here there was judicial encouragement but no appointment. Answer **(B)** is wrong because the 50-hour standard in Rule 6.1 is aspirational rather than mandatory. Answer **(D)** is incorrect because financial hardship is relevant under Rule 6.2 to declining court appointments rather than doing pro bono work. Answer **(C)** is correct.

148. **The correct answer is (A).** Under Rule 6.2, "[a] lawyer shall not seek to avoid appointment by a tribunal to represent a person except for good cause." Examples of good cause include a lack of competence and the existence of a conflict of interest, including a personal interest conflict created by the lawyer's revulsion for the client or the cause. A mere preference not to undertake the representation is not good cause. If it were, then Rule 6.2's limitation on a lawyer's ability to decline appointments only for "good cause" would in fact be no limitation at all. Answer **(B)** is incorrect because a lawyer can seek to avoid an appointment even if the lawyer is competent. For example, as Rule 6.2(c) notes, good cause exists if "the client or the cause is so repugnant to the lawyer as to be likely to impair the client-lawyer relationship or the lawyer's ability to represent the client." Answer **(C)** is wrong because Rule 6.2 does limit a lawyer's ability to seek to avoid an appointment. Unlike pro bono work, acceptance of court appointments is not merely aspirational. Answer **(D)** is incorrect because Lawyer owes the same duties to Mother that a paid lawyer would. *See* Comment 3 to Rule 6.2. Lawyer's obligation under Rule 1.1 to render competent representation should be a sufficient safeguard of lawyer's competent representation of Mother. Again, if a preference were enough to enable a lawyer to escape appointment, for this reason or any other, the "good cause" standard would mean nothing. Lawyers can be rightfully expected to rise above their preferences (if not their revulsion) and render competent and diligent representation to clients, even if the lawyers are reluctant to undertake the work. The right answer is **(A)**.

149. **The correct answer is (B).** Under Rule 6.3, Lawyer was permitted to serve on the board of a legal services organization even though the organization served persons having interests that were adverse to the interests of Lawyer's client, but Lawyer was not permitted under Rule

6.3(b) to participate in a decision of LSO "where the decision or action could have a material adverse effect on the representation of a client of the organization whose interests are adverse to a client of the lawyer." Here, the decision to discontinue funding the class action had a material adverse effect on tenants who were clients of LSO, and the interests of the tenants were adverse to Lawyer's Client, Landlord. Lawyer was required not to participate in this decision of LSO. Answer (**A**) is incorrect because Rule 6.3 permits a lawyer to serve as a board member of a legal services organization, even if the organization serves clients whose interests are adverse to the interests of a client of the lawyer. Answer (**C**) is wrong because revelation of Lawyer's representation of Landlord was not enough. Lawyer needed to refrain from participation in the decision (contrast Rule 6.4 when a lawyer is permitted to participate in a decision of a law reform organization but must reveal that the lawyer represents a client who might benefit from the decision). Answer (**D**) is incorrect because it states one of but not the only limit on a lawyer's participation in a decision of a legal services organization on whose board the lawyer sits. The other limit is the one at stake here: the lawyer may not participate in a decision that hurts a client of the organization who is adverse to a client of the lawyer. Answer (**B**) is correct.

150. **The correct answer is (D).** Rule 6.4 provides that a lawyer "may serve as a director, officer or member of an organization involved in reform of the law or its administration notwithstanding that the reform may affect the interests of a client of the lawyer" but also requires that, "[w]hen the lawyer knows that the interests of a client may be materially benefitted by a decision in which the lawyer participates, the lawyer shall disclose that fact but need not identify the client." Here, Lawyer did exactly what was required of him. Answer (**A**) is incorrect because a lawyer is permitted to participate in a decision of a law reform organization when a client might benefit, as long as the lawyer discloses that fact (contrast rule 6.3, which requires a lawyer not to participate in certain decisions when serving as a director, officer or member of a legal services organization). Answer (**B**) is wrong because Rule 6.4 requires only that Lawyer reveal that a client would benefit. It does not require a lawyer to identify the client or clients. Answer (**C**) is incorrect because it states a general rule that does not include Lawyer's obligation in this particular circumstance: to disclose the fact that a client would benefit from the rule change. The right answer is (**D**).

151. **The correct answer is (C).** Rule 7.6 provides that "[a] lawyer or law firm shall not accept a government legal engagement or an appointment by a judge if the lawyer or law firm makes a political contribution or solicits political contributions for the purpose of obtaining or being considered for that type of legal engagement or appointment." Lawyer's purpose in helping Judicial Candidate was to obtain appointments as a guardian, but giving uncompensated services is not a "political contribution." *See* Comment 2 to Rule 7.6. Lawyer did not, therefore, violate the rule. Answer (**A**) is incorrect because lawyers may participate fully in the political process and then accept appointments. *See* Comment 1 to Rule 7.6. They just cannot accept appointments if they made political contributions, themselves or through their firms or political action committees, for the purpose of obtaining appointments. Answer (**B**) is wrong because giving uncompensated services is not a "political contribution" for purposes of the rule. Answer (**D**) is incorrect because bribery is not the only way for a lawyer to commit mis-

conduct in seeking to influence a judge to make appointments. Even if the lawyer is not bribing the judge within the definition of bribery in the criminal law, Rule 7.6 forbids a lawyer from accepting appointments when the lawyer made political contributions to a judge for the purpose of getting those appointments. *See* Comment 6 to Rule 7.6 ("If a lawyer makes or solicits a political contribution under circumstances that constitute bribery or another crime, Rule 8.4(b) is implicated."). Answer (**C**) is right.

152. Lawyer violated Model Rule of Professional 8.2(b), which provides that "[a] lawyer who is a candidate for judicial office shall comply with the applicable provisions of the Code of Judicial Conduct." Under the Model Code of Judicial Conduct, Lawyer became a "judicial candidate" as soon as she made a public announcement of her candidacy (see the Terminology section of Model Code of Judicial Conduct). As a judicial candidate, Lawyer was forbidden by Rule 4.1(A)(8) from personally soliciting campaign contributions (such as by the letter that she sent). Because Lawyer violated the Model Code of Judicial Conduct as a candidate, she violated Model Rule of Professional Conduct 8.2(b).

Judicial Conduct

153. **The correct answer is (B).** Under Rule 2.9(a)(2), Judge is entitled to "obtain the written advice of a disinterested expert on the law applicable to a proceeding before the judge, if the judge gives advance notice to the parties of the person to be consulted and the subject matter of the advice to be solicited and affords the parties a reasonable opportunity to object and respond to the notice and to the advice received." Here, Judge did everything right except for the failure to give advance notice. Answer **(A)** is incorrect because judges are permitted to use disinterested experts to investigate matters of law, although under Rule 2.9(c), judges are not permitted to investigate facts independently. Answer **(C)** is wrong because the prompt report of the expert's written findings after the fact is not enough. The parties were entitled to know ahead of time of Judge's intention. Answer **(D)** is incorrect because, although Judge had the right to investigate independently a question of law, Judge had to do so in the precise manner delineated in Rule 2.9(a)(2). Answer **(B)** is correct.

154. **The correct answer is (D).** Judges are generally under Rule 3.3 supposed to refrain from testifying as character witnesses, "except when duly summoned." Here, Judge was duly summoned to testify, and therefore he did not violate Rule 3.3 by giving character witness testimony. Answer **(A)** is incorrect because Judge testified only when summoned, which is the exception to the general rule that judges should not give such testimony. Answer **(B)** is wrong because, according to Comment 1 to Rule 3.3, "[e]xcept in unusual circumstances where the demands of justice require, a judge should discourage a party from requiring the judge to testify as a character witness." Here, there were no such unusual circumstances, given that Law Student had numerous other witnesses who could testify about his character. Answer **(C)** is incorrect because it is inconsistent with the general rule against judges giving character testimony. In the words of Comment 1 to Rule 3.3, a "judge who, without being subpoenaed, testifies as a character witness abuses the prestige of judicial office to advance the interests of another." Answer **(D)** is right.

155. **The correct answer is (B).** Under Rule 3.7, generally (subject to the requirements of Rule 3.1) "a judge may participate in activities ... sponsored by or on behalf of ... charitable, fraternal, or civic organizations not conducted for profit...." The permitted activities include "soliciting contributions for such an organization or entity, but only from members of the judge's family, or from judges over whom the judge does not exercise supervisory or appellate authority...." Here, there is no indication that Judge violated the general requirements of Rule 3.1, and United Way is a charitable organization, but Judge solicited contributions from the trial judges. Such a solicitation would appear to be coercive, because Judge exercises appellate authority over these judges. *See* Rule 3.7(a)(2). Answer **(A)** is incorrect because judges are not

forbidden from all fundraising for charitable organizations. The problem is that targets of this fundraising included judges over whom Judge had appellate jurisdiction. Answer (C) is also wrong. Soliciting contributions from members of a lower court is inherently coercive, even if the text of this particular letter was not. Answer (D) is incorrect because Judge may not solicit contributions, even for a charitable organization like the United Way, from judges over whom Judge has appellate jurisdiction. Answer (B) is right.

156. **The correct answer is (D).** Comment 2 to Rule 2.8 explains that "[c]ommending or criticizing jurors for their verdict may imply a judicial expectation in future cases and may impair a juror's ability to be fair and impartial in a subsequent case." Rule 2.8(c) provides that "[a] judge shall not commend or criticize jurors for their verdict other than in a court order or opinion in a proceeding." The exception applies here and is understandable. A judge who is granting a new trial on the basis that a jury's verdict is against the great weight of the evidence would have a hard time not criticizing the verdict. Answer (A) is incorrect because the exception applies. Usually judges may not criticize verdicts, but judges may do so in court orders or opinions. Answer (B) is wrong because judges are allowed to use their life experience and knowledge in the discharge of their professional responsibilities. Although under Rule 2.9(c), judges may not gather new information by investigating matters, it is too much to ask them to forget everything they learned before becoming judges. Answer (C) is incorrect because it goes too far. A judge presumably would feel justified in criticizing any verdict with which the judge disagreed. Yet if there is no legal purpose, as there would be in a court order for a new trial, then the judge does harm even by justified criticism. As Comment 2 notes, such comments might impair the fairness of future proceedings. Answer (D) is correct.

157. **The correct answer is (A).** Rule 2.11(B) requires every judge "to keep informed about the judge's personal and fiduciary economic interests." Judge had an economic interest as a fiduciary in Acme. He could truthfully say that he did not know about it, but once it is discovered, it will cast a shadow over the result in the case that Judge decided. To prevent such circumstances, the Code requires judges to stay informed, so that they will recuse themselves when they should. Answer (B) is incorrect because Judge did not know about the interest. This economic interest was not de minimis, and therefore, it was an economic interest within the meaning of the Code. Rule 2.11(A)(3) requires a judge to disqualify himself or herself when the judge, personally or as a fiduciary, has an economic interest in a party to the proceeding, but only if the judge knows about the interest. "Knows" in the Code is defined to be actual knowledge, which Judge lacked because he did not read the broker's statements. Answer (C) is wrong because it is a separate violation for Judge not to keep informed about his economic interests as a fiduciary, even if he did not violate Rule 2.11(A)(3) due to his state of mind. Answer (D) is incorrect because the issue is whether Judge should have been presiding over the case at all, not whether Judge got it right. Here, no matter how right Judge's decision might be, his participation in the case could undermine public faith in the judicial system, because he had an economic interest as a fiduciary in the result. To prevent this eventuality, the Code requires Judge to know about his economic interests, including those he has in a fiduciary capacity, so that he will know to recuse himself when his impartiality might reasonably be questioned. Answer (A) is right.

158. Judge need not disqualify himself from the case. Under Rule 2.11, Judge must disqualify himself if his impartiality might reasonably be questioned, including but not limited to certain listed situations. It is given in the question that there are no circumstances other than the bare fact of Judge's relationship to one of the parties that might cause Judge's impartiality to be reasonably questioned. The question, therefore, is whether Judge is so closely related to the party that Judge is automatically disqualified. He is not. Under Rule 2.11(a)(2)(A), disqualification is automatic if: (a) the judge is a party; (2) the judge's spouse or domestic partner is a party; (3) someone within the third degree of relationship to either the judge or the judge's spouse or domestic partner is a party; or (4) the spouse or domestic partner of someone who is within the third degree of relationship to the judge or the judge's spouse or domestic partner is a party. The definition in the Model Code of Judicial Conduct of "third degree of relationship" does not include cousins. Therefore, Judge would be presiding over a case in which one party is the spouse of someone who is not within the third degree of relationship to the Judge or the Judge's spouse. The relationship is not close enough, and Judge is not disqualified.

159. Yes, Judge committed misconduct. Rule 2.3(C) provides that judges "shall require lawyers in proceedings before the court to refrain from manifesting bias or prejudice, or engaging in harassment, based upon attributes including but not limited to race, sex, gender, religion, national origin, ethnicity, disability, age, sexual orientation, marital status, socioeconomic status, or political affiliation, against parties, witnesses, lawyers, or others." Judge permitted Lawyer to engage in harassment of the defendant based upon "an attribute," the defendant's large nose. The size of Defendant's nose was not relevant to the proceeding. Defendant's credibility was relevant, but unless one believes that untruthfulness causes a human being's nose to grow, the references were improper, harassing theatrics. Judge had a responsibility to require Lawyer to stop.

160. Judge did not violate the Model Code of Judicial Conduct. Rule 1.3 forbids judges from abusing the prestige of their judicial office to advance the personal interests of another. Here, Judge has certainly advanced the interests of another, and presumably the prestige of Judge's judicial office made his recommendation valuable. However, this may be a *use* of the prestige of the judge's judicial office, but it is not considered to be an *abuse* of that prestige. As Comment 3 to Rule 1.3 states, "Judges may participate in the process of judicial selection by cooperating with appointing authorities and screening committees, and by responding to inquiries from such entities concerning the professional qualifications of a person being considered for judicial office."

Answers

Practice Final Exam

161. **The correct answer is (A).** Rule 5.5(d)(1) allows a lawyer who is licensed in one jurisdiction to live and work full-time in another jurisdiction, where the lawyer is not licensed, if the lawyer is providing legal services only to the lawyer's employer and those are not services for which the jurisdiction requires pro hac vice admission. Such admission was necessary for Lawyer to appear in court in State B, where she is not licensed. Therefore, the exception in Rule 5.5(d)(1) does not apply, and Lawyer is violating rule 5.5(a) by practicing law in a state without authorization. Answer **(B)** is incorrect because Lawyer could practice law in State B without a license from State B if she had satisfied any of the exceptions, such as those in Rule 5.5(c) or (d), to the general rule against practicing in a state where the lawyer is not licensed. Answer **(C)** is wrong because it is not enough under Rule 5.5(d)(1) to just represent the employer. The services rendered also must be ones that do not require pro hac vice admission. What Lawyer did for Corporation in the courts of State B were services that required pro hac vice admission. Answer **(D)** is incorrect because having a license in one state does not generally empower a lawyer to practice in other states. There are exceptions, such as those in Rule 5.5(c) and (d), but if the exceptions do not apply, then the lawyer is violating Rule 5.5(a)'s prohibition on practicing law in a jurisdiction without a license. Answer **(A)** is right.

162. **The correct answer is (C).** Rule 8.3(a) provides that "[a] lawyer who knows that another lawyer has committed a violation of the Rules of Professional Conduct that raises a substantial question as to that lawyer's honesty, trustworthiness or fitness as a lawyer in other respects, shall inform the appropriate professional authority." Rule 8.3(b) provides that "[a] lawyer who knows that a judge has committed a violation of applicable rules of judicial conduct that raises a substantial question as to the judge's fitness for office shall inform the appropriate authority." These obligations, however, are subject to Lawyer's confidentiality duty under Rule 1.6(a). Rule 8.3(c) and Comment 2 to Rule 8.3. Client's refusal to give informed consent to the reports meant that Lawyer could not make them. Answer **(A)** is incorrect because Lawyer could not report Prosecutor without Client's informed consent. Answer **(B)** is wrong because Lawyer's obligation of confidentiality superseded Lawyer's duty to report the Judge. Answer **(D)** is incorrect because Lawyer had a duty, not an option, to report Prosecutor and Judge, but only if Lawyer could have obtained the informed consent of Client. Answer **(C)** is correct.

163. **The correct answer is (B).** Under Rule 8.4(b), it is misconduct to "commit a criminal act that reflects adversely on the lawyer's honesty, trustworthiness or fitness as a lawyer in other respects." Not every criminal act falls into that category, but violent offenses do. Comment 2 to Rule 8.4. Answer **(A)** is incorrect because what matters is the commission of the criminal act, not the arrest. It is possible to be arrested for acts that one has not committed, and therefore

the mere fact of arrest cannot be misconduct. Answer **(C)** is wrong because Rule 8.4(b) does not concern just acts that relate to the practice of law. It is misconduct to commit a violent crime, regardless of whether it has anything to do with a lawyer's professional life. Answer **(D)** is incorrect because no conviction is necessary. The commission of the criminal act, rather than the conviction for it, is the misconduct. Answer **(B)** is right.

164. **The correct answer is (A).** Rule 5.5 sets forth some circumstances under which a lawyer may practice temporarily in a state other than where the lawyer holds a license, but one thing a lawyer may not do is establish an office in such a jurisdiction. Rule 5.5(b)(1). Answer **(B)** is incorrect because it would not have mattered if Lawyer engaged local counsel. Under Rule 5.5(c)(1), engaging local counsel is one way to legitimize temporary activities, but, regardless of whether Lawyer used local counsel, Lawyer was not permitted to establish an office in State B. Answer **(C)** is wrong because Rule 5.5(b) forbade Lawyer from *either* establishing an office (or other systematic and continuous presence) (5.5(b)(1)) *or* from representing that Lawyer was licensed in State B (5.5(b)(2)). Lawyer violated Rule 5.5(b)(1), even if he did not violate Rule 5.5(b)(2). Answer **(D)** is incorrect because Lawyer may not establish an office in State B even if what he is doing is otherwise a permitted temporary activity under Rule 5.5(c)(3) (activities related to alternative dispute resolution proceedings). Answer **(A)** is correct.

165. **The correct answer is (C).** Lawyer was trying to figure out whether he had the option under Rule 1.14(b) to take protective action for Client. Comment 6 describes considerations for lawyers in this position and provides that, in appropriate cases, "the lawyer may seek guidance from an appropriate diagnostician." The necessary revelation of confidential information to obtain the help of the diagnostician, for the benefit of Client, would be impliedly authorized under Rule 1.6(a). Answer **(A)** is incorrect because Lawyer's revelations were impliedly authorized. Answer **(B)** is wrong because the mere existence of an impairment does not mean that a client cannot give a lawyer instructions that the lawyer is bound to follow. In fact, Lawyer did exactly what Rule 1.14(a) required of him: he used the time, place and manner of communication to have as normal an attorney-client relationship as possible. Answer **(D)** is incorrect because Lawyer was not taking protective action under Rule 1.16(b). Lawyer was instead taking the prudent steps to determine whether he had the option to do so. Seeking the appointment of a guardian or talking to Client's children would be examples of protective action. *See* Comment 5 to Rule 1.14. Answer **(C)** is right.

166. **The correct answer is (D).** The general rule is that a lawyer must promptly comply with a client's reasonable requests for information. There is an exception, however, when doing so may harm the client. That is this case. Here, Lawyer was justified in delaying the delivery of the report until Client has a support system in place. *See* Comment 7 to Rule 1.4. Answer **(A)** is incorrect because this is a special case in which the general duty to promptly comply with reasonable requests for information does not apply. Answer **(B)** is wrong because Lawyer was impliedly authorized to share the report with other lawyers in the firm for the purpose of aiding in the representation of the client. *See* Comment 5 to Rule 1.6. Answer **(C)** is incorrect because Lawyer did have a duty under Rule 1.4(a)(4) to respond to Grandfather's request for information. In this particular case, Lawyer was justified in delaying that duty, but that does not mean that Lawyer had no duty to communicate. Answer **(D)** is correct.

167. **The correct answer is (B).** Rule 1.16(b) governs when a lawyer may withdraw from representing a client. One of those circumstances, in Rule 1.16(b)(5), is when a client fails to fulfill an obligation to the lawyer. One obligation that, if failed, frequently leads to withdrawal is the failure to pay fees. For a lawyer to be permitted to withdraw under Rule 1.16(b)(5), however, the client must have been "given reasonable warning that the lawyer will withdraw unless the obligation is fulfilled." Here, Lawyer just abruptly withdrew, in understandable frustration, but Client was entitled to a warning. Answer (A) is incorrect because a lawyer is permitted to withdraw under Rule 1.16(b)(5) even if the burden is not substantial, as long as the lawyer gives an appropriate warning. A separate provision, Rule 1.16(b)(6), permits a lawyer to withdraw when continuing the representation would cause an unreasonable financial burden, whether or not the client has failed to fulfill an obligation to the lawyer. Answer (C) is wrong because Client was entitled to a warning before Lawyer withdrew, even though Client had failed to fulfill obligations to Lawyer. Answer (D) is incorrect because a "financial burden" alone is not enough of a reason to withdraw, although an unreasonable financial burden can be a basis for doing so. Answer (B) is correct.

168. **The correct answer is (B).** The fact that Client had ceased paying Lawyer's bills was confidential information because it related to the representation. Under Rule 1.6(a), therefore, Lawyer had the obligation to keep that information confidential unless Lawyer had authorization to reveal it. Yet Lawyer had the right to seek to withdraw under Rule 1.16(b)(5), and the court may ask for or require an explanation. Comment 3 to Rule 1.16 states that the lawyer's statement that "professional considerations require termination of the representation ordinarily should be accepted as sufficient." Therefore, Lawyer was obliged in the motion not to reveal any confidential information. *See* ABA Formal Op. 476 (2016). If the court had required more information, then Rule 1.16(b)(5) or (6) would permit Lawyer to disclose Client's confidential information to the extent reasonably necessary in support of the motion to withdraw. Id. Answer (A) is incorrect because Lawyer was allowed to seek to withdraw once Client stopped living up to the obligation to pay lawyer's bills and Lawyer had warned Client that Lawyer would withdraw if Client did not pay the bills. Answer (C) is wrong because, although Lawyer was entitled to seek to withdraw under these circumstances, Lawyer was not allowed to reveal confidential information unless the court required more than the statement that "professional considerations" required withdrawal. Answer (D) is incorrect because the Court may, and often would, merely take a lawyer's word for the fact that withdrawal is permitted under the rules because of "professional considerations." Answer (B) is right.

169. **The correct answer is (A).** Rule 1.6(b)(7) is an exception to the general rule of confidentiality. It permitted Lawyer to reveal confidential information to the extent it was reasonably necessary "to detect and resolve conflicts of interest arising from the lawyer's change of employment" but not if the information revealed would "compromise the attorney-client privilege...." Lawyer told New Law Firm what his client had told him. That was privileged information, and Lawyer was not permitted to reveal it. Answer (B) is incorrect because Rule 1.6(b)(7) allows the revelation of confidential information (as opposed to privileged information) in this context (as long as doing so does not prejudice the client). Answer (C) is wrong because the exception in Rule 1.6(b)(7) does not allow for the revelation of privileged

information. Answer (**D**) is incorrect because it is not necessary that the privileged information be harmful. Rule 1.6(b)(7) permits the revelation of confidential information to detect conflicts of interest when a lawyer is changing firms, as long as the revealed information "would not compromise the attorney-client privilege *or* otherwise prejudice the client" (emphasis added). The information that Lawyer revealed might not have prejudiced Smith, but the information was privileged, and Lawyer had no right to reveal it. Answer (**A**) is the correct answer.

170. **The correct answer is (C).** Rule 4.1(b) required Lawyer to reveal the confidential information because doing so was necessary to avoid assisting in Client's fraud. Lawyer's assistance had already been rendered, but the fraud would not be complete until payment of the purchase price. The revelation was necessary, because there were no other steps that Lawyer could take to avoid assisting in the fraud. For example, a "noisy withdrawal" at that point would be unlikely to alert the Buyer in sufficient time to stop the fraud. One condition of Rule 4.1(b)'s mandatory disclosure is that the circumstances must be such that the lawyer could disclose the information under Rule 1.6. Here, Lawyer had the option under Rule 1.6(b)(3) to reveal the information in order to "prevent … substantial injury to the financial interests … of another that is reasonably certain to result … from the client's commission of a … fraud in furtherance of which the client has used the lawyer's services." Answer (**A**) is incorrect because Lawyer was required by Rule 4.1(b) to reveal the fraud and also had the authority under Rule 1.6(b)(3) to do so. Answer (**B**) is wrong because Lawyer stopped the fraud from being completed. Answer (**D**) is incorrect because Lawyer had both the option (under Rule 1.6(b)(3)) and the mandate (under Rule 4.1(b)) to reveal the confidential information. Answer (**C**) is right.

171. **The correct answer is (B).** Under Comment 6 to Rule 1.7, a lawyer may not without consent represent one client against another current client in litigation, even if the matters are wholly unrelated. Even though Lawyer had no conflict of interest until Corporation B intervened, as of that moment, a conflict existed, and Lawyer violated Rule 1.7 by continuing the representation of Corporation A without the informed consent of both Corporation A and Corporation B. Answer (**A**) is incorrect because it is overbroad. Although screening is not available in this situation, it does cure some conflicts of interest. *See* Rules 1.10(a)(2), Rule 1.11(b), Rule 1.12(c), and Rule 1.18(d). Answer (**C**) is wrong because Smith & Jones is all one firm. Under Rule 1.10(a), a conflict for one lawyer under Rule 1.7 is imputed to all the other lawyers in the firm, no matter how large, and no matter how disparate the offices. Answer (**D**) is incorrect because two matters in which current clients are directly adverse do not need to be related for there to be a conflict under Rule 1.7. *See* Comment 6 to Rule 1.7. Relatedness of claims matters with respect to former clients, but not with respect to current clients. Answer (**B**) is correct.

172. **The correct answer is (A).** Subsidiary and Parent are in the same "corporate family," but that does not automatically mean that they will be treated as one entity for purposes of conflicts of interest. ABA Formal Op. 95-930 established a "facts and circumstances" test to evaluate the question. Here, the facts and circumstances indicate strongly that Parent and Subsidiary will be treated as one entity for conflicts purposes. The two companies operate as alter egos, they have integrated management, and they share in-house legal staff. Given those factors,

Law Firm cannot represent New Client against Parent because, in effect, Parent is a client due to Law Firm's representation of Parent's alter ego, Subsidiary. Under Rule 1.7, a lawyer has a conflict of interest in suing a current client, even in an unrelated matter. *See* Comment 6 to Rule 1.7. That is the conflict that Law Firm faces here. Answer (B) is incorrect because it is not sufficient just to be part of the same corporate family to establish that two separate entities will be treated as one for conflicts purposes. One must examine the "facts and circumstances," as set forth in ABA Formal Op. 95-930. Answer (C) is wrong because, under the right circumstances (present here), separate legal entities in the same corporate family will be treated as one entity for conflicts purposes. Answer (D) is incorrect because a lawyer has a conflict of interest in acting as an advocate against a current client, even in an unrelated matter. Answer (A) is right.

173. **The correct answer is (B).** Rule 1.8(e) limits the types of financial assistance that a lawyer may provide a client in connection with pending or contemplated litigation. The limits of Rule 1.8(e) apply to court cases and to administrative proceedings. *See* Comment 11 to Rule 1.8. Paying for grocery bills is not permitted assistance. Answer (A) is incorrect because Lawyer is permitted to pay the court costs and litigation expenses of an indigent client. Lawyer has merely promised to do something that is permissible. Answer (C) is wrong because Rule 1.8(e) applies to "contemplated litigation" as well as pending matters. Answer (D) is incorrect because "litigation" includes administrative proceedings. Answer (B) is correct.

174. **The correct answer is (C).** Rule 1.8(a) regulates business transactions between lawyers and clients, but that rule's strict requirements do not apply to standard business transactions in which clients routinely engage and therefore can protect themselves. *See* Comment 1 to Rule 1.8. The client here sells art for a living and is unlikely to be taken advantage of by Lawyer. Answers (A) and (B) are wrong because they state, respectively, two of the requirements in Rule 1.8(a) for business transactions between lawyers and clients. Rule 1.8(a) is inapplicable to this transaction. Answer (D) is incorrect because it states yet another requirement of Rule 1.8(a), that the terms of the deal must be fair and reasonable. The fairness of this deal is not what makes it permissible. It is permissible because it is a standard commercial transaction in which Art Dealer is not at risk from trusting Lawyer too much. Answer (C) is the right answer.

175. **The correct answer is (B).** Rule 5.4(c) provides that "[a] lawyer shall not permit a person who recommends, employs, or pays the lawyer to render legal services for another to direct or regulate the lawyer's professional judgment in rendering such legal services." That is exactly what happened here. Insurance Co. employed Lawyer and was paying for Lawyer's representation of Shareholder, but Lawyer was nevertheless required to exercise independent professional judgment on behalf of Policyholder. As hard as it might be for a full-time salaried employee of Insurance Co., Lawyer must remember that Policyholder is the one and only client in this circumstance, and Lawyer's independent professional judgment must be exercised only for the sake of Policyholder. Answer (A) is incorrect because insurance companies are allowed to provide legal services to their policyholders directly through "captive firms" of salaried lawyers. Clients must be informed of the relationship between such lawyers and the insurance company, but there is no per se ban on the arrangement. *See* ABA Formal Op. 03-430. Answer (C) is wrong because under Rule 5.4(c), Lawyer may not allow anyone, including his em-

ployer, to regulate his professional judgment for a client. Answer **(D)** is incorrect because Rule 1.8(f) provides specifically that Lawyer may not accept payment from a third-party (Insurance Co.) to represent a client (Client) if there is "interference with the lawyer's independence of professional judgment or with the client-lawyer relationship." Answer **(B)** is right.

176. **The correct answer is (B).** Lawyer has a conflict of interest under Rule 1.11(a), because Lawyer was involved personally and substantially on behalf of Government in prosecuting Airline for antitrust violations. The suit by Government and the suit on behalf of Client are the same "matter" under Rule 1.11(e)(1) because they involve the same controversy—whether Airline by these specific acts violated the antirust laws—and involves a specific party. Because Lawyer was involved personally and substantially and the Government will not consent to Lawyer's representation of Client, Lawyer has a conflict of interest and may not represent Client. Under Rule 1.11(b), however, Law Firm may continue to represent Client as long as Lawyer is screened from participation in the case, receives none of the fees that Law Firm earns on the case, and as long as Law firm gives Government written notice. Answer **(A)** is incorrect because it is irrelevant that Client and Government are "on the same side." The issue is whether Lawyer was personally and substantially involved in a matter for the Government and now seeks to represent a private client in that same matter. Answer **(C)** is wrong because Lawyer's status as lead counsel does not matter. What matters is that Lawyer was personally and substantially involved in the matter. It is that involvement that creates the conflict of interest and requires Law Firm to screen Lawyer. Answer **(D)** is incorrect because Rule 1.11(b) allows for screening that will prevent imputation. Answer **(B)** is right.

177. **The correct answer is (D).** Rule 6.5 is a special rule regarding conflicts of interest for a lawyer "who, under the auspices of a program sponsored by a nonprofit organization or court, provides short-term limited legal services to a client without expectation by either the lawyer or the client that the lawyer will provide continuing representation in the matter." That is what Lawyer was doing for Husband. Normally, Lawyer would have violated Rule 1.7(a) by undertaking to represent Husband while he had an imputed conflict under Rule 1.7(a) resulting from Law Firm's representation of Wife. However, Rule 6.5(a)(1) provides that Lawyer was subject to Rule 1.7(a) only if he knew about the conflict of interest, and here he did not know. Answer **(A)** is incorrect because Lawyer qualifies for the protections of Rule 6.5(a)(1). Answer **(B)** is wrong because the limit on the scope of the representation was reasonable. Helping a client to complete standard, court-created forms is a common form of "unbundling" legal services and is a reasonable limit on the scope of the representation. Answer **(C)** is incorrect because the Model Rules of Professional Conduct do apply to such arrangements. There is a special rule for them, but they are not exempt from the rules of conduct. Answer **(D)** is right.

178. **The correct answer is (B).** An arbitration clause that limits the remedies that a client may have for a malpractice claim is a prospective agreement to limit the lawyer's malpractice liability. Under Rule 1.8(h)(1), it is improper to enter into any such agreement unless the client is independently represented in making the agreement. *See also* ABA Formal Op. 02-425. Answer **(A)** is incorrect because arbitration clauses are permissible if the client is fully informed and the clause does not in effect constitute a prospective agreement limiting the lawyer's liability for malpractice (unless the client is independently represented in connection with such

an agreement). <u>Id</u>. Answer **(C)** is wrong because informed consent is only one requirement. The clause also must not, as this one did, prospectively limit the lawyer's liability for malpractice. Answer **(D)** is incorrect because Rule 1.8(h)(1) provides that independent representation, rather than merely the advice and opportunity to secure such representation, is necessary for a prospective agreement that limits the lawyer's malpractice liability. Answer **(B)** is correct.

179. **The correct answer is (A).** Under Rule 1.16(a)(1), a lawyer must seek to withdraw if continuing the representation will result in a violation of the rules of conduct. Lawyer knew that continuing in the murder case would cause Lawyer not to be able to give appropriate attention to his other cases. Lawyer owed a duty of diligence under Rule 1.3 to all of those other clients. As Comment 2 to Rule 1.3 notes, "[a] lawyer's work load must be controlled so that each matter can be handled competently." *See also* ABA Formal Op. 06-441. Answer **(B)** is incorrect because the "good cause" standard under Rule 6.2 is for seeking to decline an appointment, not for withdrawing from a case once the appointment has already been accepted. Answer **(C)** is wrong because, although there was no basis upon which Lawyer could seek to avoid the appointment at the time it was made, he nevertheless had a duty later to seek to withdraw once the effect on his workload became clear. Answer **(D)** is incorrect because this was not a situation of optional withdrawal under Rule 1.16(b). These circumstance required withdrawal. Answer **(A)** is right.

180. **The correct answer is (B).** Rule 3.4(a) provides that a lawyer "shall not ... unlawfully alter ... a document or other material having potential evidentiary value. A lawyer shall not counsel or assist another person to do any such act." Lawyer violated Rule 3.4(a) by instructing Sister to delete the browser history, which altered the evidence in a way that made it less useful against Lawyer's Client. Note that any such alteration must be "unlawful," which requires reference to other law, but it is hard to imagine that the alteration of a laptop computer for the purpose of making it less useful in a criminal proceeding would not be unlawful as an obstruction of justice. Answer **(A)** is incorrect. Lawyers are permitted sometimes to take physical possession of evidence of client crime. *See* Comment 2 to Rule 3.4. Answer **(C)** is wrong because Lawyer directed Sister to alter the evidence. That violates Rule 3.4(a), even if returning the computer to its source is permissible. Answer **(D)** is incorrect because Lawyer need not personally alter, conceal or destroy the evidence to violate Rule 3.4. Lawyer also may not counsel another to do any such act, which is what Lawyer did. Answer **(B)** is right.

181. **The correct answer is (D).** Rule 3.3(d) places on lawyers who obtain an ex parte hearing the special obligation to "inform the tribunal of all material facts known to the lawyer that will enable the tribunal to make an informed decision, whether or not the facts are adverse." The reason for this special rule, as stated in Comment 14 to Rule 3.3, is that the court has a duty to "accord the absent party just consideration," and the absent party, by definition, is not there to present its side of the case. Therefore, according to Comment 14, "[t]he lawyer for the represented party has the correlative duty to make disclosures of material facts known to the lawyer and that the lawyer reasonably believes are necessary to an informed decision." That special rule, however, only applies in ex parte proceedings. Here, although the hearing was an emergency hearing for a temporary restraining order (which frequently are ex parte), the

lawyer for Opposing Party was present and could present the adverse facts. Rule 3.3(d) did not apply. Answers (A) and (B) are wrong because Lawyer had no special duty in an adversarial hearing with both sides represented to argue against Client by presenting adverse facts. That was Opposing Counsel's job. Answer (C) is incorrect because it is irrelevant whether the Court ruled for or against Lawyer. A "harmless" violation of the rules of conduct is nevertheless misconduct. Answer (D) is correct.

182. **The correct answer is (A).** Rule 3.7(a) prohibits lawyers from serving as both an advocate and a necessary witness at trial unless one of three things is true. One of the exceptions to the general rule, in Rule 3.7(b)(2), is when "the testimony relates to the nature and value of legal services rendered in the case." Because Lawyer fits within that exception, Lawyer may act as an advocate and a witness at trial. Answer (B) is incorrect because a "burden" on Client, by itself, would not be enough to enable Lawyer to be both an advocate and a witness. Under Rule 3.7(a)(3), a lawyer-advocate may be permitted to testify if the client would suffer "substantial hardship" otherwise. "Substantial hardship" and "burden" are different things. Answer (C) is wrong because it is not necessary that a lawyer's testimony be undisputed in order for that lawyer to serve at trial as both a witness and an advocate. It is true that, under Rule 3.7(a)(1), lawyers may be both advocates and witnesses if their testimony is undisputed, but there are other exceptions as well, and the exception in Rule 3.7(b)(2) applies here. Answer (D) is incorrect because there is no basis for disqualifying Lawyer. If Lawyer was disqualified under Rule 3.7(a), his associates could try the case as authorized by Rule 3.7(b), but their presence is not required. Answer (A) is right.

183. **The correct answer is (B).** Under Rule 3.4(e), Lawyer was prohibited from stating a personal opinion as to the innocence of the accused. Lawyer was not a witness and should have confined himself to arguing for inferences from the record. Answer (A) is incorrect because the usual constraint on asserting frivolous defenses does not apply in the context of criminal defense. Rule 3.1 sets forth the basic rule permitting only meritorious claims and defenses, but then the rule immediately provides that "[a] lawyer for the defendant in a criminal proceeding, or the respondent in a proceeding that could result in incarceration, may nevertheless so defend the proceeding as to require that every element of the case be established." Answer (C) is wrong because Lawyer added personal opinion to the argument from the record. The latter is fine, but the former is prohibited by Rule 3.4(e). Answer (D) is incorrect because even criminal defense attorneys are limited in some ways by the rules. Under Rule 3.1, they are not limited to meritorious defenses, but they nevertheless cannot express personal opinions about guilt. Answer (B) is correct.

184. **The correct answer is (B).** Lawyer knew that Corporation was represented. Therefore, Lawyer could not communicate (without the permission of the lawyer for the entity) with any corporate constituent who fell into any of the three categories of persons described in Comment 7 to Model Rule of Professional Conduct 4.2. One of those categories includes people whose actions may be imputed to the corporation for purposes of civil liability, and here, Lawyer spoke to the person who did the act that allegedly gave rise to the liability. Answer (A) is incorrect because not all corporate employees are off limits. Comment 7 to Rule 4.2 describes the three categories of constituents with whom a lawyer may not communicate without per-

mission of the company's counsel. All other constituents are fair game. Answer (C) is incorrect because it is not necessary for Supervisor to be personally represented. Supervisor is off limits because of his role in an entity that has representation. Answer (D) is incorrect because Lawyer was under a duty to terminate the conversation. Comment 3 to Rule 4.2 states: "The Rule applies even though the represented person initiates or consents to the communication. A lawyer must immediately terminate communication with a person if, after commencing communication, the lawyer learns that the person is one with whom communication is not permitted by this Rule." The right answer is (B).

185. **The correct answer is (A).** Under Rule 4.4(b), Lawyer was obliged to notify opposing counsel of the inadvertent receipt of an electronic communication. Rule 4.4(b) imposes no obligation beyond that, but Lawyer had a duty to inform opposing counsel. Answer (B) is wrong because a party's willingness to pay a particular price is not a "material fact" under generally accepted conventions in negotiation. Lawyer, therefore, was not violating Rule 4.1(a) by bluffing about Client's unwillingness to pay more than $800,000. *See* Comment 2 to Rule 4.1. Answer (C) is wrong because notification to the other lawyer about the email was a mandate under Rule 4.4(b) and not just an option. Answer (D) is wrong because only certain kinds of statements in a negotiation are not treated as statements of material fact. Comment 2 to Rule 4.1 lists several, but Comment 2 is not a license for lawyers to misrepresent any and all facts in a negotiation. Answer (A) is right.

186. **The correct answer is (B).** Rule 8.4(g) provides that it is misconduct for a lawyer to "engage in conduct that the lawyer knows or reasonably should know is harassment or discrimination on the basis of race, sex, religion, national origin, ethnicity, disability, age, sexual orientation, gender identity, marital status or socioeconomic status in conduct related to the practice of law." Lawyer conceded that she discriminated on the basis of race. Although 8.4(g) exempts "legitimate advice or advocacy," the Supreme Court of the United States has held that lawyers may not exercise peremptory challenges on the basis of race. *See* Batson v. Kentucky, 476 U.S. 79 (1986). This tactic is not, therefore "legitimate." Answer (A) is incorrect because a judge's finding that a lawyer has used peremptory challenges in a discriminatory manner does not automatically establish a violation of Rule 8.4(g). *See* Comment 5 to Rule 8.4. Answer (C) is incorrect because Rule 8.4 was amended in 2016 to add section (g) and define misconduct to include certain discriminatory actions, including knowing illegitimate discrimination on the basis of race. Answer (D) is incorrect because the Supreme Court has held in Batson and subsequent cases that race discrimination in jury selection violates the U.S. Constitution and is therefore not legitimate. Answer (B) is the correct answer.

187. **The correct answer is (A).** Lawyer was representing an entity and thus bound by Rule 1.13. Lawyer did the right thing under Rule 1.13(b) when he "reported up" the violations of the law by the low-level employees. However, Lawyer had a further duty once he was discharged, because Rule 1.13(e) provides in pertinent part that "[a] lawyer who reasonably believes that he or she has been discharged because of the lawyer's actions taken pursuant to paragraphs (b) or (c), ... shall proceed as the lawyer reasonably believes necessary to assure that the organization's highest authority is informed of the lawyer's discharge or withdrawal." To protect his client from the wrongdoing of the Vice President for Environmental Compliance, Lawyer

was obliged to alert the Board that Lawyer had been fired. Presumably, the Board would have inquired why and, upon learning of the dumping, could have taken actions to stop it and protect itself (not to mention the public). Answer (B) is incorrect because Lawyer had no duty to reveal the dumping. Lawyer might have eventually had the *option* under Rule 1.13(c) to reveal the dumping to protect Corporation if Corporation's board of directors refused to do anything about it, but Lawyer would not have had any *obligation* under that rule. Lawyer also had the option under Rule 1.6(b)(1) to reveal the dumping to prevent the substantial bodily harm to members of the public, but again that was an option and not a duty. Answer (C) is wrong because Rule 1.13(e) imposes a duty that not only extends beyond Lawyer's discharge but also is in fact triggered by it. He had a duty to report the firing to Corporation's board because he was fired for doing what he was supposed to do under Rule 1.13(b). Answer (D) is incorrect because Lawyer did have the option under Rule 1.6(b)(1) to reveal the dumping because Lawyer reasonably believed that doing so was necessary to prevent substantial bodily harm. Answer (A) is the correct answer.

188. **The correct answer is (A).** Rule 3.8(d) requires a prosecutor to "make timely disclosure to the defense of all evidence or information known to the prosecutor that tends to negate the guilt of the accused.…" This Evidence was known to the prosecutor and tended to negate guilt. Answer (B) is incorrect because the Model Rules of Professional Conduct do not require an "open-file policy," although many state prosecutors use that policy. The United States Department of Justice explicitly rejects the notion of an "open-file" policy in its guidance to prosecutors for compliance with disclosure obligations. Answer (C) is wrong because Prosecutor knew about the Evidence. Even if evidence is in the hands of a third party, a prosecutor must make timely disclosure of it if it is known to the prosecutor. Answer (D) is incorrect because "materiality" is not the standard under Rule 3.8(d). Prosecutor was also bound to make some disclosures by <u>Brady v. Maryland</u>, 373 U.S. 83 (1963), and its progeny, and "materiality" is the standard under that doctrine. Rule 3.8(d), however, imposes a separate and (in some ways) stricter disclosure obligation on Prosecutor. Answer (A) is right.

189. **The correct answer is (C).** Rule 1.15(d) requires a lawyer who comes into possession of property belonging to another to notify that person and deliver the property to them. Although under Rule 1.15(e) a lawyer must hold property when there is a dispute about who owns it, here there is no dispute. One-half of the proceeds belonged to Ex-Wife, and no matter what Client thought about it, Lawyer was obligated to notify her and deliver her money to her. Answer (A) is incorrect because Client's instructions cannot override Lawyer's duty under Rule 1.15(d) to notify and deliver. Answer (B) is wrong because Rule 1.15(d) imposed an explicit duty to notify Ex-Wife when Lawyer came into possession of property that belonged to her. Answer (D) is incorrect because lawyers do not have discretion to resolve competing claims. *See* Comment 4 to Rule 1.15. Here, however, there were no competing claims. Answer (C) is correct.

190. **The correct answer is (C).** Lawyer's ad made a comparison of the quality of her services with the quality of the services offered by other lawyers. There is a risk that such a statement could violate Rule 7.1, because it would mislead the public into thinking that the comparison could be substantiated. Comment 3 to Rule 7.1. The disclaimer, however, made it unlikely that the

public would be misled by the comparison. Id. Answer **(A)** is incorrect because there is nothing wrong with truthful advertising of prices. To the contrary, one reason to encourage lawyer advertising is to foster price competition (at least for routine services typically rendered for flat fees) so that the public benefits from lower fees. Answer **(B)** is wrong because Lawyer included the disclaimer. A comparison of quality would be troublesome without it, but the ad explicitly warns that the comparison cannot be substantiated. No reasonable person would be misled by the ad. Answer **(D)** is incorrect because Lawyer's First Amendment constitutional right to advertise does not include the right to be misleading. Answer **(C)** is right.

191. **The correct answer is (B).** Rule 7.2(b) forbids lawyers from paying another to recommend the lawyer's services, with certain exceptions that do not apply here. Lawyer paid Advertising Agency a flat fee for recommending Lawyer, contingent upon the caller actually becoming a client. Answer **(A)** is incorrect because the Model Rules of Professional Conduct do not regulate taste. *See* Comment 3 to Rule 7.2. As long as the commercials were truthful and not misleading, they did not violate the rules. Answer **(C)** is wrong because the truthfulness of the advertising does not excuse the underlying arrangement in which Lawyer paid Advertising Agency for recommending Lawyer's services. Answer **(D)** is incorrect because the payments to Advertising Agency, although they were not tied in any way to Lawyer's fees and thus could not be improper fee sharing under Rule 5.4(a), nevertheless were improper payments for referrals under Rule 7.2(b). Answer **(B)** is right.

192. **The correct answer is (B).** Rule 7.3(a)(2) generally permits a lawyer to solicit former clients, even if it is for a lawyer's pecuniary gain. Rule 7.2, however, contains exceptions to a lawyer's ability to solicit people, like former clients, whom lawyers generally may solicit. One of those exceptions, in Rule 7.3(b)(1), is when the person "has made known to the lawyer a desire not to be solicited by the lawyer." Smith could not have been more explicit: "Don't call me, I'll call you." Answer **(A)** is incorrect because Smith's status as a nonlawyer is not why Lawyer may not solicit him. Lawyers generally may solicit other lawyers under Rule 7.3(a)(1), but Lawyer had an alternative basis for soliciting Smith: Smith was a former client. It is only Smith's request not to be contacted that made the solicitation improper. Answer **(C)** is wrong because Smith was no longer Lawyer's client. Generally, "a representation in a matter is completed when the agreed-upon assistance has been concluded." Comment 1 to Rule 1.16. There is nothing in the question to indicate that the attorney-client relationship continued as "years" passed after the conclusion of Lawyer's work on the one discrete project, the estate plan, for which Smith hired Lawyer. Answer **(D)** is incorrect because Lawyer was not permitted to solicit a former client, despite the general permission to do so in Rule 7.3(a)(2), if that former client made it known that the former client did not wish to be solicited. Smith had done so. Answer **(B)** is the correct answer.

193. **The correct answer is (D).** Rule 6.1 provides that "[e]very lawyer has a professional responsibility to provide legal services to those unable to pay" and states that lawyers should "aspire" to render fifty hours of pro bono service per year, but Comment 12 to Rule 6.1 also provides that "[t]he responsibility set forth in this Rule is not intended to be enforced through disciplinary process." There is no discipline for failing to fulfill the so-called "professional responsibility" to render pro bono service or to meet the aspirational standard of fifty hours per year.

Answer (**A**) is incorrect because there is no discipline for failing to render pro bono service in any amount. Answer (**B**) is wrong because Supervisory Lawyer's instruction was not only reasonable, it was right. Furthermore, the lack of any enforcement of the "professional responsibility" to render pro bono service is not an arguable question. It is clear from Rule 6.1 and its comments. Answer (**C**) is incorrect because it is never enough simply for a lawyer to act at the direction of a supervisor. Under Rule 5.2(b), a subordinate lawyer can violate the rules at the direction of a supervisory lawyer and yet escape discipline only if "that lawyer acts in accordance with a supervisory lawyer's reasonable resolution of an arguable question of professional duty." Answer (**D**) is right.

194. **The correct answer is (A).** Rule 2.9(C) of the Model Code of Judicial Conduct provides that "[a] judge shall not investigate facts in a matter independently, and shall consider only the evidence presented and any facts that may properly be judicially noticed." Lawyer helped Judge conduct an improper investigation and thereby violated Model Rule of Professional Conduct 8.4(f), which states that it is misconduct for a lawyer to "knowingly assist a judge or judicial officer in conduct that is a violation of applicable rules of judicial conduct or other law." Answer (**B**) is incorrect because Lawyer's assistance with Judge's factual investigation would have been improper with or without prior notice to the parties. With prior notice to the parties, judges may under Rule 2.9(A)(2) seek the opinion of a disinterested legal expert on the law, but there is no such procedure for a judicial investigation of the facts. Answer (**C**) is wrong because, regardless of the lack of a conflict of interest, Lawyer was not permitted to help the Judge do something that violated the Code of Judicial Conduct. Answer (**D**) is incorrect because revelation of the improper investigation did not make the investigation proper. Answer (**A**) is correct.

195. **The correct answer is (B).** Rule 2.11(A)(6) requires Judge to recuse, because Judge "was associated with a lawyer who participated substantially as a lawyer in the matter during such association." Other lawyers in Law Firm represented Wife while Judge was a lawyer in the firm, and that connection was enough to require disqualification. Answer (**A**) is incorrect because judges are not automatically disqualified from cases in which their former firms appear. It would be common, especially in a judge's early days of judicial service, for the judge's connection to the former firm to be close enough that the judge's impartiality might reasonably be questioned under Rule 2.11(A), but disqualification is not automatic. Answer (**C**) is wrong because it does not matter that Judge did not possess confidential information. That fact is important when lawyers change firms and face possible conflicts of interest, but for a judge, it is enough that the matter was being handled in the judge's former firm when the judge was there. Answer (**D**) is incorrect because personal representation of Wife in the matter was not essential. Other lawyers in Judge's firm represented Wife in the matter while Judge was in the firm, and that causes automatic disqualification under Rule 2.11(A)(6). Answer (**B**) is right.

196. **The correct answer is (C).** Rule 3.4 specifically provides that "[a] judge shall not accept appointment to a governmental committee, board, commission, or other governmental position, unless it is one that concerns the law, the legal system, or the administration of justice." The State University Historical Commission is a governmental commission (note the appointment by the Governor and the fact that the University is a public university), and the Com-

mission's purpose is not to deal with any questions of law, the legal system or the administration of justice. Answers (**A**) and (**B**) are wrong because they state two of the general conditions that must be true before a judge may engage in any extrajudicial activity, but Rule 3.4 specifically prohibits this activity even if those general conditions are met. Answer (**D**) is incorrect because not all service on government commissions is prohibited. If the commission concerns the law, the legal system or the administration of justice, and the general requirements on extrajudicial activities in Rule 3.1 are met, a judge may serve on a government commission. Answer (**C**) is right.

197. The business plan would not violate the Model Rules of Professional Conduct. No legal fees are being shared with the nonlawyer lobbyists (*see* Rule 5.4(a)), and without any ownership or managerial role, the lobbyists present no threat to the independence of the lawyers (*see* Rule 5.4(b) and Rule 5.4(d)). Law Firm will need to be careful to abide by Rule 5.7, which governs the delivery of "law-related" services such as lobbying (*see* Comment 9 to Rule 5.7 for a list of examples of "law-related services"). Law Firm will want to take reasonable measures to make sure clients understand when the protections of the attorney-client relationship apply (in the provision of legal services) and when they do not (in the provision of lobbying services). *See* Rule 5.7(a). If Law Firm is not careful to make sure that clients understand this distinction, Law Firm will find that the Model Rules of Professional Conduct will apply even to the provision of the lobbying services. <u>Id.</u>

198. Client has the right to fire Lawyer, even if Client's actions are unjust. Under Rule 1.16(a)(3), Lawyer is required to withdraw from the representation, but that withdrawal is conditioned upon Lawyer's compliance with Rule 1.16(c)'s requirement that Lawyer seek court permission to withdraw. If court permission is granted, then Lawyer must comply with Rule 1.16(d)'s requirements. Lawyer must refund the $10,000 of unearned fees and surrender Client's file.

199. Lawyer has not violated any confidentiality obligation by seeking advice about how to comply with the Model Rules of Professional Conduct. Lawyer does owe a duty of confidentiality to the business partners, even though at this point they are only prospective clients, under Rule 1.18(b). However, Rule 1.6(b)(4) allows Lawyer to reveal confidential information to seek advice about compliance with the rules of conduct. With respect to what Lawyer should say to the prospective joint clients about confidentiality and privilege, Comments 30 and 31 to Rule 1.7 provide guidance. According to Comment 30, prospective joint clients need to understand that "it must be assumed that if litigation eventuates between the clients, the privilege will not protect any such communications...." Comment 31 advises lawyers to tell prospective joint clients that the lawyer will not treat information obtained from or about one client as confidential from the other, that such "information will be shared and that the lawyer will have to withdraw if one client decides that some matter material to the representation should be kept from the other."

200. Lawyer Smith is now associated with all of the lawyers in Jones & Brown. Lawyer Smith personally has a conflict of interest that would prevent him, absent consent, from representing Bank against Client. The two matters are the same (or at least substantially related), and therefore, under Rule 1.9(a), Lawyer Smith may not represent a new client (Bank) against a former

client (Client) when the interests of Bank are adverse to the interest of Client. Lawyer Smith's conflict under Rule 1.9(a) will be automatically imputed to all the lawyers in Jones & Brown unless Jones & Brown screens Lawyer Smith and provides the notices and certifications required by Rule 1.10(a)(2). This process is available to Jones & Brown, because the conflict arises out of Lawyer Smith's association at a prior firm. The only other alternative, if Jones & Brown wishes to accept the representation of Bank, is to obtain the informed consent of Client, under Rule 1.9(a).

201. Lawyer did not violate the Model Rules of Professional Conduct. Under Rule 1.2(d), a lawyer may not assist a client with conduct that the lawyer knows to be fraudulent. Lawyer did not know that the earlier deals were fraudulent when Lawyer provided assistance. With respect to the last deal, Lawyer was assisting with a transaction that was not criminal or fraudulent and therefore was not violating Rule 1.2(d). Under Rule 1.16(b)(3), Lawyer had the option to withdraw from representing Client once Lawyer knew that Client had used Lawyer's services to perpetrate frauds in the past, but withdrawal under such circumstances is optional rather than mandatory.

202. Lawyer's best defense would be that Lawyer did not owe Plaintiff a duty of reasonable care. To prevail in a malpractice action, Plaintiff will have to prove duty, breach, causation and damage. Lawyer undoubtedly breached the duty of care to Client, and clearly Plaintiff was damaged by Lawyer's negligence. But Plaintiff was not Lawyer's client. Although there are a few exceptions to the general rule that a lawyer is not liable in a malpractice action to anyone other than a client, none of those exceptions apply here. Note particularly that there is no indication that Client intended the legal opinion to be for the benefit of Plaintiff or that Client told Lawyer any such thing.

203. The best argument to disqualify Defense Counsel would be to argue that Defense Counsel would be an "unsworn witness." Defense Counsel has first-hand knowledge about the wiretapped conversations, and in the course of cross-examining Witness, is likely to reveal that personal knowledge to the jury. Effective impeachment of Witness might well require Defense Counsel to interject Defense Counsel's own recollection and interpretation of the conversations. Under Rule 3.7, Defense Counsel likely would be disqualified from being both an advocate in this trial and a witness to the conversations. Here, the same harm—jury confusion about the role of Defense Counsel—likely would be caused by Defense Counsel, in effect, testifying via cross-examination as an "unsworn witness."

204. Yes, Lawyer may interview Driver. Because Corporation is represented in the matter, Lawyer must be careful not to communicate about the case with certain constituents of Corporation without the permission of Corporation's lawyer. Comment 7 to Rule 4.2 lists the categories of constituents who are off limits. For example, Lawyer may not without permission contact a constituent whose act or omission might give rise to civil liability in the matter. If Driver were still employed by Corporation, he would be in that category, and Lawyer could not communicate with him without permission of Corporation's lawyer. However, Comment 7 to Rule 4.2 also makes it clear that *former* constituents like Driver are not off limits. Lawyer may speak with Driver without the permission of Corporation's lawyer, even though Driver's act or omission may give rise to civil liability in the matter.

205. Lawyer's client is the Corporation, not the individual Employee. Lawyer's investigation has revealed that Employee's interests are adverse to the Corporation's interests, and therefore, under Rule 1.13(f), Lawyer was obliged to explain that she represented Corporation. Furthermore, Employee's questions revealed that he was confused about Lawyer's role in the matter, because he asked Lawyer for personal legal advice. Under Rule 4.3, Lawyer was obliged to make reasonable efforts to correct the misunderstanding.

206. When Lawyer received the settlement check, Lawyer came into possession of property (the Client's share of the funds) that belonged to another. Under Rule 1.15(a), Lawyer was obliged to hold that property separate from Lawyer's property, in a separate account. When Lawyer deposited the check into Lawyer's operating account, where Lawyer kept personal funds, Client's funds were commingled with Lawyer's personal funds. Lawyer should have deposited the settlement check into a trust account. Then under Rule 1.15(c), Lawyer should have withdrawn Lawyer's earned fees from the trust account and deposited them into the operating account. Under Rule 1.15(d), Lawyer then needed to notify Client that Lawyer was in possession of Client's funds and promptly pay those funds out of the trust account to Client. Under Rule 1.5(c), Lawyer also needed to provide Client a written statement showing the outcome of the matter, the remittance to Client, and how the remittance was calculated.

207. Rule 7.5 governs firm names. Lawyer Brown of course may use her own name, and using the name of deceased partner Smith is permissible. *See* Comment 1 to Rule 7.5. Lawyer Brown may not use the attorney general's name in the firm name during Jones's term of office, because Rule 7.5(c) provides that "[t]he name of a lawyer holding a public office shall not be used in the name of a law firm, or in communications on its behalf, during any substantial period in which the lawyer is not actively and regularly practicing with the firm." Nor may Lawyer Brown use the name of the office mate, because including White in the firm name would imply that Brown and White are practicing in a partnership when they are not. Rule 7.5(d). The closest that Lawyer Brown can get to the desired name is to call her firm "Smith & Brown."

208. Judge did not violate the Model Code of Judicial Conduct. Under Rule 3.1, judges may engage in extrajudicial activities, subject to some restrictions. Teaching is one such activity, and here, there is nothing to indicate that teaching will interfere with Judge's discharge of judicial duties or compromise the judge's independence and impartiality. *See* Comment 1 to Rule 3.1. Judge is permitted to be compensated for an extrajudicial activity such as teaching under Rule 3.12, "provided the compensation is reasonable and commensurate with the task performed." Comment 1 to Rule 3.12. Because Judge received the same stipend as all the other adjunct professors, the compensation is not a problem. Judge is in compliance with the Model Code of Judicial Conduct.

Rule Index

Model Code of Judicial Conduct

Topical Index

Topic	Questions
Malpractice	75, 77, 78, 81, 82, 83, 84, 85, 86, 87, 178, 202
Agreements prospectively limiting malpractice liability	84, 178
Criminal defense	81
Insurance	86
Judgmental immunity	85
Non-clients	78, 82, 87, 202
Proof of damages	81, 83
Settlement of malpractice claim	77
Third-party beneficiaries of lawyer's work	87
Transactions	83
Mediation, duty to clarify role of lawyer as mediator	125
Misconduct	112, 114, 121, 123, 139, 145, 146, 163, 180, 194
Assisting judge in violation of code of judicial conduct	194
Attempts to violate the rules of conduct	145
Criminal acts	112, 123, 163
Stating or implying ability to achieve results through improper means	146
Through the acts of another	114, 121, 139, 145, 180
Multidisciplinary practice	5, 197
Multijurisdictional practice	2, 4, 161, 164
Continuous and systematic presence in state where attorney is not licensed	164
In-house counsel	161
Litigated matters	2
Transactional matters	4
Negotiations	113, 115, 123, 185
Bluffing	113, 115, 185
Misstatements of law	115
Threats	123
No-contact rule	109, 112, 114, 184, 204
Consent of party or witness	184
Corporate parties	184
Former employees of corporate party	109, 204